Beyond the Glass Case

Beyond the Glass Case

The Past, the Heritage and the Public

Nick Merriman

Institute of Archaeology
University College London

First published in Great Britain as *Beyond the Glass Case: The Past, the Heritage and the Public in Britain* in 1991 by Leicester University Press (a division of Pinter Publishers)

This unabridged edition published 2000 by UCL Institute of Archaeology

Institute of Archaeology
University College London
31-34 Gordon Square
London WC1H 0PY

ISBN 0 905853 37 7

Printed and bound in Great Britain by Antony Rowe Ltd., Chippenham, Wilts.

Contents

For my parents

List of tables

Acknowledgements

This book is a revised version of a doctoral dissertation submitted to the Department of Archaeology at the University of Cambridge. Research grants were provided first by the Department of Education and Science and then by St. John's College, Cambridge, and the cost of implementing the survey was funded from grants by the Historic Buildings and Monuments Commission, the Cole Charitable Trust, and the Department of Archaeology of the University of Cambridge. Without the help of these bodies none of this work could have been carried out. My current employer, the Museum of London, also very kindly allowed me a sabbatical to finish the thesis, for which I am most grateful.

Very great thanks are due especially to Cathie Marsh who supervised me through the bulk of the work. Without her expert advice and encouragement the survey would never have been viable. In addition, many thanks are due to Kate Pretty for taking over as supervisor for guiding me through the writing-up stage.

Other individuals I wish to thank are Colin Renfrew for advice and help in securing grants, and Ian Hodder for advice over many years and for helping in the initial setting-up of the project. For helpful discussions and comments during the project I would also like to thank Fred Baker, Caroline Beattie, John Bintliff, Robin Boast, Chris Evans, Eilean Hooper-Greenhill, Nick James, Susan Pearce, David Prince, Chris Tilley, Peter Vergo, Kevin Walsh and Patrick Wright. NOP Market Research Ltd kindly allowed me to view the data they gathered on museum visiting on behalf of the English Tourist Board, for which I am grateful, and the Henley Centre for Forecasting kindly agreed to the reproduction of the material in Table 5.22.

Elements of this book have appeared in interim form in *Museum Studies in Material Culture* (ed. Susan Pearce, Leicester University Press, 1989), *Archaeological Review from Cambridge*, and *The Museum Archaeologist*. I hope those who have read these will nevertheless find something of interest here.

Introduction

'The most remarkable aspect of Western ideology
is its leechlike addiction to its past'

(J. H. Plumb, *The Death of the Past*, Macmillan, London, 1969: 51)

Access to the past

The premise of this book is that the past is something that belongs to all, irrespective of the circumstances of their birth and upbringing. Consequently everyone should have the right to gain access to their history, even if they choose not to avail themselves of this opportunity. Museums and similar organisations are one of the principal means by which people can gain access to the past, and everyone should thus have the opportunity to visit them and feel at home in them. Their role as guardians of the heritage thus makes them different from other cultural institutions such as cinemas, where there is little concern to bring in a public that reflects the diversity of the total population.

For a long time museums have been seen by curators as educational institutions just as much as places as diversion, and their potential to provide universal access to knowledge has long been accepted. This aim has been adopted by the Museums Association (1945: 33) and has been enshrined in numerous international resolutions (e.g. UNESCO 1982) and in the founding charters of many museums. The British Museum Act of 1753, for example, explicitly constitutes the museum as being 'not only for the inspection and entertainment of the learned and the curious, but for the general use and benefit of the public' (quoted in Crook 1972: 39). Particular emphasis has at times been placed on the potential that museums have to be 'people's universities', acting as institutions for the promotion of lifelong learning within the community, especially giving a second opportunity for education for those who did not take full advantage of the formal schooling process (Chadwick 1980, Millas 1973). More recently, with the proclamation of a 'new museology' (Mayrand 1985) the potential of museums as a positive social force has been raised with renewed vigour. It is argued that museums should now be actively involved in their communities, helping them to build their own past for themselves whether in rural areas (Teruggi 1973) or in the inner cities

1

(American Association of Museums 1972) while at the same time raising awareness of contemporary issues such as famine, racism and drug abuse (Hancocks 1987).

There is, then, a considerable body of opinion attesting to the democratic potential of museums, and a body of recommendations and legislation enshrining the principle of public access for all. The well-documented existence of a heritage boom (Hewison 1987) might in fact be taken as a demonstration that museums are fulfilling their functions well and helping a large public to gain a sense of their history. However, the expansion in heritage presentations has not been accompanied by an expansion in the range of people visiting them. Time and time again surveys show that individuals of above average income and affluence are represented far out of proportion to their numbers in the population as a whole (English Tourist Board 1982a, HMSO 1981, Prince 1983). At present, it seems that this democratic potential of museums is still not being fulfilled. One reason for this must be that, ever since their inception, museums have been associated with the elite, and their imposing architecture and their glass cases have symbolically and literally excluded large sections of the population from them. In order to explore their full potential, we must now work to dismantle the cultural barriers that have been deterrents to wider participation in museums.

This book principally focuses on opening up access to museums, but in order to do this it has been necessary to examine the public's relationship with the past in a broader way, because the premise of accessibility raises fundamental questions concerning ideology, the role of museums, and the nature of the past, before even the premise itself can satisfactorily be accepted. At the heart of this enterprise is an engagement with the theoretical issues that concern the social context of museums and museum visiting within our society. Until recently, most literature about museums consisted of technical reports of exhibitions and equipment, proceedings of conferences, a few histories (e.g. Bazin 1967) and even fewer examinations of the social and educational role of museums (Adam 1939, Wittlin 1949). It was only the art history field, because of the nature of its subject matter and the strong academic tradition of art curators, that showed much interest in the theory of representation and interpretation in museums. Only in the last few years has it become recognised that theory has a place in museum training because hitherto the prevailing ideology amongst museum workers has been that their duties (collection, documentation, preservation, research, interpretation) are all commonsense techniques requiring perhaps discussion of method but not of underlying philosophy. The lack of debate about the nature and role of museums has led to the impression that museums are somehow different from the rest of society and not the product of specific historical circumstances, and that the knowledge they produce is in some way objective and value-free. Thankfully, over the last fifteen years or so the situation has improved greatly partly from pressures within museums from a new generation of workers schooled in these debates, and partly as a result of the increased number of postgraduate courses in museum studies. Museum studies has moved on from the learning of technical processes to a more all-encompassing enquiry of the underlying philosophies of practice.

The assimilation of debates from the wider social sciences has led to the gradual realization that both the institutional framework within which museums operate, and the information they disseminate, are not neutral or natural, but are the product of very particular social conditions and have a definite social and political role beyond that of simply telling people about the past (or present). The development and flourishing of museums in Western society has occurred under particular historical circumstances and they had, and still do have, a particular social and ideological role, which has by and large been associated with the dominant classes. Once we accept, as we must, that museums have a social role, we must then ask what this is (or indeed what different roles it plays for different groups of people). The study of this aspect of museums then becomes an exercise in the historical and contemporary sociology of a particular institution. In order to do this, then, we must study, critically, the history of museums, and combine this with an understanding of how they function in contemporary society. There can be many branches to this study, ranging from analyses of the culture of the museum profession to the ideology expressed in the exhibitions. This contribution to the debate attempts to understand how people themselves think about the past and museums and how they use them, rather than how analysts *think* they use them.

The production and consumption of the past

Western society's obsession with the past, noted in Plumb's opening quotation, has been reflected for centuries by the study and popularisation of history, and in recent years by a proliferation of organisations that present the past to the public. Most critical reaction to the latter phenomenon has been negative. In particular, the rise of the pejoratively-termed 'heritage industry' has been seen as a symptom of the failure of modern society to face the future after the decline of industry. Instead, society is looking back to a more glorious past, but this past, as portrayed in displays led by marketing policies, is a romanticised fiction. Worse, it has become a commodity devoid of specific content, that ultimately supports the dominant ideology by showing the past as being the same as the present, and thereby prevents any conception that society could be different and thus silences any potential dissent and conflict. In Chapter 2, these arguments are presented in summary form to represent current thinking about presentations of the past. Most of these analyses take the form of formal critiques of the *production* of the past in the shape of such things as museum exhibitions. The *consumption* of the past, the way in which people think about history, and visit museums and other presentations, has rarely been studied, except in the form of superficial and repetitive surveys of the characteristics of museum visitors.

The key to providing this extra dimension, and to opening up museums to a wider public, has to be the people who visit them. In order to gain a fuller understanding of the meaning of this Western obsession with the past, we must investigate the different ways in which people use the past and its material manifestations. It is only when this is done that we will be in a position to establish whether the tradition of museum visiting and the phenomenon of the rise of heritage presentations can be explained purely by successful marketing and by the power of the dominant classes to persuade people to visit these institutions and accept the ideology encapsulated within them, or whether, as is favoured here, 'heritage' can have very positive connotations as well as negative ones, and can play a crucial, creative role in the lives of different communities.

In order to provide this dimension, a survey was undertaken of 1500 adults throughout Great Britain, on the patterns of people's heritage visiting, their attitudes to them, their images of the past, and on other, non-museum, ways in which they experience the past. At a basic level this would be useful information for those working in the field, and at a deeper level it would provide some information on how presentations of the past are consumed, and what the consumers, rather than the producers, think of them. Full details of the survey are given in Appendix 1.

The results of the survey show, as a crucial benchmark, that the majority of the population attach some value to knowing about the past. However, images of the past are, surprisingly, not nostalgic but overwhelmingly adverse. Rather than wanting to retreat to the past as a haven from today's problems, most people believe they are much better off in the present. Beneath this agreement about the harshness of the past, however, lurks a great deal of variety. Clear links exist between people's current social position and their images of the past. Those who are less fortunate in the present are more likely than any others to see the past as better in many respects than the present, while those who are well-off now see few redeeming features in the past. Images of the past, then, being rarely articulated, are an important personal way in which individuals can come to terms with themselves and their circumstances, and they can also be seen as an unspoken discourse on the present. The work on people's images of the past thus shows that people use the past creatively, and this in turn opens up the possibility that museums can act as institutions which can promote this creative and non-dogmatic use of the past. If this role for museums can become established, then the ideal of opening them up to as wide a public as possible becomes less problematic.

Having established that people use the past creatively and that museums are therefore not solely to be seen as agents of the dominant ideology, the rest of the book proceeds with exploring the aim of opening up heritage presentations to the community. Chapters 4 and 5 present central data on museum and heritage visiting on a national scale. It is confirmed that visiting is still primarily the preserve of those who are better educated and more affluent than average, but that participation has widened greatly in recent years. Deterrents to visiting are examined in detail, and it is found that cultural barriers are far more important than structural ones in influencing whether someone thinks of a visit to a museum or historic building as being a worthwhile leisure activity.

Explanations for these patterns are reviewed in Chapter 6, where it is argued that the psychological and sociological approaches both have valuable elements in them. The work of Bourdieu is particularly useful in providing a social theory which can accommodate museums, although he is unable to explain their recent popularity. A fusion of both approaches is attempted by looking at related developments in leisure theory, and by examining the history of museums. Museums still suffer from their historical associations with power and authority, which manifest themselves in the persistence of a negative image. This image is still true, to a certain extent, as museums still act as symbols of social divisions. Broadly, society can be divided up into those who see museum visiting as part of their culture, and those who reject it. More and more people, however, are taking up museum visiting as a result of their improved social status: the connotations of museum visiting make it an appropriate leisure activity with which to signal a change in status. While museums are still at root socially divisive, then, their openness allows more people to visit them, but these increased visits are to a large extent taking place because of museums' persistent social connotations.

How then are we fully to dismantle these cultural barriers around museums that still signal their association with the dominant fractions of society? One way in which this might be done is by examining non-museum approaches to the past to see if they offer any clues as to how museums might widen their appeal. In Chapter 7, a case study is made of attitudes to, and participation in, an academically sanctioned activity (archaeology) and ones that are not sanctioned (treasure hunting, beliefs in UFOs and the like). This finds that participants in both are very much like one another in terms of demographic characteristics. What distinguishes those who participate in non-sanctioned activities tends to be their enjoyment of the romantic elements of the past and its discovery, and, in some cases, their disillusionment with the present. None of the activities, however, is regularly participated in by the sort of people who tend not to go to museums and other heritage presentations.

The same is true of the other non-museum activities reported on in Chapter 8. It is the heritage-keen 'culture vultures' who are also most likely to research their family tree, collect old objects and join history and collectors' societies. When it comes to conventional means of gaining access to the past, it seems that there is a great gulf between those who undertake a wide range of activities, and those who do nothing. Crucially, it is discovered that the main way that the latter group prefers to experience the past is at home, and that the most important sense of the past for them is personal and local.

This suggests that we can best conceive of the past as two distinct fields. The first, common to all, is the personal sense of the past which relies on memory and attachment to places and things. The second, which is dominated by the educated and affluent, is the sense of an impersonal heritage which overlays the personal sense of the past. The impersonal heritage is that which has no direct connection with one's personal past, being expressed in terms of the history of other people, of the region, the nation, or the world.

With the discovery that those who do not visit museums find the personal sense of the past most appealing, a further dilemma then arises for the museum worker attempting to break open the museum beyond its narrow confines. Until recently, museums were associated with the educated bourgeoisie and aristocracy, from amongst whom the staff were recruited, and whose history was portrayed in the displays. There was thus a congruence between the public, the staff, and the contents of the presentations. Now, however, it has become abundantly clear that history cannot entirely be constituted of this world view, and that a plurality of pasts exist, often conflicting with each other. This development has now been accepted by a great many museum staff, who then have to work with this within a framework which sees little of this development reflected in recruitment into the profession, or in museum displays. Now that history has been burst open to reveal this plurality of conflicting views, how do museum curators reflect this in their work? If they do nothing, museums will be seen as shipwrecked bastions of monolithic history, peripheral to the debates raging around them, and continuing to reflect outdated ideas and practices. If the curator does wish to open up museums to reflect the diversity of historical viewpoints, he or she is then faced with the dilemma of being accused of appropriating and taming the history of non-white and non-middle class culture into an institution associated with the dominant groups of society.

Possible solutions to this dilemma are suggested in the final chapter, which looks at practical ways in which museums might change from being institutions which produce a single past to be consumed uncritically by a restricted public, to being services which enable a broad public to produce, in a critical way, diverse pasts of their own. When we begin to move along this road, the marvellous potential envisaged for museums for well over a century, may begin to be realised.

The scope of the book

This book is based on a large-scale postal survey, and the desire to achieve nationwide coverage of the survey has meant that analysis has had to be conducted at a very broad level, as is the case with all large surveys. Consequently, the book has only dealt with the concept of 'the museum' rather than with specific types of museums or individual museums. Deliberately, too, an undefined and generalised sense of 'the past' has been studied rather than particular periods of the past. For similar reasons, the broadness of the data means that the complexity and fine-grain of people's images of the past or their attitudes to museums have been glossed over. Thus, not all who read this book will find here the detailed answers to specific problems that they might have been expecting. Most will be able to find examples of individual museums that do not conform to the patterns described here: it can only be stressed that the general national patterns revealed here have some validity and usefulness of their own. This work was designed to examine museums as a social phenomenon at a very broad level, and ideally this now needs to be supplemented with complementary in-depth analyses of specific elements of museums, conducted in the manner of the ethnographer.

Reflecting the author's background as a prehistorian, the focus of analysis has been on the past and on museums and other insitutions that present the past. Despite this, it is recognised that not all museums concern themselves wholly or even partly with the past, and good museums should also concern themselves with the present and future. It is to be hoped, nevertheless, that some of the conclusions arising from the book apply equally to those areas of museums that are not concerned with the past.

The presentation of the data

Over 12,000 simple crosstabulations are possible with the survey data; 800 using only the main explanatory variables. Clearly some sort of selection process has to be undertaken. Tables that are essential to the argument have been presented in the main body of the text to enable easy inspection. Others that are important are found in an appendix and referred to in the text. Finally, all of the survey data are on deposit at the SERC Data Archive at the University of Essex, where they are available on-line to researchers.

All statistics presented in the tables are significant at the $p = \cdot 05$ level except where indicated. All percentages are rounded up to the nearest whole number, and for ease of discussion the five-fold percentages in Likert scales (Strongly Agree—Agree—Neither Agree Nor Disagree—Disagree—Strongly Disagree) have been collapsed into three, although they remain in expanded form in the tables for inspection.

The demographic variables used are mostly self-explanatory or explained in the text as they are used. The status variable is a composite one, based on educational background, housing tenure and access to a private vehicle. Those of high status stayed on at school, own their own home, and possess at least one vehicle, while those of low status left school at the minimum age, rent their accommodation, and do not have access to a vehicle. Those of intermediate status possess a mixture of these characteristics. Owing to an interaction of age with status, low status is divided into those who are over sixty years old and those who are under sixty.

2 The death of the past and the growth of heritage

The growth of heritage

One particular phenomenon that has exercised critics in the last few years has been the proliferation of representations of the past that have come to be termed 'heritage'. Although it is easy to understand at an intuitive level what is meant by 'heritage', closer examination shows that it is extremely difficult to define. At root the word means 'that which comes from the circumstances of birth; an inherited lot or portion; the condition or state transmitted from ancestors' (*Oxford English Dictionary*), but since the 1970s it has come to be applied more concretely to cultural and natural heritage such as historic buildings and landscapes that are to be preserved and passed on for future generations (eg UNESCO 1972). All attempts to define exactly what constitutes heritage have, however, met with failure because ultimately heritage can be 'anything you want' (Hewison 1989: 15). Part of the confusion over what constitutes heritage lies in the fact that the word is applied to two different sorts of phenomena. On the positive side the word is used to describe culture and landscape that are cared for by the community and passed on to the future to serve people's need for a sense of identity and belonging. In this context, the use of the term 'heritage centre' in, for example, natural parks, covers institutions which aim to explain the different facets of the landscape and encourage understanding and care for them. These positive values of care and identity are in sharp contrast to the more negative and pejorative uses of the term 'heritage'. In this sense, as used in 'the heritage industry', the word has become synonymous with the manipulation (or even invention) and exploitation of the past for commercial ends. These are usually characterised as 'heritage rides', 'heritage experiences', or are part of theme parks. The divide between the two can be difficult to discern, although it may as a rule of thumb be possible to distinguish between those institutions which aim primarily to enable the public to understand the past and secondarily to make money or not at least lose it, and those whose prime aim is to make money and whose secondary aim, if it exists at all, is to provide an educational experience. Fowler (1989) has suggested that the presentations of the latter group can be characterised by their eclecticism, their discontinuity with the present, and their inaccuracy, parody and commercialisation. Unfortunately, because so

8

much critical attention has been focused on 'heritage experiences', museums and other similar institutions have been tarred with the same brush, and many of their positive connotations have been forgotten. It is now time that the balance was restored.

A genuine growth in institutions, practices and objects that are used in some way to represent the past has occurred in the last two decades. Both Lowenthal (1985) and Hewison (1987) have noted how Britain and the USA have been affected by 'creeping heritage' in the form of revivalist architecture, the burgeoning of the antiques market, genealogy, historical fiction, historical radio and television series, and fashions for old films, clothes and music. In the latter two categories there is already a fashion for the 1970s: cultural nostalgia in areas of rapid change is currently lagging only fifteen years behind the present! In particular there has been a great growth in the number of museums and of other institutions purveying representations of the past in varying degrees of accuracy. This has included a virtual doubling of the number of museums in Britain since 1971 (Prince and Higgins-McLoughlin 1987: 12). At the last count (1987) there were 2,131 of them compared with a figure of 217 a hundred years ago (British Association 1887). Until recently they were opening at a rate of thirty a year, or more than one a fortnight (Museums and Galleries Commission 1984: 46), although there are now signs that saturation point has been reached, as growth has apparently outstripped demand (Middleton 1990). One problem in estimating the growth or decline of museums accurately is that no overall figures are available for museum closures.

One of the newest phenomena is the heritage centre, defined by the Civic Trust as 'a permanent exhibition with the evolution of a whole community as its theme' (BTA/ETB 1989). These have increased in numbers from 5 in 1978 (English Tourist Board 1979: 4) to 51 in 1988 (BTA/ETB 1989: 32) As well as the increase in museums, there are now 1,783 historic buildings open to the public in England alone (*ibid*: 26), compared with 1,280 in 1978 (ETB 1979 :4), and over the past fifteen years they seem to have been opening at an average rate of around one every three weeks (ETB 1983: 2). At least 1,168 of these historic buildings include a museum, exhibition or collection as part of their attractions (BTA/ETB 1989: 30). In addition to these buildings open to the public in England, there are 200 others open by appointment, over 8000 Anglican churches open without appointment, and thousands of historic hotels, pubs, banks and town halls to which the public have access (*ibid*: 26).

As the number of heritage presentations opened for display to the public has increased in recent years, so have attendances to them. Overall, the number of annual visits to historic properties have increased from 52 million in 1977 (ETB 1978: 3) to 78 million in 1989, and visits to museums and galleries have increased from 57 million to 72 million (BTA/ETB 1990: 1). Two museums, the British Museum and the National Gallery, are among the top five most-visited attractions in Britain, with 4,400,000 and 3,368,000 visits respectively (*ibid*: 6). The three most popular presentations with archaeological content are the Roman Baths and Pump Room at Bath (931,832 visits — many no doubt attracted primarily to the Pump Room), the Jorvik Viking Centre (904,483 visits) and Stonehenge (681,657 visits).

The direct and indirect revenue earned by these historic attractions has also increased in recent years. For example, in 1988, historic buildings earned a record £153 million in Britain, an overall rise of eight per cent on the previous year, and supported a total of 10,875 paid jobs (BTA/ETB 1989: 41). In a wide-ranging survey, Myerscough noted that there were 251 million attendances at arts events in Britain during 1984/5, generating a consumer spending of £433 million, of which £18 million was accounted for by admissions to museums, and £34 million on the built heritage. He found that the turnover of museums and galleries in Britain for the same year was £230 million, of which £23 million was from earned revenue, and £189 million from public funds and that museums and galleries employed around 19,000 people (Myerscough 1988). Overall, tourist attractions (rather than tourism as a whole) saw 330 million visits and supported 64,281 full- and part-time paid jobs in 1989, as well as 35,946 volunteers, and brought in a gross revenue of around £700 million (BTA/ETB 1990). In 1987, tourism supported around 1.4 million jobs in Britain and brought around £14 billion into the economy, making it one of the most important industries in the country (BTA 1988: 3). In particular, the total arts turnover, estimated at £10 billion (Myerscough 1988: 61) is comparable to the market for cars, motorbikes and other vehicles. Myerscough's figures show that tourism with an arts ingredient generates around a quarter of this revenue, and that museums and galleries are a very important element in this, particularly as 31 per cent of all museum visits (44 per cent in London) are by overseas tourists (Myerscough 1988: 80).

The heritage debate

On the surface, this expansion in the number of heritage attractions and of people visiting them is encouraging: it seems to indicate that museums and related institutions are carrying out with great success their task of presenting the past to the public and stimulating interest in it. For critics, however, there is a darker side to this phenomenon, represented by the negative values noted above, whereby the past is seen simply as a marketable product, devoid of any intrinsic meaning. It is this more critical approach to heritage that is examined here.

The first stage in a critical examination of the growth of heritage must be to ask why the past is so pervasive in its evocations in the late twentieth century. Writers who have examined the problem are united in seeing it as a reaction to the scale and extent of social and environmental dislocation, although they disagree as to when exactly this process began.

In his book '*The Past is a Foreign Country*' (1985), Lowenthal traces the gradual process by which he feels a 'breach with the past' has occurred (cf Plumb's '*Death of the Past*' dealing with the same phenomenon). In pre-industrial society, he suggests, for the great mass of people the past was not distinguished as a separate realm but was continuously reproduced in the present through the traditional patterns of people's everyday lives. The pace of change was slow enough for most people to feel that the past had been the same as the present. The pattern for change began in the Renaissance with the gradual development of science and the slow move towards rationality, but it was in the Victorian period that the past was turned to on a large scale. Both he and Plumb see the cause of this as being industrialisation, which created a new kind of society with no precedent and no roots in the past. At the same time, the scale and pace of change gave people a greater need than ever to understand the past in order to give them a perspective and a sense of stability amongst the disorientations of modern life. Thus it is in the Victorian period that we see the proliferation of antiquarianism, museums, historical and archaeological societies and the beginnings of systematic academic study of the past. This basic need for the past as a means of coping with change is a genuine phenomenon and one that is still with us. This phenomenon was also isolated for more recent times by Alvin Toffler in his influential book *'Future Shock'*. He describes 'future shock' as 'the shattering stress and disorientation that we induce in individuals by subjecting them to too much change in too short a time' (Toffler 1970: 2). Like Plumb, he characterises the pace of change that has occurred within living memory in the form of a 'break with the past', and argues that society will increasingly need enclaves of the past, such as museums and preserved villages in order to cope with this change (ibid: 391-2).

However, the fundamental paradox at the heart of the breach with the past is that, although the pace of change creates a strong need for a sense of the past, it removes at the same time any possibility of this need ever being satisfied. This is because the breach with the past has also meant that history, devoid of its previous role in the active constitution of the present, is seen as completed and becomes a matter for curiosity or nostalgia. All attempts to bring back the past only serve to emphasise its separation from the present (MacCannell 1976: 83).

A consequence of this putative death of the past is that attitudes to it become primarily nostalgic: 'The new methods, new processes, new forms of living of scientific and industrial society have no sanction in the past, and no roots in it. The past becomes, therefore, a matter of curiosity, nostalgia, a sentimentality' (Plumb 1969: 14).

In the Victorian period, the main impetus behind this nostalgia for the past was the need to find solace, and virtues that were no longer to be found in 'the dreadful present' (Lowenthal 1985: 97). The contemporary obsession with medieval England was thus expressive of a desire to return to a rural idyll with a shared and ordered life. Wright similarly argues that modernity has its own nostalgia for a pastoral golden age, which expresses the genuine tensions and aspirations of everyday life. He suggests that nostalgia will be specifically shown for traditional and deep seated communities, for the more authoritative and sufficient family, for lost crafts, for the Second World War as 'a righteous war', and for a sense of 'the unique' (Wright 1985: 19-24).

Heritage as index of decline

While the origins of the supposed death of the past are held to lie in the consequences of the *rise* of industrialism, a few writers have attempted to identify why it is that a heritage boom should have occurred specifically in the course of the last two decades. They too are united in seeing it as a consequence not this time of the *rise* of industrial society, but of its *decline*. In complete contrast to the experience of Victorian Britain, contemporary heritage and tourism is seen as an expression of loss of confidence in the future: society turns towards the past in order to understand how it arrived at the present. MacCannell (1976: 85) suggests that there comes a point where modern societies become so differentiated that they can develop no further and 'they turn in on themselves, elaborating ever more refined internal reflections of their own structure'. Similar sentiments have been expressed by a number of 'postmodern' writers, notably Eco (1986) and Jameson (1984) and these are usefully summarised by Walsh (forthcoming).

In response to this feeling, Bommes and Wright formulate the concept of 'history as entropy', in which historical time in modern societies is experienced as a process of degeneration and decline: 'National Heritage is the backward and predominantly hindering glance which is taken from the edge of the abyss' (Bommes and Wright 1982: 21).

Wright (1985) and Hewison (1987) have suggested specific influences on the formation of the contemporary national past. The strongest of these are held to be recent economic and imperial decline, together with post-war depopulation of the countryside and the dislocation of city communities by the demolition of housing and subsequent resettlement in New Towns (Wright 1985: 25). In addition Hewison feels that the social and sexual revolutions of the 1960s, the decline of religion and traditional authority, and the experiences of immigration, crime and unemployment have all contributed to Britain's climate of decline. In particular, a watershed is seen to have occurred in the late 1960s and early 1970s, when the positive atmosphere of renewal and modernisation within which initial post-war socio-economic and environmental changes had taken place was replaced by one in which change took place in an atmosphere of decline (Hewison 1987: 41). He sees specific catalysts as being the devaluation of the currency in 1967, the oil crisis of 1973 and Britain's submission to the dictates of the international monetary fund in 1976. It is difficult to take such sweeping causal assertions seriously, and he offers no evidence to support his arguments, but there seems a clear consensus that the rise of heritage industry occurs at a time of the decline of manufacturing industry and acts as a replacement of it.

Heritage as commodity

A further consequence of the death of the past and its separation from everyday life is that it becomes little more than a commodity, a package offering a sanitised version of the past for public consumption as heritage in museums and other 'experiences' (Bommes and Wright 1982: 291). Shanks and Tilley have dealt most comprehensively with this 'commodification' of the past. They argue that in museums artifacts all become treated as identical and are merely props in an experience which is bought in the present. Objects, once with distinctive meanings in particular social systems, become homogeneous commodities for study and display in a process described as 'shopfront commodification'. Artifacts thus become static and removed from history, avoiding any suggestion that history is a dynamic process involving conflict and change. A consequence of this static portrayal of the past, they argue, is that the present, and the capitalist mode of thought, are made to appear inevitable, thus maintaining the social status quo: 'in the museum the past becomes the death mask of the present' (Shanks and Tilley 1987: 53).

This is a point made earlier by Horkheimer and Adorno in *Dialectic of Enlightenment* (1973). Mass culture is seen to be produced by a 'culture industry', which reproduces the economic industry in its standardisation and commodification of culture and its treatment of human labour in terms of exchange value (ibid: 131). In other words, the culture industry gears itself almost entirely to the development of cultural forms which are compatible with the preservation of capitalism (Held 1980: 92). The implication of the commodification of the past is its recruitment to an ideological function, which is to legitimate contemporary social relations in favour of the dominant groups. It is this aspect of museums that has caused most concern amongst curators and critics in recent years.

Museums and ideology

Historians and archaeologists have long known that the interpretations they put on the past reflect contemporary circumstances. Historiography was first introduced into the fields of art history and history with the publication of Kenneth Clark's *'The Gothic Revival'* (1928) and Butterfield's *'The Whig Interpretation of History'* (1931). Museum theory, however, has been most closely influenced by developments in archaeological theory through their common interest in material culture (Pearce 1990: 57-8), so it is instructive to follow how this has impinged on both areas of study. Historiography in archaeology did not make its mark until 1950, with the publication of Daniel's treatment of the history of archaeology and Piggott's work on Stukeley, both of which clearly showed how previous archaeological interpretations reflected the social conditions in which they were produced. This insight has been best expressed in Hawkes's aphorism 'Every age has the Stonehenge it deserves — or desires' (Hawkes 1967: 174).

The discovery of ideology

In the 1960s and 70s, the aim of the New Archaeology to formulate a general cultural science and an objective, value-free approach to the writing of the past (Watson, LeBlanc and Redman 1971: 162) led to a feeling that the historiography of archaeology would no longer be relevant. However, the general failure of the programme of the New Archaeology, together with the increasing theoretical awareness of archaeology and its assimilation of debates in related disciplines has led to a resuscitation of interest in the subjective nature of interpretation.

In the early 1980s the critique of functionalism that had taken place earlier in social theory, particularly in the work of Giddens (1976, 1979) began to have its impact in archaeological theory and subsequently in museum studies (Hodder 1982, Tilley 1982, Pearce 1986a,b,c). One of the main consequences of this critique has been the engagement of theory in these two areas with structuralism, Marxism and their various derivatives. A key concept to emerge from consideration of these wider debates has been that of ideology.

The study of ideology has a long and chequered history, but it is possible to extract two basic definitions from an analysis of the way it has been used in recent social theory (Thompson 1984). The first is a 'neutral conception' where the term is used in a descriptive sense to mean systems of thought or belief which are allied to social actions or to particular projects. The second is a 'critical conception', and it is this which is most widely used in critiques of museums. This sees ideology as acting to maintain domination through asymmetrical power relations, by representing sectional interests as universal, by denying contradictions, and by naturalising the present (Giddens 1979: 193-5).

The dominant ideology thesis

The classic formulation of what has become known as the dominant ideology thesis was made by Marx and Engels in trying to explain why revolution was *prevented* from happening spontaneously in all countries in Europe:

> The ideas of the ruling class are in every epoch the ruling ideas, i.e., the class which is the ruling material force of society, is at the same time its ruling intellectual force. The class which has the means of material production at its disposal, has control at the same time over the means of mental production (Marx and Engels 1864: 61).

According to this formulation, the dominant ideology penetrates and permeates the consciousness of the working class, who come to see and experience reality only through the conceptual categories of the dominant class. They therefore fail to understand their exploited position in the capitalist system and revolution is not conceived of as a possibility.

The actual content of the dominant ideology is difficult to determine because it might not be consciously expressed (Abercrombie *et al.* 1980: 130). One of its main tenets, however, is progressivism (cf. Bowler 1989), because the inculcation of a belief in progress and improvement is an effective way of maintaining the power of dominant groups. People are led to believe that the betterment of their lot is best achieved by letting the social process run its course unhindered. Members of the Frankfurt School of critical theory have written extensively of the role played by the ideologies of science and progress in legitimating capitalist society. The processes inherent in the culture industry act to affirm the status quo by preventing any conception that society could be different (Adorno 1975). Ideology becomes absorbed into reality (Marcuse 1968: 26), leading to the 'freezing' of the status quo, a lack of understanding of social and historical context, and the absence of any sense that society can be changed (Held 1980: 169).

One of the major consequences of this conceptualisation of ideology is that interpretations of the past can no longer be regarded as neutral and unproblematic (Hodder 1984a). In particular, museums, as one of the principal means by which the results of archaeological and historical work are communicated to the public, have been seen as ideological institutions, acting to maintain the hegemony of dominant social groups.

Although the classic Marxist definition of ideology has been used in a number of criticisms of museum presentations (see below), it is the reformulation of the concept by Althusser that has provided a clearer framework for their ideological analysis. He insists that 'an ideology always exists in an apparatus, and its practice, or practices', and he terms these 'Ideological State Apparatuses', or ISAs (Althusser 1971: 127-8). The ISAs, which inlude the communications media and cultural institutions, act in tandem with 'Repressive State Apparatuses' (RSAs), such as the police, the courts and the army, to ensure the continual reproduction of the capitalist mode of production in favour of the dominant class.

As far as heritage presentations are concerned, this showed the way in which seemingly peripheral institutions such as museums could be seen not simply as reflections of ruling ideas but as actually constituting one of the apparatuses which ensure the maintenance of the present social system. Museums could be seen as important by this very peripherality: their messages could easily be assimilated because of their seeming uncontentiousness. In this way, Althusser's scheme offered a way in which heritage presentations could be linked to wider socio-political processes in a way that was far more specific than the original Marxist concept of ideology. These views of ideology have important implications for the analysis of museums and other heritage presentations. If museums do act as apparatuses which inculcate an obeisance to the dominant order, then curators might rightly question whether they should be encouraging wider participation in such a potentially nefarious institution. Chapter 6 provides a historical overview of museums' social role which shows that they have always had a role in society which can be termed ideological. In the Victorian period in particular, ideas of social improvement and control were combined in a strong way in museum provision, and this saw a clear expression in the architecture of museum buildings and in the layout of displays.

As the concept of ideology has become more refined in social criticism, formal analyses of modern museum displays have come to similar conclusions about their ideological role. The most explicitly Marxist interpretation of a historic presentation is that given by Wallace (1981) of the reconstructed eighteenth century township of Williamsburg in Virginia. He notes that the original presentation as formulated by Rockefeller commemorated the planter elite in whom were seen to reside the timeless values of Americanism and who presided over a harmonious social order with no dirt, no signs of conflict and particularly no reference to the fact that half of Williamsburg's population in the eighteenth century were black slaves. Now, although slavery, black history and the existence of different classes have been nominally recognised, it is argued that presentation has remained at the level of surface phenomena such as productive techniques rather than exploring class relations or processes such as capitalism and trade union movements. Museum presentations thus select certain material for emphasis and remain silent on others in such a way as to falsify reality and become 'instruments of class hegemony' (Wallace 1981: 88). Leone has similarly analysed Williamsburg, seeing the presentation as naturalising the present social order by locating it in history (Leone 1973, 1981a). Museums thus become 'the empirical substantiation of national mythology' (Leone 1973: 129).

Meltzer's study of the National Air and Space Museum in Washington, DC uses what he sees as an explicitly Althusserian framework (Meltzer 1981). The concept of the Ideological State Apparatus is used to suggest that 'the museum contributes to the legitimization of the state by applauding its accomplishments and lauding its efforts and showing its future' (Meltzer 1981: 118).

In its presentations of the development of air and space technology over the past century, the museum is seen to naturalise and legitimise the ideas of change and progress, particularly by the way in which the American Dream is extended into space through its portrayal as the final frontier. Certain aspects of aviation development — those relating to the Korean and Vietnam wars — are excluded, in order to demonstrate that 'all is good, all has been good, and all always will be good' (*ibid*: 121). He argues that visitors collude in this view by touching the piece of moon rock that is displayed, an act he sees as a 'sanctification' of the extant order. In its role as an ideological state institution, the NASM is not all it seems: 'the museum is about air and space, but only on a superficial level: it is more properly about us' (*ibid*: 125).

Finally, an analysis of the cultural meaning of tourism and the museum visit is presented in Horne's *The Great Museum* (1984). He sees tourism as being chiefly concerned with the appropriation of the past as a commodity, which is reflected in the central role of purchase, especially of souvenirs, in tourism, which is seen as an experience 'drained of cultural meanings' (ibid: 249). In terms redolent of the Frankfurt School, he suggests that: 'A visit to a museum is a reaffirmation of the values of the industrial world, values reflected in the organised tour with its imposed order, its planned movement of bodies, its concern with time-tabling' (Horne 1984: 116).

From such a point of view, the past presented in museums is essentially meaningless, an experience in commodity form that is purchased by the tourist. It is also a commodity whose message propagates the dominant ideology. All tourists are portrayed as duped by this ideology, whose 'true' nature is only revealed to the analyst, and there appears to be no escape.

A reconsideration of the heritage debate

The examples cited above, and others (e.g Leone 1981b, Shanks and Tilley 1987), suffice to make the point that a dominant ideology thesis in the analysis of museum presentations does exist, whether it is couched in its original Marxist terms or in terms derived from the structural Marxism of Althusser. This thesis can be combined with arguments concerning the death of the past and its subsequent commodification as a meaningless heritage to portray museums and other institutions purveying representations of the past entirely in negative terms. This viewpoint of heritage is a fundamentally pessimistic one because its exponents can offer few solutions other than the adoption of 'a critical culture' (Hewison 1987: 144-6) or a more creative use of the past. These are themselves admitted to be dependent on wider changes in society, so that the analyses given can only serve as warnings. However, there are many reasons for taking issue with this analysis and suggesting that the situation may not be as bleak as it seems. This is principally because such an analysis only presents one side of the story, which are outsider analyses by critics of the production of the past. If we examine the other side of the story — through insider analysis of the consumption of the past by the public — we reveal a much more positive and potentially liberating role for museums and similar bodies.

The first objection that can be raised against the bleak analysis presented above is that it is based on an inadequate conception of the nature of the dominant ideology, both empirically and theoretically. Surveys show that museums are most likely to be visited by those who are of above average education and affluence. Those who would be considered to be 'the dominated' (the unemployed, certain sections of the elderly, those of low status, housewives) tend not to go to museums. The effectiveness of the dominant ideology in effecting social reproduction depends on its message being received and assimilated by all sections of the population. If the very group who are supposed to be kept in place by the dominant ideology do not go to museums, then their effectiveness as ideological institutions must be strongly questioned.

These doubts are supported by a number of penetrating theoretical and empirical criticisms of the dominant ideology thesis in general made by Abercrombie and his colleagues (1980). They suggest that the role of the dominant ideology in maintaining class hierarchy has been consistently over-emphasised. In particular, it is argued that political stability is maintained primarily by 'the dull compulsion of economic relations', i.e. the fact that the system, on which workers depend for their wage, relies on their conformity. They thus have a vested interest in maintaining the existing system of production. In addition, other stabilising factors include the reforms that have made large sections of the working class relatively affluent, the disciplinary threat of the police and courts, the bad image of Soviet-style communism and the failure of the working class to integrate politically.

Though the agencies of ideological transmission are well developed, there is a considerable body of evidence to show that they do not incorporate all groups as successfully as they are seen to do by many theorists. Work on youth subcultures, for example, demonstrates the existence of ideologies oppositional to the dominant ideology (Hall *et al.* 1976, Willis 1977). The coherence of the dominant ideology is thus greatly overestimated, as even the dominant class itself is fragmented into different economic interest groups. Abercrombie and his colleagues are finally only prepared to accord dominant ideology the role of incompletely binding together a section of the dominant class.

As with the arguments that the past is a meaningless heritage commodity, the inherent portrayal in the dominant ideology thesis of the public as unthinking dupes is a symptom of a much wider failure in functionalist social theory to accommodate the role of the sentient individual in social practice (Giddens 1979: 5). The implication of the approach is that all members of the public have the same reason for visiting museums and that all receive and similarly assimilate the messages contained in its presentations. Not only is this theoretically inadequate, it has strong political implications because 'it implies a derogation of the lay actor' (Giddens 1979: 71). As Wright has written: 'If the culture of the nation is only so much wool, then the eyes over which it is pulled must belong to sheep. And so everything disappears, except the possibility of farming' (Wright 1985: 5).

Rejection of the dominant ideology thesis for museums does not, however, mean that museums can no longer be considered as ideological institutions. It is perfectly possible to argue that all representations of the past are ideological in that they do not represent universal truths. Indeed, one can broadly agree with some of the above critiques of presentations of the past without detracting from the essential point about the non-universal nature of the dominant ideology. Rather, the evidence suggests that the dominant ideology is restricted to the dominant, who tend to be the sort of people who regularly visit museums. We therefore have to reconsider the ideological role of the museum, which now seems not to be to inculcate general obeisance to the dominant order, but in some way to bind members of the dominant stratum together.

The root of the problems with all of these arguments lies in an unthinking transfer of theories of the *production* and dissemination of the past to its *consumption*. If it is agreed that 'all social actors, no matter how lowly, have some degree of penetration of the social forms which oppress them' (Giddens 1979: 72), then it is clear that a more accurate theory of the use of the past has to focus on the consumption of the past rather than on its production, and this theory has to take into account the possibility of creative individual action, i.e. that people might see the past and use its presentations in different ways.

Concepts of the death of the past and of its consequent commodification have both been over-emphasised in the literature because they ignore the different and creative ways in which individuals construct their own past from their personal experience and memories, and from the materials, such as museum presentations, that are given to them by others. This raises the exciting possibility that museums and other similar institutions promoting a non-commercial representation of the past based on the positive values of stewardship and scholarship, might have a vital role to play in providing materials for people to creatively construct the past. To explore this possibility we must begin by examining how people view the past and what a sense of the past means to them in their lives.

3 The past as discourse

'Those who talk of the past as "dead" fail to recognise its organic nature and to appreciate that, despite its physical existence as monuments and muniments, essentially it lives in the mind' (Fowler 1981: 67).

In his classic work on historical method, E.H. Carr (1961) argued that history is 'a continuous process of interaction between the historian and his facts, an unending dialogue between the present and the past'. To illustrate this point, as many before and since him, he noted how both the personal background of individual historians and the wider social circumstances of which they are a part, affect the kind of past that they write. While there can be basic agreement about core 'facts' in history, the selection of historical evidence and its interpretation have always been a source of debate and have always changed through time. There is thus no single objectively true history: indeed the number of different sub-fields of enquiry currently existing in history can scarcely have been greater.

Responsible academic historians may pursue their particular specialisms in, for example, industrial or constitutional history, but they will probably agree on certain key elements which consensus will designate as to all intents and purposes 'objective', and will conduct their arguments according to the conventions of scholarly debate. Others, however, may not be so rigorous, and a certain 'fuzziness' as to what constitutes legitimate representation of the past has led to its being used in unusual ways (some deliberately manipulative) which have revealed the aims and circumstances of those putting forward the interpretation. At its worst, the malleability of the past has led to its distortion for political propaganda purposes by, for example, the Nazis as a legitimation of their expansionism (Arnold 1990, Clark 1947). The study of the re-use of the past by subsequent generations has become a field in itself, which encompasses anything from the forgery of the grave of King Arthur by medieval monks at Glastonbury, to the invention of recent 'traditions' of behaviour (Hobsbawm and Ranger 1983). In other words, it is possible to analyse history, and the past in general, as a form of unconscious discourse about the present, which may reveal just as much, if not more, about current concerns as it reveals about the past.

Indeed, scrutiny now at some distance in time invariably shows that attitudes to the past demonstrated in the last century or earlier directly reflected the different aspirations of different groups of people. Dellheim, in his study of the various uses of the medieval past in Victorian England (1983) shows clearly that restorations of the past can be masks for innovations just as much as they can express a desire to escape from the present. The Gothic style of architecture used on Manchester Town Hall and on the Bradford Wool Exchange, for example, can be seen as an attempt to invest the institutions of the industrial bourgeoisie with historical weight and dignity. For this group, the appropriation of the past in the form of architecture and in other activities such as genealogy and antiquarianism was one way of legitimating their new status. By identifying the institutions of the present with the past, a myth of historic continuity was preserved and progress was made to appear inevitable and valuable. In this sense, 'these links to the past were bridges to the future more than detours from the present' (Dellheim 1983: 31).

These insights revealed at some distance from the present show that what we think about the past is also a reflection of current concerns. In other words, our images of the past are just as much a discourse about contemporary life as they are about what the past was 'really' like. In the sections below, various aspects of this past-present linkage are examined.

Popular images of the past

As a prelude to seeking to understand the social role played by heritage and visiting heritage attractions, we must attempt to understand the role played more generally by the past in people's lives. While we may not be able to pinpoint the diverse derivations of people's images of the past, we can at least attempt to understand how people view the past and try to examine the importance people place on it. If people's images of the past express something about the way they feel about the present, it could be that their visiting or rejection of representations of the past in museums may fulfil a similar role, or alternatively they might be entirely unrelated. At a more practical level, it is only by finding out the content of people's images of the past that we can begin to assess where misconceptions lie and where approaches to the exhibition of the past might be modified.

In fact, the ways in which ordinary people think about the past, and the extent to which their images of the past may reflect their contemporary concerns, is an area that has been relatively neglected. The little work that has been done has principally been conducted in the field of environmental psychology, the framework in which the work of Tuan (1974) on landscape perception and of Morris (1981) on townscape images has been developed. One of the most influential methodological pieces of work in this area has been conducted by McKechnie (1974) who developed a set of environmental 'dispositions', amongst which was an 'antiquarianism' or 'environmental nostalgia' scale. This was characterised by, for example, approval of older buildings rather than modern ones, an enjoyment of antiques and collecting, and a liking of historical places. He found that people scoring high on the environmental nostalgia scale tended to be young rather than old, and to indulge in artistic, intellectual and cultural pursuits in their leisure time.

Taylor and Konrad (1980) used McKechnie's findings as a starting point to explore public dispositions towards the past in more detail, by means of a general population survey of residents of the Toronto area (1214 in total). The respondents were asked to indicate their level of agreement or disagreement with various statements about the past and its physical remains. Analysis of the answers to these statements isolated four basic areas: the conservation of (pre)historical resources, appreciation of the past as cultural heritage, appreciation of direct experience of the past, and general interest in the past, all of which were rated positively by most respondents.

A different and more far-reaching approach has been adopted by Szacka (1972) as part of a wider project on historical consciousness in Poland (conducted in 1965). Her survey consisted of 12,855 questionnaires sent by post to university-educated people, of which only 26 per cent were returned. Her results are thus not representative of all Polish people, but of a segment of the better-educated and more articulate population, which was her intention. From the answers to questions such as 'If you had the choice, when would you choose to live?' and 'Do you think that a knowledge of history is necessary to contemporary man?', she isolated two different orientations to the past. In the first, 'historicist' orientation towards the past, interest in earlier periods of history is combined with interest in the twentieth century (Szacka 1972: 68). Here, conception of time is linear, and there is a clear continuity and link between past and present.

The second, which she labels 'escapist' is primarily expressed by a desire to live in some time other than the present, either long ago or in the future. In this orientation, the past is imbued with values not found in the present: people subscribing to this view feel that, for example, people were happier, better off, more free, and individuals were more valued. In particular, no great interest is shown in historical knowledge, and some breach in continuity is observable between past and present, suggesting to Szacka that the present is not a continuation, but a negation of the past (1972: 69). Concepts of time amongst this group seem to be mythical, and oppositional to the generally accepted linear view of time.

Szacka's research is significant because it clearly shows that images of the past can be idealized even if they contradict the accepted historical wisdom, such that 'the past is endowed with values which the respondent longs to enjoy but cannot find in the present' (Szacka 1972: 66). This serves to demonstrate that what may be expressed in the content of individuals' ideas about the past is a veiled discourse about the present, because it is only in relation to the present that the past can be formulated, and generally the latter must serve as a contrast to highlight attributes of the former. This is very close to Davis's analysis of nostalgia (1979). He traces the development of the term, coined from the Greek 'nostos' and 'algia' ('a painful yearning to return home') in the late seventeenth century by the Swiss physician Johannes Hofer to describe the condition of Swiss mercenaries fighting far from their native land. Davis points out that, in contrast to 'antiquarian feeling', nostalgia expresses a *personal* relationship to the past. Like all relationships to the past, it of necessity encompasses some inner dialogue between past and present, and in the case of nostalgia, it is always the past which is viewed in a more favourable light than the present. Nostalgia therefore expresses something quite powerful about an individual's feelings about the present in relationship to their feelings about the past.

In Britain, a first attempt at linking public attitudes to the past with contemporary concerns was made by Ian Hodder and a group of colleagues. Their survey was carried out in Cambridge, Southampton, York and Lancaster, and 301 interviews were completed (Stone 1986: 16). Hodder reports that when people were asked about their views of the past, they immediately compared it with the present. The great majority of the sample (70 per cent) felt that people needed to know about the distant past, but many had quite ambivalent attitudes, recognising the advantages of modern technology while at the same time feeling that change was happening too fast and people were losing a sense of place in the world (Hodder 1986: 167-8). He concludes that individuals are not duped by a dominant ideology because people view the past in many different ways, and argues that 'the past as constructed and experienced in contemporary life may reveal as much about the present as it masks' (*ibid*: 167).

While these conclusions are stimulating, there are a number of problems concerning the representativeness of the survey, as Stone (1986: 15-16) notes. It was conducted in university towns with a strong archaeological presence, so the opinions may not be representative of people in the country as a whole. In addition, the sample taken was small, the quality of the interviews was variable, the sampling was not truly random, and statistical analysis was made difficult by the use of open-ended questions. As a result, the conclusions of the survey can only be regarded as tentative propositions to be investigated further. The larger-scale survey reported here was in part designed to explore the validity of the results of Hodder and his colleagues on a national scale.

Survey Results

Value put on the past

The first attitude that must be established as a fundamental baseline in such a study is the value that the public puts on knowing about the past, and by implication, their level of interest in the past as a whole. If a large proportion of the population places a low value on knowing about the past, then we must attribute other motives to the expansion in visits to museums and other heritage presentations, and non-visiting might simply be explained by lack of interest.

In fact, 79 per cent of respondents thought that the past was definitely worth knowing about and 12 per cent thought it 'probably' worth knowing about (Table 3.1). The middle age group (those aged 35-59) most enthusiastically endorsed the value of knowing about the past, while those aged sixty and over or under thirty-five were more likely to express reservations. Nevertheless, in all age groups, those placing little or no value on the past were in a small minority. A similar range of opinion was found by respondents' status, with 9 per cent of low status respondents who are over 60 feeling that it is not worth knowing about the past (while 68 per cent feel it definitely is worth knowing about).

Table 3.1 Attitudes to the value of knowing about the past, by age and status

	'Do you think it is worth knowing about the past?'					
	Definitely	Probably	Perhaps	No	(%)	N
Age (%)						
< 35	77	14	7	1	100	300
35–59	83	10	4	3	100	375
> 60	73	14	7	7	100	259
Status (%)						
High	86	7	4	2	100	149
Middle	79	12	5	3	100	602
Low < 60	73	17	8	2	100	83
Low > 60	68	17	6	9	100	81
All (%)	79	12	6	4	100	934

This finding confirms the much smaller scale results of Hodder and his colleagues, and Taylor and Konrad's finding amongst the Toronto public that 54 per cent strongly disagreed with the statement that 'The past is not worth saving' (Taylor and Konrad 1980: 302). The confirmation of an interest in the past amongst the vast majority of the population, even those of low status, is important in the context of the rest of this work, first because it suggests that what might be called 'the turn to the past', expressed by the millions of visits to presentations of the past, is a genuine phenomenon, born out of real needs and interests, and not simply the result of a mass persuasion of people to visit by successful marketing strategies. Second, and most important, it suggests that non-visiting of museums and other organisations cannot be entirely explained by lack of interest in the past.

Reasons for studying the past

Having established that the great majority of people value knowing about the past, we need to know next why people feel it is worth knowing about. In gauging this, an open-ended question, 'What do you think is the main reason for studying the past?' was asked in order to gain unprompted responses. In attempting to make sense of these, the overall answers can be distilled into three categories, which can be described as present-, past- and future-oriented respectively. Categorisation was a difficult task, because of the great variety amongst the 961 answers given, and the fact that many people gave several different answers. What are presented, then, are subjective groupings devised by the researcher for purposes of analysis and they should be treated only as a rough guide to attitudes (Table 3.2).

Table 3.2 Reasons for studying the past

'What do you think is the main reason for studying the past?'		
Frequencies	**%**	**N**
To understand the present and how we got here	49	382
For curiosity, knowledge of 'life in the past'	43	336
To learn from our mistakes and predict the future	26	205
Other reasons	4	38

(Percentages add up to over 100 because many respondents gave more than one answer)

The first, present-oriented, group of answers, expressed by half of the respondents, suggests that the main reason for studying the past is to orientate people in the present. The study of the past and the exploration of historical roots is valued by many because it gives a sense of stability in their lives. A selection of verbatim responses is given here to capture the variation in replies:

- 'The past is the key to the present'
- 'Comparison with present day'
- 'To discover what made the world the place it is now'
- 'To establish origins and the development of humanness'
- 'To understand formation of society today'
- 'So we know where we came from'
- 'One must know of the past to appreciate the present'
- 'Without a knowledge of the past you are living in a vacuum'
- 'Increased understanding'
- 'As background for today & interesting in its own right'

Almost as frequently mentioned (by 43 per cent of respondents) is the belief that we should know about the past for no particular purpose other than innate interest and sheer curiosity about what life was like then. This can be labelled a 'past-oriented' reason for knowing about the past:

- 'Curiosity'
- 'It is interesting for us to know what happened in the past'
- 'To find out about places and people who lived years ago'
- 'Interest'
- 'Because man's curiosity will never be satisfied'
- 'It is worth learning how people in the past did things'
- 'To know more about history and what happened years before our time'
- 'It is nice too know how people lived like, and too know what their lived in and the things they used'
- 'Curiosity about the past'
- 'See how people lived'

Finally, a quarter of the respondents felt that studying the past has the definite pragmatic purpose of helping society to plan the future (future-oriented reasons). The idea that history can instruct humanity about the future, by providing models, in particular for bad situations to avoid, is a current that runs deep in public perceptions of the value of history, and is contradictory to the views of the majority of historians who have abandoned the idea of a moral and instructive role for history. Typical responses are as follows:

- 'To help the future'
- 'To learn for the future'
- 'Because lessons can be learned'
- 'To enable us to make a *better* future'
- 'To see where we went wrong'
- 'To gain knowledge to help in the future'
- 'We need to know our past history in order to re-arrange the course of our future'
- 'To learn from our mistakes'
- 'With knowing the past helps the future'
- 'Ideally that we should learn from the struggles of past civilisations the way to a more harmonious existence with our fellow men'

The present- and future-oriented groups of responses therefore see knowledge of the past as bringing definite benefits to the individual or the community, while the other group sees it as an end in itself, for pure knowledge devoid of any functional purpose.

These different responses are by no means mutually exclusive, and the fact that many people gave several replies to the question shows that present-, past- and future- orientations can coexist within a single individual. There was no significant variation in these attitudes amongst the various demographic indicators used. This may be an effect of collapsing the actual answers into three main categories with a consequent loss of their variability, and also an indication that many respondents may subscribe to all three views. Later in this chapter, when a greater range of views are studied, it is shown that significant variations in approaches to the past do exist, with, for example, higher status people being more present- and future- oriented than past-oriented.

The public thus exhibit an overwhelming agreement that the past is worth knowing about and put forward a variety of reasons for knowing about it, the majority of which suggest that history provides useful knowledge in showing people how we arrived at the present, and providing lessons for the future. We can now start to weigh up some of the issues outlined at the beginning of the chapter by examining the actual content of people's images of life in the past.

Images of life in the past

The source of people's images of the past is a huge research topic in itself, and one that is not guaranteed success if only for the reason that most people find it very difficult to pinpoint the source of any long-held ideas or attitudes. Among the influences on attitude formation in general are family, peer group, teachers, and media. It is media images of the past that are most often selected for study and usually approbation, as they are more concrete than verbal attitudes passed on by friends and relatives. Typical instances that could be cited of film images of the past are 'medieval' knights from Hollywood, Raquel Welch's famous anachronistic portrayal of a prehistoric woman in leather bikini fleeing from dinosaurs in 'One Million Years BC', Egyptian mummies in horror films, and the Indiana Jones series. On television many series have been set just before the Second World War when, it is implied, deference and tradition still ensured that everyone knew their place. Much contemporary advertising refers to the past in unashamed soft-focused romanticism in seeking to imbue new products with the authority of the past. Most critics have indeed focused on the inaccurate portrayal of the past as a happy, romantic place by such advertisers and other heritage merchants (Hewison 1987, Wright 1985). If their arguments were correct we would expect the public's attitudes to the past to be primarily nostalgic: the past would be seen as something 'other', something bearing little relation to the present, but viewed as a time when life was better in many ways than it is now. The questions designed to examine this proposition, however, elicited answers which clearly showed that these views are unfounded, and highlighted the danger of treating the public as passive receptacles for ideological messages.

The first three questions were open-ended, respondents were asked to put themselves in the position of 'the ordinary person', and 'the past' was given the explicit definition of 'any time from before your grandparents were alive, as far back as the first people'. These criteria were put forward in an attempt to gain a general non-personal image of the past unfiltered by respondents' own experiences and memories; accordingly 'the past' was set in a time with which they have had no personal contact. As might have been expected from previous work, however, the answers given strongly suggest that people's images of the past are primarily coloured by their own personal experiences. This is no doubt inevitable in the process of thinking about the past because, although the sources of individuals' images of the past are many and varied, in order to be assimilated they must mean something to the individual, and so the most powerful ones must be those that fit in with personal experiences. Again, the answers to the open-ended questions were difficult to use statistically, and had to be classified for purposes of analysis according to convenient categories devised by the researcher.

The broad categories of answer are laid out in Table 3.3, where each category comprises the percentage of total respondents mentioning the category. The most surprising finding was that the images of the past articulated by most people (82 per cent of respondents mentioned it) were overwhelmingly negative. Specific negative aspects of the past that were mentioned repeatedly included hard physical toil, the threat of violence, the prevalence of disease, the difficulty of obtaining food, and the continual struggle for survival. In addition, a quarter of those replying noted the lack of amenities taken for granted today such as medical care, sanitation, electricity and mechanised transport. The existence of poverty, greater social divisions,

Table 3.3 General images of life in the past

'Please describe what you think life in the past was like for the ordinary person'		
Frequencies	(%)	N
Hardness of life in general	82	705
Lack of modern amenities	25	211
Poverty	13	110
Lack of personal fulfilment	8	23
Greater social divisions	7	61
Short Life	5	44
Poor education	3	23
Various positive aspects	43	365

(Percentages add up to over 100 because many respondents gave more than one answer)

poor education and the lack of ability to get on in life were also frequently mentioned. A random selection of verbatim responses is given below to indicate the range of answers given to the question on what life was like in the past for the ordinary person:

- 'Hard manual graft for little mony or food, very good craftmanship'
- 'Physically more demanding and unsure'
- 'The ordinary person worked very hard. Family was very important also the neighbours helped each other in times of need. Life was slower people much more contented'.
- 'Dark, life nowadays is made so much easier by mechanization'
- 'Longer hours at work less pay very hard on the women to make ends meet'
- 'Life must have been very hard with no medication, light and sanitation'
- 'Very hard and unrewarding'
- 'The ordinary person had to work very hard to maintain a bare existence'
- 'Extremely bad, lack of dignity and poor education'
- 'Long hours of labour and very hard times'
- 'Hard, poor, cold, dirty'

These negative images are confirmed and amplified by the answers to a question specifically aimed at gauging the worst aspects of life in the past (Table A2.1). The most frequently mentioned theme (noted by a third of all respondents) was the lack of medical facilities and the consequent prevalence of illness and shorter life expectancy. This was followed by the problems of poverty and hunger (28 per cent), the absence of modern amenities (25 per cent) and social exploitation (24 per cent).

Although the disadvantages of life in the past accounted for the majority of responses, many people felt at the same time that it held a number of advantages over that in the present. In Table 3.3 these were classified together as they were very varied. They often revealed an ambivalence towards life in the past, expressed by such phrases as 'hard work, little money, but family ties [closer] and happy'. In order to explore specifically the issue of nostalgic images of the past, another question asked respondents to suggest what they thought the best thing about life in the past was. A selection of verbatim responses to the question on the best thing about life in the past is as follows:

- 'Family's were a lot closer'
- 'Very little poloution'
- 'There were few or no cars'
- 'Life was at a slower pace'
- 'Common bond of neighbourliness'
- 'Less emphasis was placed on money earned'
- 'The rate of change, both technically and socially, was slower and meant a greater degree of stability'
- 'There was no nuclear weapons'
- 'Life was simple with no economic worry'
- 'Values were higher'

When all answers were combined into discrete categories, two main themes stood out (Table 3.4). The feeling that life in the past was peaceful and ordered, so that everybody knew their allotted place (for example, 'people were more contented with their lot') was mentioned by 38 per cent of respondents, and a third felt that family and community ties were much closer (for example, 'everyone got on better with each other'). The other main issues mentioned were the feeling that the environment was less polluted and built-upon, and that personal and spiritual values such as honesty, respect and piety were greater.

These unprompted answers clearly show that, aside from the qualifications noted above, the vast majority of attitudes to the past are not of a nostalgic or a romantic nature. Almost all of those questioned have a generally hard-headed attitude to what they see as the harshness and squalor of the past and would not like to live in any time other than the present. Another of the preliminary findings of Hodder's survey is also confirmed in that people instinctively and inevitably compare and contrast the present with the past in their answers. Images of the past are very frequently couched in terms of the absence of certain things which are valued in the present, such as material comforts, or

Table 3.4 Favourable images of the past

'The best thing about life in the past was that...'		
Frequencies	(%)	N
Life was peaceful and ordered	38	294
Closer relations amongst family and community	33	255
Environment was less spoiled	13	100
Personal and spiritual values were greater	11	85
Other	14	110

(Percentages add up to over 100 because many respondents gave more than one answer)

people see in it elements which are perceived to be missing from the present, such as closer family relationships or a harmonious environment. Thus images of the past directly reflect current social and political concerns such as those expressed by the Green movement, the Church, and pressure groups from all hues of the political spectrum. The past is a resource, not just in material terms (buildings, monuments and so on) but also in imaginative terms; in the way it can express ideas, hopes and fears, and as such it can mean a great deal of different things to different people. One important way in which the past is used, as Szacka has suggested, is as a contrast with the present, allowing people to assess their relative well-being. It seems that for most people the advantages of the present outweigh the disadvantages.

Relationship of attitudes to the past to current position

If it is true that people use their images of the past as an unconscious way of orienting themselves in the present, it would be expected that people's images differ according to their circumstances in the present: those who are in a fortunate position might be expected to see the past less favourably than those who are in a less fortunate position.

The most significant differences in images of the past are reflected in people's current age and status. The youngest age group is more likely than other age groups, especially the elderly, to mention the absence of the material advantages which they enjoy today such as medical care and amenities such as electricity, plumbing and transport; those of high status mention the same things. These attitudes are most clearly seen in feelings about the worst aspects of the past (Table 3.5) but are also demonstrated in general images of life in the past (Table 3.6). For both groups, images seem to be centred on how their personal lives would be materially changed for the worse if they lived in the past. For those under 35 this might be a reflection of their relative youth and their orientation to the future (see below). In the case of those of high status the

Table 3.5 The worst thing about life in the past, by age and status

	'The worst thing about life in the past was that...'						
	Age (%)			**Status** (%)			
	<35	35-59	>60	High	Middle	Low <60	Low >60
Illness, death, lack of medicine	40	35	20	37	33	32	20
Poverty and lack of food	23	24	40	23	28	27	38
Lack of modern amenities	28	23	24	32	25	12	23
Exploitation	20	24	29	19	24	22	35
General hardness of life	7	10	6	4	8	15	8
Other	9	14	16	20	11	12	15

past seems to be viewed unfavourably as representing the loss of those aspects of their present life which they most value.

In contrast, when asked about the worst aspects of life in the past, the elderly were more likely than other age groups to mention general poverty, lack of food and social exploitation (Table 3.5). These were similarly noted by those of low

Table 3.6 General images of life in the past, by status

	'Please describe what you think life in the past was like for the ordinary person'			
	Status (%)			
	High	Middle	Low <60	Low >60
Hardness	87	83	82	67
Lack of modern amenities	40	25	13	21
Poverty	14	13	7	14
Social divisions	5	9	7	5
Lack of fulfilment	10	7	13	12
Poor education	3	2	2	7
Shorter life	6	4	7	5
Positive aspects	50	41	38	56

(Percentages add up to over 100 because many respondents gave more than one answer)

status, who in their general images of the past were also slightly more likely to mention the lack of opportunities for education and personal fulfilment, although the differences are not statistically significant (Table 3.6).

The sort of images likely to be held by the elderly and those of low status are things that they might themselves have had experience of, and might have seen alleviated in their own lifetime. Being elderly and/or of low status, they are less likely to have the advantage of modern comforts enjoyed by other groups, and they are more likely to suffer from poor health (OPCS 1990: 60), which is why they are less likely to see life in the past as characterised by illness and a lack of modern conveniences. As Szacka's work has already suggested, the most prominent images of the past, rather than being a direct reflection of the present, seem to be those which most strongly contrast with it.

In view of this, it is not surprising that the elderly are least likely to stress the negative aspects of the past and most likely to point out the positive qualities that were also to be found in it (Table 3.6). When asked specifically about the best aspects of life in the past, both the elderly and those of low status agreed in stressing the warmth and closeness of family relationships and the feeling that personal values were higher (Table 3.7).

Table 3.7 Best thing about life in the past, by age and status

| | 'The best thing about life in the past was that...' | | | | | | |
| | **Age** (%) | | | **Status** (%) | | | |
	<35	35-59	>60	High	Middle	Low <60	Low >60
Life peaceful and ordered	36	40	38	46	39	28	32
Closer personal relationships	25	34	41	30	33	19	50
Environment less spoiled	16	14	8	15	13	17	8
Higher personal values	10	9	16	8	10	14	26
Other	22	12	10	12	16	22	3

In contrast, those of high status were far more likely to stress that life in the past was more ordered and peaceful than that of today (as were the 'establishment' middle age group). For such dominant groups a return to a time when everyone knew their place and there was deference to the established order is no doubt an attractive proposition: the fact that they are most likely to mention it as the best aspect of life in the past shows that it is perceived to be a problem in the present.

As has been mentioned, the answers to these open-ended questions are difficult to use in statistical terms because of the great range of variation masked by the broad categories used for analysis. In order to check some of the patterns evident in the answers to these questions, it is therefore useful to compare them with answers to a series of closed statements on a similar range of subjects (mostly chosen verbatim from the initial exploratory interviews) which respondents were asked to evaluate. These clearly show how favourable or unfavourable images of the past are influenced by individuals' feelings about their present situation.

For example, 68 per cent of the elderly thought it true to some extent that people were actually happier in the past, compared with only 37 per cent of those under 35. Almost exactly the same differences were shown between high and low status respondents (Table 3. 8). Similarly, the elderly and those of low status were far more likely than anyone else to think it true that there was less crime in the past, that life was more peaceful, and that families were much closer (Tables 3.9-11).

Table 3.8 Attitudes to whether 'people were generally happier' in the past, by age and status

	True	— | —	Neither	— | —	False	(%)	N
Age (%)							
<35	16	21	36	16	11	100	295
35–59	19	24	33	12	12	100	355
>60	55	13	14	8	9	100	276
Status (%)							
High	16	20	38	14	11	100	146
Middle	24	21	30	14	11	100	588
Low <60	28	17	28	11	17	100	81
Low >60	72	14	4	2	8	100	86
All (%)	28	20	29	13	11	100	918

Table 3.9 Attitudes to whether 'there was less crime' in the past, by age and status

	True	— | —	Neither	— | —	False	(%)	N
Age (%)							
<35	25	20	17	22	17	100	300
35–59	29	24	23	15	9	100	361
>60	55	17	10	8	10	100	264
Status (%)							
High	19	21	21	25	15	100	146
Middle	31	22	19	16	12	100	593
Low <60	42	17	15	10	17	100	83
Low >60	73	16	4	2	6	100	88
All (%)	35	21	17	16	12	100	926

Table 3.10 Attitudes to whether 'life was more peaceful' in the past, by age and status

	True	— | —	Neither	— | —	False	(%)	N
Age (%)							
<35	24	21	21	24	9	100	300
35–59	36	26	17	12	9	100	358
60+	62	14	9	6	9	100	261
Status (%)							
High	28	27	21	18	7	100	147
Middle	36	22	19	15	8	100	589
Low <60	34	21	9	19	17	100	81
Low >60	82	8	–	4	6	100	86
All (%)	39	21	16	14	9	100	922

Table 3.11 Attitudes to whether 'the family was closer' in the past, by age and status

	True	— | —	Neither	— | —	False	(%)	N
Age (%)							
<35	56	27	11	4	2	100	300
35–59	68	23	6	2	1	100	363
>60	86	10	2	–	2	100	261
Status (%)							
High	62	31	4	2	1	100	146
Middle	66	21	8	3	1	100	596
Low <60	73	23	4	–	–	100	83
Low >60	96	2	–	–	2	100	85
All (%)	69	21	6	2	1	100	926

The strength of these associations shows that different social groups can hold quite different perspectives on the past. The elderly, for example, whilst also acknowledging the hardship in the past, seem to see the past in a much more favourable light than the young, as a place of happiness and closer relationships. Their belief, for example, that families were closer in the past shows that this is one of the things whose absence they most feel in the present. The elderly also fear crime more than any other group (Hough and Mayhew 1983: 22-25) and seem to see the past as a haven of peace and security from such worries. It is interesting to speculate whether the differences in replies between young and old is a period effect (due to the time they were born into) or a biological age effect (which would imply that the young might change their views as they become older) but a longitudinal study would be required to ascertain this.

Thus, the less-privileged are likely to see the past as a time in which current anxieties and disappointments would not have existed, while the more privileged are much less willing to accord it such a role. For those who are in some ways disadvantaged in the present one role of the past seems to be as a source of covert, probably unconscious, criticism of the present for its perceived absence of certain valued qualities. At the same time, images of life in the past can serve as a refuge from these very problems: criticism and escape are closely linked.

So far, then, the survey has shown that most attitudes to the past are far from nostalgic. There is also no evidence that the past is a meaningless heritage commodity. Instead, the ways in which people view the past seem to be very varied, and their images play a very active role in the way in which they come to terms with their own lives.

Attitudes to the present and future

As well as gauging attitudes to the past, it is necessary to investigate people's feelings about the present as a control. In particular, gauging attitudes to technology and progress is important because of the way in which the past has been used to affirm the march of progress (Hobsbawm 1972: 11, Shils 1981: 88) and because, as noted earlier, faith in technological rationality and belief in progress has been seen as one of the ideological cornerstones of modern society (Horkheimer and Adorno 1973: 130, Marcuse 1968: 12).

If a progressive and instrumental ideology, as outlined in Chapter 2, were widespread, one would expect to find a firm belief in progress and a strong endorsement of the value of science and industry amongst all sections of society. The survey shows however that attitudes are ambivalent and strongly influenced by current social position.

Progress When given the choice, almost all respondents would prefer to live in the present than in any other period in the past. They were asked to indicate the desirability of living in different historical periods and, although the periods were jumbled up in the question, the answers came out in exact

Table 3.12 Rank order of attractiveness of different periods

'Please put these periods in order, depending on how much you would like to live in them'
1. The Present
2. Victorian Period
3. Elizabethan Period
4. Middle Ages
5. Roman Period
6. Prehistoric Period

chronological order (Table 3.12). This would seem to be a clear confirmation of general public endorsement of the concept of progress.

The fact that attitudes to the past were predominantly unfavourable, and that people felt that the more recent the period, the more desirable it was to live in, might suggest that the ideology of progress is successfully preached amongst the public. Whether or not 'progress' has occurred is not at issue here, not least because of the difficulties that would be associated with its definition and measurement. However, it is important to investigate the extent to which people *believe* in progress because of its effect of legitimating the current social system. It is also relevant to studies of the past because progress can only be gauged by reference to history. In fact, the findings revealed evidence that individuals can and do hold mutually inconsistent attitudes to the past without any great 'cognitive dissonance' (Festinger 1957). Those who tend to exhibit some degree of romanticism in their images of the past can also seem to affirm ideas of progress, and those who tend to be more unfavourable in their images can also question the idea of progress. This seeming contradiction is explored below.

The majority of people (54 per cent) agreed with the statement 'mankind is always progressing to better things', compared with 35 per cent who disagreed. Crosstabulations with the age and status variables produced no

Table 3.13 Attitudes to progress, by age, status and education

	'Mankind is always progressing to better things'						
	Strongly Agree	Agree	Neither	Disagree	Strongly Disagree	(%)	N
Age (%)							
<35	14	38	12	27	8	100	300
35–59	11	40	11	30	7	100	366
>60	18	40	11	26	5	100	265
Status (%)							
High	14	35	15	32	5	100	147
Middle	14	39	11	28	8	100	601
Low <60	15	46	10	25	4	100	83
Low >60	16	46	10	22	6	100	86
Education (%)							
Received minimum	15	41	9	27	8	100	637
Stayed on at school	13	38	10	36	3	100	103
Received tertiary education	10	34	21	28	7	100	170
All (%)	14	40	12	28	7	100	935

significant variation, although in percentage terms the elderly and those of low status were actually more likely to agree than other groups (Table 3.13). The only variable that produced significant results was that of education, with those who had received the minimum formal education most likely to believe in progress.

These results are somewhat surprising bearing in mind the attitudes to the past revealed by the survey. It might have been expected that those of high status, tending to have unfavourable images of the past and being well-off in the present, would be most likely to endorse the idea of progress enthusiastically. Instead, it is more likely to be believed in by those who are worst-off in the present, and who are more likely to have romantic images of the past.

One way of explaining this would be to suggest that those of low status are being successfully duped by an ideology of progress, while those of higher status, being better educated, take a broader view and realise that in many ways progress has not necessarily been a linear phenomenon.

However, this apparent affirmation of progress by the least privileged seems to be contradicted by answers to another question. Low status respondents are over three times more likely than those of high status to agree that 'the lot of the average person is getting worse, not better' (Table 3.14). Those with minimum education are twice as likely to agree as those who went to university or college, and the elderly are also more likely to agree. This now suggests that

Table 3.14 Attitudes to the lot of the average person, by age, education and status

| | 'In spite of what people say, the lot of the average person is getting worse, not better' | | | | | | |
	Strongly agree	Agree	Neither	Disagree	Strongly disagree	(%)	N
Age (%)							
<35	12	31	16	32	8	100	98
35–59	12	29	12	38	9	100	369
>60	14	38	8	29	10	100	270
Education (%)							
Minimum	15	36	13	28	8	100	645
Stayed on at school	6	31	12	45	6	100	103
Tertiary	7	19	9	50	15	100	171
Status (%)							
High	5	15	11	55	15	100	148
Middle	12	34	12	34	8	100	604
Low <60	19	38	17	25	2	100	83
Low >60	19	48	12	12	10	100	90
All (%)	13	33	12	34	9	100	943

the ideology of progress is *not* successfully inculcated amongst dominated groups. This contradiction is best resolved if the answers to the questions are seen as evidence of genuinely inconsistent beliefs, with educational background producing an intervening effect.

There is considerable evidence from other surveys that non-dominant groups will answer personal and general questions from different frames of reference. Parkin isolates two levels of normative reference amongst subordinate classes, the 'abstract' and the 'situational'. He argues that questions posed in general and non-situational terms will produce findings that emphasise class consensus on values, because 'the moral standards and evaluations which make up the abstract framework originate within another, more powerful, social class' (Parkin 1972: 95); in other words they answer in the way they feel they *should* answer. Situational questions, on the other hand, produce evidence of a much more class-differentiated value system, because they are answered in personal terms[1].

It is likely that the answers to the question on progress are couched in abstract, global terms, and that those to the question on the lot of the average person are expressed in situational terms, i.e. from the individual's personal point of view. In general, then, it could be that the majority of people, irrespective of their circumstances, believe that the overall march of history has been progressive. The fact that those who have been to college are more likely to be unsure about progress may be a reflection of their longer education. They may be more aware of, and more able to articulate, doubts concerning progress because of, for example, the destruction of the global environment and the existence of chemical and nuclear weapons. It could however be that groups such as the elderly and those of low status are only paying lip service to dominant values here in giving the answer that they feel is expected from such a generalised question. They may be showing their real feelings in their answers to the question about the lot of the average person.

If this interpretation is taken together with the fact that non-dominant groups are more likely than others to have a romantic view of certain aspects of the past, it seems that a considerable body of people are not being duped by the ideology of progress, and are using their views of the past to indicate their dissatisfaction with their current lot. This confirms a similar tentative suggestion arising from Hodder's survey (Hodder 1986: 167). Therefore, even if producers of the past are held to be agents of the dominant ideology, their message is not being assimilated by all sections of the public. This confirms what was suspected earlier in a theoretical critique of the dominant ideology thesis: outsider analyses of productions of the past can argue convincingly that they act as agents of the dominant ideology, but an insider examination of the consumption of these productions of the past suggests that the ideology is not being assimilated. People are not dupes, but instead use the past in multifarious ways to suit their own particular needs and feelings about the world.

Technology The value of industrialisation to society is supported by nearly half of the public. 48 per cent thought life in the past was worse because there was less industry, but 36 per cent thought it was better for the same reason (Table

3.15). The only significant variation was with status. Those of low status, irrespective of their age, were more likely to think life in the past was better because there was less industry. This may be interpreted as indicating that those who most benefit from the products of industry (those of higher status) are most likely to endorse it, while those who have more contact (social or practical) with the process of industry are more likely to see its disadvantages. In this case, then, industrialization has not prevented either dissent or the conception that things can be different.

Table 3.15 Attitudes to whether life in the past was better or worse 'because there was less industry', by status

	A lot better	A little better	Not sure	A little worse	A lot worse	(%)	N
Status (%)							
High	10	24	15	30	23	100	145
Middle	10	25	16	26	24	100	599
Low <60	10	31	13	21	25	100	83
Low >60	26	15	17	22	20	100	80
All (%)	12	24	15	23	25	100	925

Table 3.16 Attitudes to whether life in the past was better or worse 'because there were no computers', by age

	A lot better	A little better	Not sure	A little worse	A lot worse	(%)	N
Age (%)							
<35	19	15	23	25	18	100	293
35–39	19	17	25	22	17	100	361
>60	42	17	22	9	9	100	256
All (%)	26	16	24	19	15	100	913

Respondents in fact gave clear indications that they felt technology was going too far, in their answers to a question about computers (Table 3.16). By far the most significant differences were found with age, with 59 per cent of the elderly feeling that life in the past had been better because there were no computers, compared with only 34 per cent of those under 35. The age effect was found to be so strong as to explain most of the status differences. For those over 60, who are much less likely than younger people to have had experience of computers, modern technology evidently is seen as incomprehensible and even threatening. In the face of such developments, the past may be seen as a haven of simpler life. To add support to this, those over 60 were significantly more likely to agree to the statement 'The rate of change in society is too fast these days' than those under 35 (77 compared with 58 per cent).

Relationship between attitudes to the past and present

The question now arises as to whether the attitudes to the past and present displayed here are individual and unrelated attitudes or whether they form part of wider belief systems. If the latter is true then it might be possible to characterise different social groups by their different orientations to the past and present, and then investigate whether these have an important influence on participation in heritage activities.

In order to examine this problem, the large number of attitudes have to be reduced to smaller groups based on a common theme. The technique used is factor analysis (Kim and Mueller 1978, Norusis 1985: 125-63)[2], and results of the regression analysis for attitudes to the past are presented in Table A2.2. They show that positive (favourable) attitudes to the past are associated with older age and lower status, and, conversely, that negative attitudes to the past are associated with young age and higher status. The analysis confirms that consistent attitudes to the past are held by different groups, and that the image held by non-dominant groups is more likely than that of other groups to include a favourable or nostalgic component.

Attitudes to the present are also consistently held. This time, however, the significant factors are status and sex, with age not having any significant independent effect (Table A2.3). A favourable attitude to the present is associated with males and those of higher status, while having an unfavourable attitude is associated with women and those of lower status. The possible reasons for this are explored in Chapter 7 where it is also shown that women are more likely to espouse non-sanctioned views of the past than men.

Finally, the generalised attitudes to the past and the present were considered together in a regression analysis in order to explore their interrelationship. This shows that people who have favourable attitudes to the present are likely to have unfavourable attitudes to the past, while those who have unfavourable attitudes to the present are likely to have more favourable attitudes to the past (Table A2.4), and confirms the role of the past in serving as a contrast by which to assess life in the present.

In assessing these analyses is should be borne in mind however that the 'attitude to the past' variable does not include the answers to the open-ended questions, which showed that the overall image of life in the past was of its unpleasantness. The attitudes presented here thus exist beneath an umbrella of overall unfavourable images. They do nevertheless demonstrate distinctly different tendencies in the conceptualisation of the past amongst different social groups, and show the existence of quite different ways of thinking about it.

Conclusions

Cumulatively the public's attitudes to the past and present as demonstrated in the survey have strong implications for the arguments about heritage summarised in the previous chapter. Contrary to the assertions of most writers, people's images of the past are not primarily of a nostalgic nature.

Almost all of those questioned have a generally unromantic attitude to what they perceive as the harshness and squalor of the past, and would not like to live in any time other than the present. This in turn might be interpreted as evidence that the ideology of progress is successfully inculcated amongst all sections of the population. The survey shows however that substantial parts of the population, especially those who are in less privileged positions, feel that, in personal terms, progress has not occurred. Whilst overall seeing the past as harsh, this group is also likely to see positive things in the past. This is not to deny, however, the existence and assimilation of an ideology of progress amongst the dominant sections of society.

The possible contradiction of the same individual having both favourable and unfavourable images of the past (with the latter dominant) can be most easily resolved once it is understood that attitudes to the past are only nominally about the past. They only have existence and meaning when considered alongside people's attitudes to the present, of which they are contrary reflections. As a return to the past is impossible, people reassure themselves by their belief that 'really' the past was much worse than the present and that they are better off now. Apart from the fact that they are less certain about the future, people essentially view the past in the same way that Dellheim feels that Victorians did: 'Few Victorians wanted to return to the past for more than a visit; but many found in their historic legacy a source of values and a sense of continuity that they used as signposts as they mapped out the road to the future'. (Dellheim 1983: 69).

In the case of current attitudes to the past, however, it seems that people find in their historic legacy not so much a sense of continuity as a sense of loss and a source of roots in a disorientating world. Broadly speaking, the attitudes to the past revealed in the survey can be divided into those that are concerned with personal qualities such as relationships and values, and those that are concerned with impersonal, material commodities. High status groups are more concerned with material things because this is what they would lose by a return to the past. In other words, their images of the past can be a projection of their fears: a return to the circumstances of the past would result in the loss of their current position. In their case ideas about the past may therefore be used as an affirmation of progress and a mental model of the problems they feel we have escaped from. Their dominant position can be legitimised, at least to themselves, by pointing to the harshness of the past.

Lower status groups, less likely to have the material advantages anyway, concentrate on the more personal aspects of the past. While they might not necessarily want to return to the past, they are more likely than other groups to see it in a more positive light, as a time when the disadvantages they have now, or the changes they perceive to have happened in their lifetimes, had not occurred. In this way their ideas about the past can be both a refuge from the present and at the same time a means of criticising it for the absence of certain values. Later chapters show that this is just one manifestation of two different ways of approaching the past that broadly characterise high and low status groups.

The survey evidence therefore suggests that, if the past is not a commodity and if attitudes to the past are not primarily nostalgic, the idea of 'the death of the past' should also be challenged. It is possible, indeed probable, that the experience of industrialisation and its attendant changes have caused severe social and environmental dislocations which have produced a great desire for the past. This past is however not merely a romantic source of comfort, neither is an experience of the past unattainable: the evidence of the survey suggests that the past still has meaning and relevance in people's everyday lives. The range of attitudes to the past expressed, and their clear variation along lines of age and status show that the past cannot simply be viewed as a meaningless heritage commodity to be bought and sold. Instead, because images of the past are personal and can be controlled by each individual they can be used as a form of discourse about the present. The past is a convenient arena for this because of its vastness and its malleability: images of the past, because they are held in the head and may not even be articulated, cannot easily be controlled or challenged and they can thus be used by the individual as a very personal way of coming to terms with his or her own situation. This fact, together with the perceived position of representations of the past, such as museums and galleries, as unthreatening, makes the past an excellent area for dominated groups whose expression is normally muted, to express themselves: the past has the potential to be creative at a personal level. The past does not die, because it is intimately tied to the present; new traditions are continually being invented to replace ones that no longer have contemporary relevance (Hobsbawm and Ranger 1983). In turn, this has important implications for the way in which museums are viewed. It suggests that their analysis principally in terms of their use as ideological apparatuses is inappropriate: instead, they can be seen as vehicles for creating a sense of the past amongst people. In this case, this experience should be available to all, and not just the relatively restricted sections of the population that currently form the backbone of the museum visiting population.

4 Patterns in museum and heritage visiting

Introduction

Having demonstrated that museums need not be analysed purely in terms of ideology, and thus that there is a potential role for them to enable people to produce their own sense of the past in a creative way, it now remains to examine ways in which museums can become more responsive to this role. In particular, we have to look at how barriers that deter people from visiting museums might be removed. In the next three chapters, an attempt is made to do this, first, by providing information on contemporary patterns of visiting and the characteristics of visitors, and then by explaining why these patterns occur through an analysis of attitudes to museums and an examination of theoretical schemes to explain them.

Previous work on museum visiting

Arguments about the contemporary role of heritage have proceeded primarily by assertion and have concentrated on the production of the past by designers, curators and marketing people, rather than the consumption of these productions by a very diverse group known as 'the public'. This is somewhat surprising as detailed information on broad aspects of the visiting of heritage presentations such as museums, galleries and historic houses has been available for many years in the form of survey data.

The development of the visitor survey

Simple counting of numbers of visitors to museums has occurred since at least the beginning of the last century. The British Museum, for example, is recorded as having had around 50,000 visitors for the year ending March 1818 (Boulton n.d.:12), compared with a current total of over 4.4 million (BTA 1990). Although useful for administrative purposes, simple counting gave no information on the personal characteristics of the visitors themselves. This did not become an interest until the 1930s when various American museum curators began to observe the behaviour of their visitors or to ask them a few simple questions about their visit (Pennsylvania Museum 1930). However, it was not until the early 1950s that a more comprehensive visitor survey was developed.

In a survey over the course of the summer of 1952, Niehoff interviewed 400 visitors to the Milwaukee Public Museum on the type of exhibit they enjoyed, how much of the museum they had seen, how long they had stayed, and how often they went to the museum. Importantly this was supplemented with questions on the visitors' age, sex, occupation and educational background which allowed a comparsion of the overall demographic profile of visitors with that of the general population shown by the census (Niehoff 1968a). This survey was then followed up by another over the winter of 1952-3 so that seasonal variations in visitor characteristics could be detected (Niehoff 1968b).

Niehoff's work set the pattern for all subsequent in-house surveys of museum visitors, although it was not until fifteen years later that the first full-scale survey was conducted in Great Britain (Doughty 1968). Since then, visitor surveys have become established as the principal method of collecting information on the museum's clientele. However, the apparent ease with which surveys can be carried out has led to many low standards, criticised to great effect by Loomis (1973). His main criticism is their frequent lack of thoroughness: questions are often not pre-tested and not neutrally phrased, untrained interviewers are used, or inadequate sampling is carried out so that the results are unrepresentative of all visitors. In addition, surveys only tend to be 'snapshot' profiles of visitor composition at a certain period. A full picture can only be obtained if visits on different days of the week, different times of the year, and even over different years are taken into account.

The contemporary context

Review of the published surveys of visitors to British national and provincial museums enables the general characteristics of museum visitors to be established. Males are usually in slightly greater proportions than females (though this varies with the subject of the museum); students and socio-economic groups A, B and C1 are over-represented in proportion to their numbers in the population, while the retired, the unemployed, and groups C2, D and E are underrepresented (Cruickshank 1972, Mason 1974, McWilliams and Hopwood 1973). The majority of visitors tend to be educated beyond the minimum school leaving age or are still in full-time education (Heady 1984). Where visitors under the age of 16 have been counted or interviewed, they have generally comprised the largest group of visitors (Griggs and Alt 1982), and the elderly have been under-represented (Digby 1974).

Individual surveys do nevertheless show a considerable degree of variation. Certain kinds of museums, particularly industrial and technology ones such as the National Railway Museum, attract a visitor profile much closer to that of the general population (Heady 1984). At the other end of the scale, certain museums, particularly large art galleries, attract an even more exclusive audience. For example, 45 per cent of visitors to the Victoria and Albert Museum finished their full-time education after the age of 21, compared with 8 per cent of the general population (Heady 1984), and at the Tate Gallery, only

2 per cent of visitors are from socio-economic groups D and E, which comprise around a third of the British population (Klein 1974).

These surveys have therefore been able to determine the demographic characteristics of museum visitors, the pattern of their visits, and some have studied their attitudes to the museum experience. Few, however, have been able to suggest why certain groups consistently tend not to go to museums, because they have not directly questioned non-visitors. Where they have been considered, their characteristics have simply been inferred as the opposite of those of visitors.

In order to understand the cultural role of museum visiting, it is essential to understand non-visiting as well. Accordingly, a survey representative of the *general* population has to be conducted, outside the museum, so that the behaviour and attitudes of museum visitors and non-visitors can be systematically compared.

General population museum surveys

Local Surveys The first general population survey in Britain was conducted in Belfast, as a continuation of Doughty's (1968) work (Erwin 1971). 650 interviews were conducted in the six postal districts of the city, with selection of interviewees done on a non-probability basis in the street, which makes errors and biases in the selection method unquantifiable. The survey found that 61 per cent of the sample had visited the Ulster Museum at some time in their lives. The lowest attenders were the unskilled and semi-skilled manual labourers, 56 per cent of whom had never been to the museum, and the highest attenders were the skilled manual workers and the clerical workers (78 per cent attendance). As Erwin's project surveyed the general population, it was possible to distinguish the characteristics of non-visitors from those of visitors. Although his survey does confirm that non-visitors are more likely to be from the lower socio-economic groups, it does not suggest why they do not visit museums, because it did not question respondents on their attitudes to museums. Furthermore, it was based only on a small, non-probabilistic sample which is not generalisable outside Belfast itself.

An attempt to gauge public attitudes to museums on a wider scale was made by Chadwick (1980). His survey bears the closest resemblance to the one reported here, in that it was based on a general population sample of 1500 implemented by post, although restricted to electors from Derby, Leicester and Nottingham, and the directors of the three major museums there. The survey was concerned with exploring the potential role of museums and galleries in community education. He found overwhelming agreement amongst respondents that museums provide a form of education for those who had left school early. Most people, however, were found to go to museums for enjoyment rather than education, and to see them as little help in solving real life problems. Using the survey results and information provided by the museum directors, Chadwick suggests ways in which museum educational services might become more community-oriented. His discussion and conclusions are useful, but he does not study the nature of museum visiting itself, and the data on which his work is based is fundamentally flawed by the low response rate (30 per cent) of his survey. Such a low rate of returns almost certainly means that the survey results are not representative of the total population, because those who replied might comprise only a certain section of the community. 50 per cent has been stipulated as the minimum response rate for a feasible survey (Erdos 1970: 144). Chadwick does not comment on this bias and does not attempt to compensate for it. Consequently his survey does little to advance our understanding of museum visiting in its social context.

The only general population survey in Britain that studies attitudes to museums with any rigour is one conducted in Kingston-upon-Hull (Prince 1985a, Prince and Schadla-Hall 1985). Interviews were completed with 217 residents selected on a non-probability basis. No details are given on the precise sampling method, the exact wording of the questions, the relative proportions of visitors and non-visitors, nor of the criteria by which the two groups were distinguished. This, together with the small size of the sample and the fact that it was restricted to Hull make it a preliminary study only. Nevertheless it was valuable in isolating, for the first time, two groups of museum visitors and non-visitors and comparing their attitudes to museums in an attempt to understand what deterred non-visitors from visiting them, and it backs this up with a theoretical scheme derived from cognitive psychology to interpret the results. Briefly, this postulates that attitudes to particular activities, reflected in interest in the subject and image of the institution, will be the most crucial determinant of participation.

The attitudes of non-visitors towards museums were, perhaps unsurprisingly, much more adverse than those of visitors. For example, four times as many non-visitors as visitors agreed that museums were boring places, and nearly twice as many agreed that they were for intellectuals only. It is concluded that a visit is not within non-visitors' scheme of perceived leisure choices because of the negative image they have developed of museums (Prince 1985a: 247-8). The importance of the image of the museum in shaping visiting or non-visiting choice is also emphasised by Eisenbeis (1972) for West Germany and by Bourdieu and Darbel (1991) for France. The Hull study, although limited in the ways described, points the way in which a fuller understanding of museum visiting and non-visiting might be achieved at a national scale by surveying attitudes of both visitors and non-visitors, and by having an explicit interpretive theory. In order to gain a more representative picture, however, it is essential to conduct surveys at the national scale.

National Surveys In recent years, four surveys have been conducted at a national scale in Britain which have included at least some questions on museum-visiting. These are the General Household Survey (OPCS 1990), the Time Use Survey (*Leisure Futures*, quarterly), and two surveys conducted primarily to gauge attitudes to admission charges (English Tourist Board 1982a, Touche Ross 1989). The first two are conducted on a regular basis, while the other two were implemented once only. All the surveys find that, nationally, museums are more likely to be participated in by the better educated and the more affluent.

Only the Touche Ross survey included questions on attitudes to museums and their facilities, but the survey is rather disappointing. The report actually combines the results of two different surveys asking different sets of questions. One is a public opinion poll of 1872 people 'in the street' and the other of 2819 visitors interviewed at twelve different museums around the country. Most of the questions were of a fairly low level and general kind such as 'Do you think any additional facilities are needed?' (Touche Ross 1989: 36). Most of the results are produced as a summary of general trends without any statistics so it is difficult to assess the validity of the statements that are made. Specific findings from the survey are addressed below in relation to the findings of the survey presented here.

For more extensive work we have to turn instead to studies conducted outside Britain to find large-scale systematic coverage of the general population's attitudes. The only statistically representative sample of a national population's participation in, and attitudes to, museums has been conducted in Canada (Dixon, Courtney and Bailey 1974). 7230 interviews were completed in a sample designed to represent all regions of Canada and all major demographic groups. 4128 self-completion questionnaires on leisure time and attitudes to museums were also returned as supplements to the interviews. Respondents were asked questions concerning the frequency of their museum-visiting, their other leisure activities, and their feelings towards a large number of attitudinal statements about museums. Specific findings will be discussed when presenting the findings of the present survey, but the general conclusions can be summarised here. Dixon and his colleagues argue that the survey shows that museum-visiting is a mass phenomenon rather than a pastime reserved for the elite. They do however acknowledge that 'the likelihood of being a museum-goer and a frequent visitor increased with education and income, decreased with age, and was influenced significantly by region of Canada, community size and language spoken' (Dixon *et al* 1974: 94), which, despite their earlier statements, can be taken to mean that museums still retain their elitist connotations.

They divide the museum-visiting population into two groups: the large majority who visit infrequently (averaging less than one visit per year) and a small core group who visit frequently. Museum visitors tend to participate in a wider range of leisure activities than non-visitors. The non-visitors are distinguished from the visitors not only demographically (tending to be less educated, less affluent and/or elderly) but also by their attitudes to museums. Attitudes are not different in kind, but non-visitors tend to have stronger negative attitudes towards museums than visitors (Dixon *et al* 1974: 194). In particular, most non-visitors thought that museums never change, and 50 per cent of them agreed that they have little interest in museums, compared to 21 per cent of visitors (*ibid*: 135). The museum's unsympathetic image amongst non-visitors was felt to be a deterrent to visiting, but, it was argued, was only a product of lack of exposure to museums. They felt that the availability of museums locally was a more important factor in determining visiting in Canada (*ibid* :246), and conclude that efforts to increase attendance should concentrate on persuading infrequent visitors to visit more often.

Although this is one of the most comprehensive surveys on attitudes to museums ever undertaken, and has produced data that are intrinsically extremely interesting and useful, its discussion of museum visiting remains at an essentially descriptive level. Like most other museum visitor surveys it again lacks an explicitly-stated theoretical framework with which to interpret its results. This chapter and the next will concentrate on presenting the results of the national survey carried out as the major part of this project, and Chapter 6 will outline approaches to the interpretation of these results.

Survey results

Who visits museums?

Incidence The survey found that 58 per cent of respondents claimed to have visited a museum or art gallery at least once in the last year (Table 4.1). This is not so different from the average of 47 per cent which can be gleaned from the Time Use Survey (*Leisure Futures* 1983-86), but is in complete contrast to the figure of 24 per cent reported in a survey carried out for the English Tourist Board (ETB 1982a). The figures for the Touche Ross report suggest that 44 per cent of the population have visited a museum in the last two years, but no figure is given for visits over a twelve month period.

Table 4.1 Annual frequency of museum visiting

Frequency	(%)	
None	42	
1-2 times	40	
3-10 times	16	
11+ times	2	
	100%	(N=930)

All of the surveys were carried out by different means and asked slightly different questions, which makes them subject to different degrees of bias. The Time Use survey, for example, is carried out on a sample of 500 adults selected by quota sampling, and combines participation in museums, art galleries and other exhibitions in one question (Henley Centre for Forecasting, pers. comm.). Because of the sampling method used, sampling error and degree of representativeness cannot be ascertained, but the consistency of its quarterly results over several years does suggest that there is little sampling error.

The English Tourist Board survey and the Touche Ross national poll, on the other hand, were carried out as one section of large omnibus surveys conducted by interview, in the ETB case on a stratified random sample and in the Touche Ross case on a quota sample. As omnibus surveys tend to be long and tedious, there might be a temptation for respondents to answer negatively to a question on museum visiting in order to avoid answering further questions. Both surveys asked about museums and art galleries separately, while the present survey asks about them together, which could account in part for the low figure. The ETB survey also found 13 per cent of respondents had visited an art gallery in the previous twelve months, and the Touche Ross survey found that 25 per cent had visited one in the last two years. However, these figures cannot of course be combined with those for museums, because museum and gallery visitors may be one and the same people.

The strongest indication of the possibly anomalous nature of the ETB survey is a comparison with the incidence of museum visiting in other Western countries. The Canadian national museum visiting survey reports an incidence of 48 per cent, which is subsequently revised to an estimated 55-60 per cent upon analysis of the self-completion questionnaires (Dixon *et al.* 1974: 99). In the USA, a survey by the Associated Council of the Arts found that 56 per cent of the adult public visited a history museum at least once a year, 49 per cent a natural history or science museum, and 48 per cent an art museum (National Research Center of the Arts, n.d.: 48). For individual cities, the figures may be even higher, such as the 68 per cent incidence of annual visiting quoted for Sheffield (Lewis, G. 1975: 21).

The average figure for other countries seems to be around 50 per cent. The figure of 58 per cent found by the current survey is within the range of figures quoted, but may be a little high due to the weighting system used. This is outlined in Appendix 1, where it is noted that weighting to make the sample demographically representative of the whole population might lead to a slight overestimation of museum visiting. If, as the small telephone sample of non-respondents indicated (Appendix 1), up to 80 per cent of non-respondents are non-visitors, then the absolute figure for museum attendance would be reduced to 47 per cent. However, as the representativeness of this sample is not known, it is perhaps best to state that yearly incidence of museum visiting amongst British adults, in Britain, is between 47 and 58 per cent.

Frequency Of those people who do visit a museum at least once a year, the largest group (40 per cent) visit just once or twice, 16 per cent visit between three and ten times, and a keen 2 per cent visit over ten times a year (Table 4.1).

On the basis of visits per year, one could thus follow the criteria used by Marilyn Hood in a survey of museum-visiting in Toledo, Ohio (Hood 1981: 52-54) and define the last two groups as frequent visitors, the next group as occasional visitors, and the other as non-visitors. However, as noted above, the Canadian survey by Dixon and his colleagues found that the majority of people space their museum visits at an interval of more than one year. Under Hood's criteria, though, they would be classified as non-visitors. In order to refine the classification of museum visitors to reflect actual visiting practice, respondents were asked when they had last visited a museum (Table 4.2). This showed that 68 per cent of the population has visited a museum within the last four years, and 82 per cent have visited at some time in their lives. This figure is midway between the finding that 68 per cent of the French population have visited a museum at some time (Le Roux 1970, quoted in Eisenbeis 1972), and that of the Canadian survey which claims that 84 per cent of the population have visited a museum just within the last five years (Dixon *et al.* 1974: 100). It is closest to that found for residents of the city of Cologne, 79 per cent of whom had visited a museum at some time in their lives (Eisenbeis 1972: 112).

Table 4.2 When respondents last went to a museum

'When did you last go [to a museum]?'		
Frequencies	(%)	
Within last 4 years	68	
5-10 years ago	5	
11-20 years ago	4	
21+ years ago	4	
Never	18	
	100%	(N=956)

As noted in an earlier publication relating to this work (Merriman 1989: 150), it is not certain whether those who have not visited a museum for several years can still be classified as potential visitors, or whether they would no longer consider visiting. 18 per cent of the population have never visited a museum, and are probably unlikely to ever go. To these might be added 4 per cent who last went over twenty years ago, and possibly the 4 per cent who last went over ten years ago, and the 5 per cent more who last went over five years ago.

Types of museum visitor

From the patterns of museum visiting through time examined above, it seems more accurate to eschew simple divisions into 'visitors' and 'non-visitors', and to devise a typology of visitors which expresses a little better the complexity of visiting patterns. By combining the results of Tables 4.1 and 4.2, the following five groups of visitors (and non-visitors) can be devised:

Type of visitor	% of sample
Frequent: Visits three or more times per year	17
Regular: Visits once or twice per year	37
Occasional: Last visited between one and four years ago	14
Rare: Last visited five or more years ago	14
Non-visitors: Has never visited a museum	18

It should be borne in mind that these are not absolute figures for museum visiting in Britain because the sample does not cover the total population of museum visitors. The first problem, as has been noted above in the discussion of incidence of visits, is that the visiting patterns of the non-respondents to the survey are not known to any degree of accuracy, except that a substantial proportion of them are not likely to be active museum visitors. The second problem is that two important groups of museum visitors, those under the age of eighteen (in school groups or privately) and overseas visitors, have not been surveyed because of the problems faced in obtaining an accurate sampling frame. The former may account for up to a third of visits to local authority and independent museums, and a quarter of visits to national museums (Prince and Higgins-McLoughlin 1987: 135), and the latter may account for a fifth of visits to museums and galleries (ETB 1983). It is therefore perfectly possible that surveys such as this one are only analysing about half of the total museum-visiting population.

In view of this problem, it is perhaps prudent to abandon the aim of producing absolute figures for museum visiting pending the availability of a representative sampling frame, and concentrate instead on the production of a database which will allow systematic *comparison* of the attributes and attitudes of a representative sample of different adult participant groups. The first step in this direction must be to examine the basic demographic

Table 4.3 Museum visiting by age, sex, status, education and activity status

	Frequent	Regular	Occas-ional	Rare	Non-visitor	(%)	N
			Type of Museum Visitor				
Age (%)							
<35	20	39	16	14	11	100	300
35–59	20	42	12	9	16	100	374
>60	10	25	15	21	29	100	271
Sex (%)							
Male	19	35	13	13	20	100	478
Female	15	37	15	15	17	100	471
Status (%)							
High	25	41	14	10	9	100	150
Middle	17	40	13	13	17	100	605
Low <60	12	25	22	16	25	100	85
Low >60	8	19	13	23	38	100	92
Education (%)							
Minimum	13	35	15	16	21	100	651
Stayed on at school	22	40	14	11	13	100	150
Tertiary education	32	41	10	11	6	100	123
Activity status (%)							
Full-time work	20	42	13	11	14	100	435
Part-time work	18	35	4	3	3	100	88
Housework	11	39	11	18	21	100	117
Student	56	19	13	6	–	100	16
Unemployed	16	35	20	13	14	100	69
Retired	12	25	15	19	28	100	221
All (%)	17	37	14	14	18	100	949

characteristics of the different types of museum visitor isolated, in order to see what sort of people have particular museum visiting patterns.

The characteristics of museum visitors and non-visitors

The characteristics of the different types of museum visitor have already been discussed elsewhere (Merriman 1989) and are reproduced here for purposes of comparison (Table 4.3). They confirm the results of the other surveys that have been discussed above, in that it tends to be those who are elderly and of lower socio-economic status who visit museums least. Crucially, as far as subsequent argument is concerned, those who would seem to have the free time to visit museums visit no more frequently than those in employment. Indeed, those who are retired are less likely to visit museums than any other group. In many surveys education seems to be the strongest factor influencing museum visiting (Bourdieu and Darbel 1991), but here the status variable, which encompasses educational background, seems to be a more powerful explanatory factor.

Patterns in heritage visiting

Incidence and frequency of visiting

Castles, historic houses and ancient monuments are all visited at least once a year by a slightly narrower range of people than museums, with 50 per cent, 46 per cent and 44 per cent participation per year, respectively (Table 4.4)

Table 4.4 Incidence and frequency of annual visits to castles, historic houses and ancient monuments

	Number of visits per year (%)					
	None	1-2	3-10	11+	(%)	N
Castles	50	39	10	1	100	928
Historic houses	54	34	12	1	100	928
Ancient monuments	56	33	10	2	100	928

Figures on heritage visiting are also produced by the Time Use Survey, but these only cover quarterly visiting. In 1990, 25 per cent visited a historic building in the autumn, while 40 per cent visited in the summer (*Leisure Futures*, February 1991). The Touche Ross survey, which asked separately about visits to stately homes and National Trust properties, found that 35 per cent of the population had visited each type (however they might be distinguished) in the last year (Touche Ross 1989: 14).

Characteristics of heritage visitors

As is the case with museums, the elderly are significantly less likely to visit castles, historic houses or ancient monuments than any other group. The young and middle age groups are equally likely to visit historic houses, while the young are more likely to visit ancient monuments and the middle aged to visit castles (Table 4.5)[3].

Table 4.5 Visitors to castles, historic houses and ancient monuments by age, status and access to vehicle

	Percentage of visitors		
Age (%)	Castles	Historic houses	Ancient monuments
<35	53	50	52
35-59	57	49	48
>60	37	40	29
Status (%)			
High	57	68	60
Middle	52	46	45
Low <60	47	34	34
Low >60	28	28	20
Vehicle access (%)			
None	39	34	34
One or More	57	54	49

Again, there are strong status effects, some of them partly explained by age, with the low status elderly being much less likely to participate, and those of high status most likely to. Some of this might be accounted for by the strong effects (between 15 and 20 percentage points) of access to a vehicle because, as we have seen earlier, the over 60s are less likely than other groups to have access to one. Castles and historic houses are generally less accessible than museums, tending often to be in present-day rural areas, and consequently access to a vehicle is a more important factor in visiting than it is for museums (See Table A2.5).

Characteristics of the last museum visit

Having determined the incidence and frequency of museum visiting, and the characteristics of visitors, it is now useful to explore specific patterns of museum visiting, such as the reasons why people go to museums, who they go with, and what sort of museums they go to. In order to concentrate respondents' minds, they were asked to take their last museum visit and answer specific questions about it.

Type of museum visited

In numerical terms, the last museum most people visited was a local authority or independent museum (Table 4.6). However, national museums are visited far out of proportion to their numbers. 30 per cent of last visits were made to the 107 national museums of England, Scotland and Wales, which comprise only 6 per cent of the total museums (Prince and Higgins-McLoughlin 1987: 24). This imbalance was also noted in the English Tourist Board Survey (ETB 1982: 5).

Table 4.6 Type of museum last visited (%)

National museum	30
Local Authority or Independent museum	57
Military museum	3
University Museum	3
Museum abroad	5
	100
	N = 775

There were no significant differences between the various types of museum visitor on which kind of museum they had last visited, except that frequent visitors were more likely than any other group to have visited a museum abroad recently. This may be an effect of the implementation of the survey in October, presumably quite soon after many respondents' annual holiday.

Who the visit was made with

The museum visit is essentially a social occasion which the visitor conducts with family or friends. Most visitors (59 per cent) went with members of their family such as parents, their own children, their grandparents, cousins or aunts and uncles (Table 4.7). 20 per cent went with friends, 11 per cent went alone, and the rest went with their school (6 per cent) or another organisation such as boy scouts or girl guides (4 per cent). There were significant differences among the different types of visitor, with frequent visitors more likely to visit museums alone, and rare visitors far more likely to have last visited with the school, over five years ago. The finding that museum visiting is for most people a social occasion is confirmed in the Canadian survey (Dixon *et al.* 1974: 167), and by the English Tourist Board survey, although this found that 22 per cent visited alone (ETB 1982: 7).

Individual studies do however show substantial variation, and suggest that the subject and accessibility of the particular museum has a bearing on the way in which the visit is conducted. For example, a survey at the Norton Priory

Table 4.7 Who the last museum visit was made with, by type of museum visitor

	Family/ relatives	Friends	Alone	School	Other	(%)	N
Type of visitor (%)							
Frequent	56	22	17	2	4	100	159
Regular	63	19	12	2	4	100	345
Occasional	62	23	5	6	4	100	132
Rare	48	18	9	21	4	100	128
All (%)	59	20	11	6	4	100	783

Museum found only 3 per cent came alone (Greene 1978), possibly because visiting may be primarily by day-trippers in cars, while 27 per cent visited the Ulster Museum alone, possibly because it is in a city and might attract casual passers-by (Doughty 1968: 47). Heady (1984: 15) in his survey of visits to national museums, shows that an art museum, the Victoria and Albert, attracts 26 per cent lone visitors, while the Science and National Railway Museums attract 10 per cent and 5 per cent respectively. It is possible that the more academic and art-oriented a museum is (and thus the more restricted a visitor profile it attracts), the greater number of single visitors it receives, although clearly a city centre museum or gallery will attract significant numbers of casual passers-by.

Holiday visiting

54 per cent of museum visitors last visited a museum when they were away on holiday or a day trip, which again confirms the social nature of much museum visiting (Table 4.8). This is a higher proportion than the 36 per cent reported for Canada (Dixon *et al* 1974:158) and around the average reported for a sample of French art museums, where the rates were 45, 61 and 63 per cent for the working, middle and upper classes respectively (Bourdieu and Darbel 1991: Table A3.17). In the present survey there were no significant variations among the different types of museum visitor.

Table 4.8 Proportion of last museum visits made on holiday

	(%)	
Visited last museum while on holiday	54	
Visited last museum while not on holiday	46	(N=923)

Reasons for visiting the museum

The answers to the open-ended question 'Why did you go to that particular place?' exhibited a great deal of variety, and a sample of verbatim responses is given below:

- 'Interesting for daughters'
- 'Personal interest'
- 'We stayed near it'
- 'We were all interested in the same'
- 'Interests'
- 'I had never been before and felt that it was a deficiency in my general knowledge'
- 'Had visited this small museum on an earlier occasion and knew my friend would enjoy it'
- 'Day trip for wife and children'
- 'My grandson has a great interest in Railways'
- 'School Project'

These answers were classified into eleven basic categories devised by the researcher for purposes of analysis (Table 4.9). The clearest pattern to emerge from this classification is that a substantial proportion of people visit museums either because they have a specific interest in some aspect of the particular

Table 4.9 Reasons for last museum visit, by type of museum visitor (%)

Reason for visit	Type of visitor				
	Frequent	Regular	Occasional	Rare	All
General interest	13	20	23	14	18
Specific interest	35	22	18	18	23
Sightseeing	8	16	10	7	12
Because nearby	10	11	15	9	11
Self education	2	1	1	3	1
For work/study	6	3	8	22	8
To take others	11	13	13	13	12
A return visit	5	6	–	–	4
To use facilities	–	–	2	–	1
Casual reasons	6	5	7	10	7
Recommended	4	3	2	3	3
	100	100	100	100	100
(N)	(156)	(341)	(132)	(122)	(762)

museum they are visiting, or because they are generally interested in museums and the sort of topics they cover. This was also the most common reason for visiting museums given in the Touche Ross survey (1989: 16).

As the findings about companions on the visit have already made clear, motivations to visit museums also have a strong social element. 12 per cent specifically mentioned that they went as part of their sightseeing of the area, (and of course we have already shown that over half of all visits were undertaken on holiday or a day trip), and 12 per cent went to take others. Similarly, almost half of those interviewed in the Touche Ross survey would either visit museums as part of a holiday or day trip, or because it would be entertaining (*ibid.*). Motivations of interest and sociability, of course are not mutually exclusive, nor did the verbatim answers imply this. Instead, it is likely that, while the general decision to visit a museum is taken for social reasons because, by definition, it is undertaken in leisure time, often on holiday and with others, the particular museum that is chosen for the visit is selected either because of a positive interest in its subject matter or because of a general interest in that type of museum. Casual reasons for using the museum, such as to shelter from the rain or to use the toilets, which are frequently anecdotally quoted by the sceptical, in fact only account for 7 per cent of reasons given for visiting.

People's reasons for visiting museums vary with the frequency of their visiting. This may be a genuine difference, or may be produced by the intervening effect of the different educational characteristics of visitor groups. Bourdieu and Darbel, for example, find that upper class visitors are far more likely to declare 'noble' reasons for visiting than working class visitors (1991: Table A3.17). Nevertheless, there does seem to be a scale of interest, from the particular, through the general, to the virtually non-existent, from the frequent visitors who express specific interest in the subject of the museum, to the more generalised interest of the occasional visitors, and, significantly, to the rare visitors who were most likely to have gone for part of a course of work or study. This pattern has been confirmed by the Touche Ross survey (1989: 15), and ties in well with the findings in Table 4.7 that the largest group of rare visitors last went with their school, which suggests that few of them will return to visit museums in the future. The rare visitors are also more likely than any other group to have visited for casual reasons.

The important conclusion to emerge from these statistics is that most people who visit museums do so for specific reasons of interest in the individual museums they go to. In this sense, individual museum visits cannot be ascribed to some ideological compulsion, although the question of why some people are interested in museums and others are not itself begs a wider question which will be dealt with in succeeding chapters.

5 Public attitudes

So far in the survey statistics have been presented on the demographic composition of museum visitors, and the patterns and motivations of their visiting. This is the point where most surveys usually finish, having satisfied their specific market research aims, and leaving further interpretation of the findings to the reader. However, if we wish to understand the place of museum visiting within contemporary British culture we have to understand why these visiting patterns occur. In particular we have to examine why some groups consistently go to museums and other heritage presentations less than other groups.

Constraints on museum visiting

In studying this problem, it is important to distinguish between structural and cultural deterrents (Prince 1983: 240-43). Structural constraints might include such things as the availability of museums and of transport to reach them, and the amount of leisure time, money and energy at the individual's disposal. Cultural constraints might include an individual's attitudes to the past and to museums, where negative images might be a deterrent to visiting. Structural deterrents have to be dealt with before cultural ones, because the simplest explanation of the behaviour of those who rarely or never visit museums might be that they do so because they are physically unable to get to them or cannot afford them. As the focus of attention is on deterrents to those who tend not to go, the explanatory variable used in the analysis is 'type of museum visitor', bearing in mind the demographic characteristics of these types as presented in Table 4.3.

Age

Age, the most significant demographic influence on museum visiting (Table 4.3) is both a structural and a cultural constraint. Very often it is considered to be structural because, it is suggested, the elderly tend to be more physically frail and more prone to illnesses than other groups, and are therefore less able to get out of the house to visit museums. However, the converse of the figures in Table 4.3 is that over a third of those over 60 have visited a museum in the last year, and half have visited one within the last four years. It is unlikely that the remaining 50 per cent of the elderly who are rare- or non-visitors are housebound and physically unable to visit museums.

While frailty and some other structural factors (the need to nurse others, lack of money) may explain the non-visiting of part of the elderly population, there is strong evidence that old age and retirement is often accompanied by a withdrawal from many previously-practised social activities. There will thus also be a substantial cultural deterrent to visiting museums consequent upon old age. This will be explored in greater detail in the next chapter.

Structural constraints on museum visiting

Availability of museums It would be difficult to determine the availability of museums locally for each individual without a complex series of questions unsuitable for a self-completion questionnaire. The perception of availability is also likely to vary from person to person; for example, a museum might be considered available by one person if it is in the same town, while for another it might only be available if it were within a short walking distance. Nevertheless, it is important to attempt to gauge the effect of the distribution of museums on museum-visiting patterns. In the Canadian survey, for example, visiting patterns are strongly related to the proximity of museums, possibly because of Canada's great size and the relatively large distances between museums (Dixon *et al.* 1974: 156).

An attempt was made to address this problem by taking a sample of a hundred respondents and examining the range of distance they had travelled from their home address to the last museum they visited. Only 35 per cent had visited a museum which could be described (by them or by inference) as local. 34 per cent had visited a national museum in London (of whom the majority were from the South-East of England but only seven were from London itself). 26 per cent had visited a non-local museum outside London, and 5 per cent had visited a museum abroad. About two-thirds of museum visits, therefore, seem to be to museums which are at some distance from the home.

Without exhaustive analysis of the distance travelled by each individual respondent from his or her home to the last museum visited (a task beyond the research programme) it is difficult to gauge accurately the extent to which the availability or non-availability of museums affects patterns of visiting. If the small sample examined reflects general patterns, however, it seems that the availability of museums locally has some effect on visiting, but not a very strong one. It might be hypothesised that the availability of local museums would have an important effect on those without private transport or with reduced mobility.

Availability of transport Access to a private vehicle might also be regarded as an important factor in determining participation in museums. It is not noted in the Canadian survey or in Hood's work in Toledo, but work on visitors to countryside trails (Prince 1983: 241), and in leisure studies in general suggests it can be a major factor in participation in some activities (Kelly 1983: 49). As Table 5.1 shows, there does seem to be a relationship between access to vehicles and museum visiting. The effect is only marginally significant, however, and a large proportion of those without access to a vehicle still manage to visit at least one museum a year, which shows that non-availability of transport by no means explains all museum non-visiting.

Table 5.1 Effect of availability of vehicle on museum visiting by type of museum visitor

	Type of museum visitor						
Vehicle Access (%)	Frequent	Regular	Occas-ional	Rare	Non-visitor	(%)	N
None	15	32	14	15	24	100	374
One	17	39	14	13	17	100	417
Two	21	41	14	13	10	100	116
Three +	22	43	16	12	6	100	43

Time Museum visiting is a leisure time activity, but this does not mean that those who have the most leisure time visit museums the most. This has been hinted at by the break-down of visiting by occupation (Table 4.3). In a study of museum visiting and the unemployed Prince (1985b) suggests that, in order for participation to occur, an activity has first to be seen as an appropriate leisure choice and 'time to visit' has to be perceived as such. In other words, as long as people have *some* leisure time, the amount of time available does not affect museum visiting; rather it is how people choose to spend this time that is the crucial determinant of museum visiting.

Admission charges At the last accurate count, in 1987, nearly half of the museums in Britain charged an admission fee (Prince and Higgins-McLoughlin 1987: 137). Availability of money to pay the entrance charge might therefore be a factor influencing visiting. Table 5.2 shows that overall, 59 per cent of respondents would be prepared to pay a fee, but that there is a marked fall-off in willingness to pay between the different visitor groups. However, there is only one percentage point separating those who never visit museums who would pay £1.00, and those who would not; in all of the other visitor types the majority would pay the fee. A similar finding is made in both the English Tourist Board and the Touche Ross surveys. Dealing with attitudes to admission charges is however difficult because of the acquiescence bias effect whereby people tend to give answers expected of them. Reluctance to pay admission charges should therefore be magnified to a certain extent to gain an accurate picture; certainly, if the majority of people do not object to them, we would not have seen the sometimes drastic fall-offs in visiting that have been experienced where museums have introduced charges (Feist and Hutchinson 1989: 7).

Income is an important factor in participation in certain leisure activities such as foreign holidays and specialized sports (Roberts 1981: 59), but it does not seem to be a major factor in determining participation in all leisure

Table 5.2 Attitudes towards paying for entry to museums, by type of museum visitor

	'Would you be prepared to pay, say £1.00, to go into a museum?'				
Type of visitor (%)	Yes	No	Don't Know	(%)	N
Frequent	64	28	8	100	159
Regular	64	31	5	100	347
Occasional	59	32	10	100	134
Rare	57	40	3	100	128
Non-Visitor	44	45	10	100	158
All (%)	59	34	7	100	928

activities. For example, Alton Towers leisure park, which is only accessible by car and coach and has a £10.00 admission charge, received 2,382,000 visitors in 1989 (BTA/ETB 1990: 6). Over half of all museums are free, and, of those that charge, the modal payment of all museums is 50 pence (Prince and Higgins-McLoughlin 1987: 142), so in comparison with Alton Towers, for example, the actual price of admission is unlikely to be a crucial factor in determining participation. It is more likely that, as with time, it is the initial perception of museum visiting as a worthwhile leisure acitivity that is more important; only then might financial factors come into consideration. This, it should be stressed, is not an argument for the introduction of admission charges. Where charges have been introduced, it is the less wealthy and less well-educated visitors who fall off in numbers. These are precisely the visitors that museums should be attracting more of in order to serve a representative public. The introduction of admission charges runs counter to this aim. The deterrent effect of admission charges *amongst those who are already museum visitors* is seen in the following selection of comments appended, unprompted, to the survey questionnaire.

- 'I feel that the interest is definitely abundant, but sometimes the pocket can't stand too many visits'
- 'Being a pensioner the cost is prohibitive'
- 'As a family of four we cannot afford entry prices at many places of historical interest'
- 'The ordinary person...cannot afford to make a visit to these places'
- 'Price of visits to castles etc. often puts us off going'

Cultural deterrents to museum visiting

Value placed on the past It is possible that the strongest cultural deterrent to museum visiting might be the individual's valuation of the past, and his or her images of what life in the past was like. It is possible, for example, that many people do not visit museums simply because they are not interested in the past. We have seen in Table 3.1 that there is a high general level of interest in the past, but Table 5.3 shows that different types of museum visitor have significantly different degrees of interest in the past. While only 1 per cent of frequent visitors and 3 per cent of regular visitors express doubt about the value of knowing about the past (by answering 'perhaps' or 'no' to the question), 18 per cent of rare visitors and 27 per cent of non-visitors express doubts, and this relative undervaluation of the past may explain why they tend not to visit museums. The value placed by an individual on knowing about the past does therefore have some effect on museum participation, but the fact that 73 per cent of non-visitors and 83 per cent of rare visitors do think the past worth knowing about shows that it too by no means determines visiting entirely.

Table 5.3 Interest in the past, by type of museum visitor

Type of visitor (%)	'Do you think it is worth knowing about the past?'					
	Definitely	Probably	Perhaps	No	(%)	N
Frequent	93	6	1	–	100	158
Regular	88	10	2	1	100	348
Occasional	84	10	4	2	100	133
Rare	68	15	10	8	100	128
Non-visitor	49	24	16	11	100	160

Attitudes to the past It is possible that an individual's attitudes to life in the past could also have an effect on their museum visiting. In particular, as was suggested in Chapter 3, someone with a more positive or nostalgic view of the past might tend to visit museums more than someone with a negative view. Regression analysis of the 'attitude to the past' variable used in Chapter 3 shows that attitude to the past has roughly the same effect as educational background in influencing museum participation (Table A2.6). Attitude to the past is therefore significant, but contrary to expectations, it is negatively related to museum visiting. This means that individuals who visit museums regularly or frequently are more likely to have an *unfavourable* view of the past than people who rarely or never visit them. Museum visiting is not therefore primarily indulged in by those who may have a nostalgic view of the past, but by those who tend to stress its harshness. This paradox may best be explained by seeing museum visiting, like attitudes to the past, as being a complex cultural phenomenon occurring in the present, in which the visitor's relationship to the past is just one of the factors influencing the visit. What seems clear is that museum visiting is not undertaken just in order to escape from the present; it might also be undertaken to affirm that one is better-off in the present.

The museum's image as an institution As well as attitudes to the past in general, the other cultural factor in museum visiting that must be investigated is attitudes to museums themselves. Borrowing from cognitive psychology, Prince (1982, 1985a) shows that attitudes to an activity will be the strongest influence on whether that activity is undertaken, and he shows that those who do not visit museums tend to have much less favourable images than those who do visit them. Despite the apparently common-sense nature of this finding, it is important to assess the relative role played by attitudes to museums in determining visiting. If, for example, they are found to be the strongest factor, then efforts can be made to remedy specific components of negative attitudes. Hood's survey in Toledo, for example, looked at the leisure expectations of different groups, surveyed their attitudes to museums, and found that those groups who had negative attitudes to museums did not feel that these expectations were being fulfilled by them (Hood 1983).

In the initial unstructured interviews conducted in the preparatory stage of the survey (Appendix 1), respondents were asked to talk generally about their images of museums. Images were taken from these interviews, together with images noted from other surveys, supplemented by two provided by the researcher ('community centre' and 'department store')[4].

Responses divided equally into three groups: those seeing the museum as a monument to the dead, those associating it with a library, and those seeing it as one of the other choices (Table 5.4). The problem then is to interpret the meaning of the images. The association of the museum with a monument to the dead is clearly a negative one, and the fact that this is held most strongly by the rare visitors and non-visitors is a good indication that this off-putting image is a strong factor in deterring visiting (bearing in mind that a significant proportion of rare visitors last went to a museum with their school some time ago). It is significant that this image is so strongly held amongst non-visitors, who by definition have never visited a museum. This confirms the persistence of a general 'deathly' image of museums popularised by film, books and other

Table 5.4 Image of museums, by type of museum visitor

'Which of these things do museums remind you of most?'						
Type of institution	**Type of visitor** (%)					
	Frequent	Regular	Occasional	Rare	Non-visitor	All
Monument to the dead	17	28	43	48	47	34
Community centre	6	3	1	2	2	3
Church or temple	10	8	8	13	14	10
School	12	12	10	6	12	11
Library	44	40	32	23	24	35
Department store	4	–	–	1	–	1
Other	9	9	6	6	2	7
	100	100	100	100	100	100

media, and passed on by family and peers. The derivation of this image is discussed in the next chapter. The image of the library is more likely to be chosen, the more frequently someone visits museums. As noted above, this may be a positive or negative image, but it rather tends to confirm the quiet and scholarly associations of the museum.

This difference in attitude towards museums between those who are most and least likely to be visitors has been seen in a number of other surveys. Specifically, in Canada, non-visitors were found to be much more likely than visitors to agree that museums never change and that they remind them of old fortresses (Dixon *et al.* 1974: 152). In France, Bourdieu and Darbel found, on a sample of 250 visitors to art museums, that the majority (44 per cent) associated it with a church, followed by 26 per cent who saw it as a library (figures calculated from Bourdieu and Darbel 1991 Table A5.8). In their analysis, working class visitors are far more likely than other classes to associate the museum with a church, and far less likely to associate it with a library. In West Germany, in a sample of Cologne residents, Eisenbeis (1972: 119) found that the most common association of the museum was with a palace (30 per cent), followed by a monument (19 per cent) and then a library (16 per cent). In Britain, Prince and Schadla-Hall (1985: 42), although not asking a question on the associations of the museum as a building, did find that non-visitors were much more likely to see museums as boring, old-fashioned and for intellectuals only.

Answers to a question on the atmosphere of the museum were consistent with the distribution of these positive and negative images. The great majority (78 per cent) of frequent visitors agreed that museums have a pleasant atmosphere and only 7 per cent disagreed, compared with 58 per cent of rare visitors who agreed and 22 per cent who disagreed (Table 5.5). The answers of non-visitors again demonstrated the existence of a generally-disseminated negative image of museums, as only 39 per cent of them agreed with the question and 20 per cent disagreed, with the largest group (41 per cent) neither agreeing nor disagreeing. Given the presence of acquiescence bias on such questions, there is thus quite a strong degree of feeling amongst rare visitors and non-visitors that the atmosphere of museums is not very conducive to visiting.

Table 5.5 Attitudes to atmosphere of museums, by type of visitor

	'They have a pleasant atmosphere'						
Type of visitor (%)	Strongly Agree	Agree	Neither	Disagree	Strongly disagree	%	N
Frequent	21	57	15	7	—	100	156
Regular	11	63	16	10	1	100	335
Occasional	9	52	23	16	—	100	121
Rare	8	50	20	20	2	100	123
Non-Visitor	8	31	41	18	2	100	132
All (%)	12	54	21	13	1	100	867

A clue as to why museums should still suffer from such a negative image is given by answers to two further questions. The answers to the first, on the relevance of museums, produced a very great range of variation. While only 11 per cent of frequent visitors and 13 per cent of regular visitors agreed that 'museums have nothing to do with our daily lives', a startling 55 per cent of non-visitors and 38 per cent of rare visitors agreed with the statement (Table 5.6). In addition, non-visitors and rare visitors were significantly more likely to agree that museums are too middle class (Table 5.7). As these visitor groups are much more likely to be of low status, they may legitimately feel that museum visiting is a middle class activity and therefore not something which is part of their cultural repertoire. Taken together, the answers to these two questions strongly suggest that the perceived irrelevance and exclusivity of museums are important deterrents to those who tend not to visit them. These images may be part of a wider feeling that museums are not aimed at certain groups of people, and tend unconsciously to exclude them.

Table 5.6 Attitudes to the relevance of museums, by type of museum visitor

	'Museums have nothing to do with our daily lives'						
Type of visitor (%)	Strongly agree	Agree	Neither	Disagree	Strongly disagree	(%)	N
Frequent	1	10	7	61	23	100	160
Regular	2	11	10	67	11	100	344
Occasional	2	27	15	47	9	100	132
Rare	6	32	9	50	3	100	126
Non-Visitor	14	41	12	27	6	100	155
All (%)	4	21	11	54	11	100	917

Table 5.7 Attitudes to the exclusiveness of museums, by type of museum visitor

	'They are too middle class'						
Type of visitor (%)	Strongly agree	Agree	Neither	Disagree	Strongly disagree	(%)	N
Frequent	2	8	20	45	26	100	160
Regular	2	10	14	24	12	100	343
Occasional	3	8	25	54	10	100	132
Rare	7	18	13	53	10	100	124
Non-visitor	3	28	29	35	5	100	147
All (%)	3	13	19	52	13	100	907

Attitudes to museum services When it comes to looking at the specific services offered by museums, there is much general agreement. There is a strong feeling, for example, that museums are places where you learn a lot (Table 5.8). Although differences in attitudes between the various types of museum visitor are statistically significant, a total of 80 per cent of non-visitors still agree, compared with 98 per cent of frequent visitors. The answers to this question should perhaps be qualified by observing that a place where 'you learn a lot' might be a positive attribute for some groups but a negative one for others. In addition, as will be argued in the next chapter, museums, as part of the dominant culture, tend to be recognised as legitimate even by large numbers of those who do not participate in them.

Table 5.8 Attitudes to the museum as an educational establishment, by type of visitor

	'You learn a lot in them'						
Type of visitor (%)	Strongly agree	Agree	Neither	Disagree	Strongly disagree	(%)	N
Frequent	53	45	1	1	–	100	159
Regular	38	56	5	2	1	100	343
Occasional	34	59	7	–	–	100	134
Rare	29	54	10	7	–	100	129
Non-visitor	21	59	16	3	2	100	150
All (%)	36	55	7	2	1	100	916

Similarly, 58 per cent of respondents agree that presentation in museums can be dull, and only 34 per cent disagree, with no significant variation amongst the various visitor types (Table 5.9). It might be a genuine truth that many museums do have displays that are boring: even most curators would recognise this, and visitors are quite capable of discriminating between different types of presentation. Thus, individuals who tend often to choose to visit museums in their leisure time can still be quite critical of their experience. This recognition combines with the genuine reservations of those who tend not to visit museums, to produce a general consensus that museum displays tend to be perceived as potentially dull. It is therefore perhaps in the area of exhibition design that museum developments can do much to dispel this image.

Table 5.9 Attitudes to museum presentations, by type of visitor

	'The presentation can be dull'						
Type of visitor (%)	Strongly agree	Agree	Neither	Disagree	Strongly disagree	(%)	N
Frequent	4	54	9	29	5	100	161
Regular	5	50	11	28	7	100	345
Occasional	8	52	12	27	2	100	132
Rare	10	47	11	29	3	100	129
Non-visitor	9	50	17	21	3	100	149
All (%)	7	51	12	27	4	100	916

It is also the regular and occasional visitors who are most likely to disagree that museums provide plenty for children to do. This is possibly for similar reasons to those advanced above: certain people have visited museums with their children and found little for them and so their answers are based on experience (Table 5.10). Some support for this interpretation is gained when answers are crosstabulated with age. Those under 35, who are perhaps the group most likely to have young children, are significantly more likely than the other age groups to disagree that museums provide plenty for children.

Table 5.10 Attitudes to provision for children, by type of museum visitor and age

	'They provide plenty for children to do'						
Type of visitor (%)	Strongly agree	Agree	Neither	Disagree	Strongly disagree	(%)	N
Frequent	15	43	22	18	2	100	158
Regular	8	35	31	24	3	100	335
Occasional	11	29	34	21	5	100	129
Rare	10	40	28	15	9	100	128
Non-visitor	12	43	25	12	9	100	148
Age (%)							
<35	6	31	32	23	8	100	159
35–59	12	37	25	22	3	100	343
>60	14	45	28	10	3	100	134
All (%)	11	37	28	19	5	100	897

The answers to other questions demonstrate again the persistence of the negative image of museums amongst those who tend not to visit them. There are, for example, significant differences in attitudes towards the amount of text presented in museum displays. 27 per cent of rare visitors and 40 per cent of non-visitors agreed that there are too many words to read, compared with only 8 per cent of frequent visitors (Table 5.11). In addition, non-visitors and rare

Table 5.11 Attitudes to the amount of text in museums, by type of museum visitor

	'There are too many words'						
Type of visitor (%)	Strongly agree	Agree	Neither	Disagree	Strongly disagree	(%)	N
Frequent	1	7	13	53	26	100	160
Regular	1	16	12	58	12	100	344
Occasional	3	11	19	60	6	100	132
Rare	4	23	16	53	4	100	125
Non-visitor	6	34	23	33	5	100	148
All (%)	3	18	16	53	12	100	909

visitors were significantly more likely than the other groups to agree that 'the attendants are like guards' (52 and 46 per cent agreement respectively). However, around a third of regular and frequent visitors also agreed with the statement, showing that the image of museum attendants is a problem even with a large section of committed museum visitors (Table 5.12).

Table 5.12 Attitudes towards museum attendants by type of museum visitor

Type of visitor (%)	'The attendants are like guards'						
	Strongly agree	Agree	Neither	Disagree	Strongly disagree	(%)	N
Frequent	5	25	15	49	6	100	160
Regular	5	28	15	44	8	100	344
Occasional	5	27	15	48	5	100	133
Rare	6	40	11	39	4	100	126
Non-visitor	9	43	18	29	3	100	150
All (%)	6	32	15	42	6	100	913

The strengths of the different deterrents

The different structural and cultural deterrents to museum visiting so far examined all have some effect, but no single one overwhelmingly explains visiting patterns. What is needed now is a way of comparing the strength of all the deterrents with each other. This can be achieved, as it was for the section concerning images of the past, by using regression analysis. The results of the regression analysis are presented in Table 5.13, where those that are statistically significant appear in their order of importance.

The most striking thing to emerge from this analysis is that the first four

Table 5.13 A model of museum visiting

Stepwise regression analysis			
Dependent variable = Type of museum visitor			
Variable	**Beta**	**F**	**Sig F**
Value placed on past	.254300	66.871	.0000
Attitude to museums	.181939	38.626	.0000
Age	−.169118	24.201	.0000
Image of building	.168914	22.986	.0000
Education	.119079	14.383	.0000
Housing Tenure	.094804	9.332	.0047
Attitude to present	.093397	8.726	.0058

significant factors are all cultural ones, and most of the structural ones, including access to a vehicle and feelings about paying for admission, do not appear at all in the equation. This confirms that it is the cultural factors, to do with upbringing and education, that are the most important in determining museum visiting in a general sense. The structural factors will only come into play at a lower level, in influencing which particular museum to visit, once the decision to visit a museum is made.

The table shows that the strongest factor in determining museum visiting is the value that an individual places on knowing about the past. This is perhaps best seen as a *precondition* for museum visiting, because the strong effect is almost certainly caused by those people who do not value the past, who also, unsurprisingly, do not visit museums. In other words, there are those who do not value the past and thus will never visit museums, whereas there are others who do value the past but are deterred from visiting by other cultural factors.

Attitudes to museum services seem to be the next most influential factor, which shows the fundamental importance of the nuts and bolts of museum work (welcoming attendants, clean toilets, pleasant atmosphere and so on) in determining the public's perception of museums in general. Just one unsatisfactory experience in one museum could potentially lead someone to reject museums in general.

This is followed in importance by age, which is negatively related to visiting. In other words the older someone is, the less likely they are to visit a museum. As we have seen earlier, however, the main effect of this is amongst those over sixty. This is followed very closely by the image of the museum as an institution: the more positive these are, the more frequently visiting is undertaken. This in turn is followed by education: the longer the formal education received, the more frequently visiting occurs. Housing tenure, as an approximate indicator of affluence, comes next, with home owners more likely to visit museums than those who rent their accommodation. Finally, the only other significant variable is attitudes towards the present. Attitudes to the present are a stronger predictor of visiting than attitudes to the past, which as we have seen are paradoxically valued negatively by museum visitors, all of which adds to the suggestion that museum visiting is mainly about the present rather than the past.

It is, then, the cultural factors which dominate the reasons for visiting museums or staying away from them. In order to explain why this is, then, we need to look at museum visiting as a cultural phenomenon; in other words, to place museum visiting back into the historical and social context that has for so long been lacking in visitor studies. To achieve this we have to begin to cast the net wider by looking, first, at the social patterning for other 'heritage' activities, and for related leisure pursuits.

Attitudes to heritage presentations

The pattern of attitudes to historic buildings[5] was similar to that found for museums. People who visit castles are more favourable in their attitudes towards them than people who do not visit, and the same applies to visitors and non-visitors to historic houses. Where attitudes to historic buildings in general (castles and houses together) are considered, it becomes clear that both the actual quality of the presentations, and their general image, act as deterrents to non-visitors. For example, while 49 per cent of people who visit both castles and historic houses disagree that 'not enough information is provided', only 23 per cent of those people who visit neither, disagree with the statement (Table 5.14).

Table 5.14 Attitudes to level of information provided in castles and historic houses, by type of visitor

Type of visitor (%)	'Not enough information is provided about their history'						
	Strongly agree	Agree	Neither	Disagree	Strongly disagree	(%)	N
Visits both	5	33	13	46	3	100	287
Visits one	5	32	20	41	2	100	296
Visits neither	5	38	35	22	1	100	303
All (%)	5	35	23	36	2	100	886

Rather than suggesting that visitors are kept away mainly by a perceived lack of information in the historic presentation, these differences might in fact be taken to indicate that they have a generally negative attitude to formal heritage presentations. For example overall, 70 per cent of respondents agreed to some extent that castles and historic houses bring the past to life better than museums (Table 5.15), but only 63 per cent of non-visitors agreed compared with 79 per cent of people who visit both. This does not necessarily imply that non-visitors are more likely to prefer museums; it gives an indication of their relative lack of willingness to approve of any heritage institutions.

Table 5.15 Attitudes to the authenticity of castles and historic houses, by type of visitor

Type of visitor (%)	'They bring the past to life better than museums'						
	Strongly agree	Agree	Neither	Disagree	Strongly disagree	(%)	N
Visits both	19	60	10	10	2	100	287
Visits one	12	58	13	16	1	100	299
Visits neither	11	52	21	16	–	100	308
All (%)	14	56	15	14	1	100	894

This interpretation is given additional strength when considered alongside attitudes to the exclusiveness of castles and historic houses. While 42 per cent of people who had visited a castle and/or a historic house agreed with the statement 'They only show the life of the rich', 67 per cent of non-visitors agreed, implying that an image of exclusiveness is a strong deterrent factor for those who tend not to visit them (Table 5.16).

Table 5.16 Attitudes to the exclusiveness of castles and historic houses, by type of visitor

Type of visitor (%)	'They only show the life of the rich'						
	Strongly agree	Agree	Neither	Disagree	Strongly disagree	(%)	N
Visits both	9	33	4	49	5	100	289
Visits one	7	36	9	46	4	100	298
Visits neither	17	50	8	24	1	100	309
All (%)	11	40	7	39	3	100	896

Indeed, as far as people who do not participate on a yearly basis are concerned, it seems to be the other attractions sometimes laid on at such presentations that would provide the main interest for a visit, not the historic building itself: 62 per cent of non-visitors agreed that such things as zoos, parks and fairs were the main attractions at castles and historic houses, compared with 31 per cent of people who visit both (Table 5.17).

Table 5.17 Attitudes to other attractions, by type of visitor

Type of visitor (%)	'One of their main attractions are the other things there (e.g. fair, zoo, park)'						
	Strongly agree	Agree	Neither	Disagree	Strongly disagree	(%)	N
Visits both	4	27	8	45	16	100	288
Visits one	5	41	12	37	5	100	296
Visits neither	10	52	16	20	2	100	303
All (%)	6	40	12	34	8	100	887

Factors influencing visits to castles and historic houses

Taken together, the attitudes demonstrated by visitors and non-visitors to heritage presentations suggest that, as was found with museums, attitudes towards the experience itself, and particularly the general image of the institution, have an important effect on whether or not visiting occurs. Regression analysis can again be used to determine the relative effects of attitudes and variables such as age, status, and vehicle access. This found that attitudes were the most important predictor of historic building visiting, as they were for museums (Table A2.5). Unlike museums, however, the next most important factor was access to a vehicle, demonstrating the important structural effect that the distribution of historic buildings has on participation, as predicted by Prince (1983) for the visiting of countryside interpretation centres.

Although structural factors are more important in historic building visiting than they are for museums, and level of education has a stronger effect than age, the important point emerging from the above analysis is that attitudes to the presentation are again the strongest factor in influencing visiting. In the next chapter it will be argued that, at least to a certain extent, the negative image of museums amongst non-visitors could be blamed on the physical environment and evangelising social mission of early museums which would have been intimidating to those unfamiliar with it. This kind of argument might also be extended to historic buildings in that they also tend to be large and imposing, and are associated with an aristocratic way of life, such that they might be viewed as intimidating by many people because of their historical associations.

Heritage and high culture

In view of the similarity between visiting patterns to different types of heritage presentation, a typology of heritage visitors was built up on the basis of annual visiting to each attraction. Five visitor types were isolated, ranging from those who visited none of these kinds of attraction in the course of a year, to those who visited all four. The characteristics of heritage visitors are similar to those of visitors to the various individual attractions, but in a more accentuated form (Table 5.18).

Table 5.18 Characteristics of types of heritage visitor

	Visits none	Visits one	Visits two	Visits three	Visits all	(%)	N
Age (%)							
<35	19	13	20	26	22	100	298
35–59	17	15	25	19	24	100	367
>60	39	17	16	16	12	100	256
Status (%)							
High	11	11	20	27	31	100	148
Middle	21	15	23	21	20	100	597
Low <60	34	19	21	11	15	100	81
Low >60	57	13	7	13	11	100	801
Education (%)							
Minimum	28	16	22	17	17	100	630
Stayed on	18	12	18	30	21	100	149
Post-school	9	11	21	25	35	100	121
All (%)	24	15	21	20	20	100	906

People over 60 years old are by far the least likely to visit any heritage presentation at all, while the other two age groups are likely to visit at least two per year. These differences are even greater where status is concerned, with those of high status most likely to visit all heritage presentations (31 per cent visit all four). Those of middle status show a fairly even spread of preferences, while those of low status are most likely not to visit any. Within the low status group, differences are especially strong between those under 60 and those over 60, with 57 per cent of the latter visiting nothing, compared with 34 per cent of the former. Finally, length of education also has a significant effect on heritage participation, with those who left school at the earliest opportunity most likely to visit none of the attractions listed (28 per cent do not visit anything), compared with those who had some form of tertiary education who are most likely to visit all four heritage presentations (35 per cent visit all four).

Table 5.19 Frequency of visits of heritage visitors to museums and historic houses

	Number of times that visitors visit (%)							
	Museums				**Historic houses**			
Type of visitor	1-2 Times	3+ Times	(%)	N	1-2 Times	3+ Times	(%)	N
Visits one	90	10	100	61	88	12	100	26
Visits two	86	14	100	125	95	5	100	81
Visits three	68	32	100	168	76	24	100	136
Visits all	50	50	100	185	57	43	100	185

Incidence of heritage participation is also related to frequency; in other words, the greater the range of presentations visited, the more frequently they are visited as well. The example of museum and historic house visiting suffices to make this point (Table 5.19): those who visit all four heritage presentations also visit them more frequently than any other group. Participation in heritage presentations thus increases with education and status both in terms of the range of institutions visited and the frequency of visits.

Individuals of high status are most likely to visit all four types of heritage presentations, and to visit them often, such that they might reasonably be nicknamed 'culture vultures'. It is in this rather pejorative term that the key to understanding heritage visiting lies, encompassing as it does the idea of a high culture devoured perhaps with little feeling for its content. Heritage is beginning to appear as just one element in a wider package of cultured leisure activities participated in predominantly, but by no means exclusively, by higher status, better educated individuals who are socialized into perceiving these activities as a legitimate and worthwhile use of their time. This point is best brought out by considering the participation of heritage visitors in a range of activities specifically chosen for their high culture associations (Table 5.20).

Again, those who visit all heritage presentations (the 'culture vultures') are far more likely than any other group to visit the theatre or attend classical

Table 5.20 Incidence of attendance of heritage visitors of theatre, classical concerts, opera and ballet

Heritage visiting	Participation (%)			
	Theatre	Concerts	Ballet	Opera
Visits none	18	4	2	1
Visits one	37	10	2	4
Visits two	43	13	7	3
Visits three	59	20	9	4
Visits all	75	29	21	22
All	46	18	8	7

concerts, ballet, or opera, and again, they also visit them more often (Table 5.21). This is a pattern also found for France by Bourdieu and Darbel (1991: Tables A4.7 & A4.8) and for Canada by Dixon *et al.* (1974: 117-8).

Table 5.21 Frequency of attendance of heritage visitors of theatre and classical concerts

Type of visitor	Number of times that visitors visit (%)							
	Theatre				Classical Concerts			
	1-2 Times	3+ Times	(%)	N	1-2 Times	3+ Times	(%)	N
Visits none	90	10	100	40	70	30	100	10
Visits one	74	26	100	53	92	8	100	13
Visits two	72	28	100	81	81	19	100	26
Visits three	72	28	100	112	66	34	100	38
Visits all	50	50	100	139	64	36	100	72

Discussion

The participation patterns noted above are consistent with findings from surveys of other leisure activities: the better educated and more affluent people are, the wider are their opportunities and consequently a wider range of activities are undertaken. The behaviour of the 'culture vultures' (who tend to be well educated and affluent) is explained by the fact that they are 'doers', and will participate in many activities. This does not mean, however, that they are indiscriminate in their leisure activities. Although the more active they are, the more they are likely to straddle taste cultures (for example, by both going to a football match and visiting a museum), there are definite class based trends in leisure activities. *Leisure Futures* (Summer 1985: 38), for example, summarises participation in various leisure activities by socio-economic group and finds that there are certain pursuits much less likely to be participated in by the normally active and wide-ranging high status groups, such as bingo and darts (Table 5.22).

Table 5.22 Participation in class-based leisure activities

Activity	Socio-economic group (%)			
	AB	C1	C2	DE
Indoor sport	53	46	31	24
Further education	39	25	13	10
Home computer	33	22	16	6
Museums	60	52	35	36
Betting & gambling	27	35	35	39
Watching sport	17	35	30	34
Darts	19	25	26	33
Bingo	4	8	19	29

(*Source: Leisure Futures*, Summer 1985: 38)

This chart clearly shows the class basis of many leisure activities. The culture vultures, then, may participate in a wide range of activities, but their sallies onto the common ground of, for example, pub-going, are done from the home ground of higher or middle-brow culture.

This chapter has shown that the visiting patterns to heritage presentations are biased towards those who are of higher status, and that patterns are similar to those for other high culture activities. At the same time it has been shown that it is not structural factors such as time, money and transport which primarily influence whether people visit museums or not, it is cultural factors such as people's image of museums and the service they provide, coupled with age and education. It seems likely that the historical and contemporary associations of museums with high culture, and the existence of cultural deterrents to visiting are highly interlinked. The nature of this link will now be explored by examining theoretical approaches to the explanation of museum- and heritage-visiting, and thus of the patterns detected in the survey.

6 Explaining the consumption of heritage

The previous chapters have demonstrated how, historically, the museum has been seen as part of high culture and how, in contemporary society, its visiting patterns are similar to other high culture activities. It has been suggested that museum visiting, and heritage visiting in general, might be part of a group of leisure activities expressive of a cultivated lifestyle. In order to explore the implications of this, we have to move beyond inadequate surface explanations of leisure, and examine wider theories which will allow museum visiting to be placed in its historical and contemporary context.

Theories of museum visiting

Discussion will now focus on two contrasting models that have been put forward to explain museum visiting patterns. The first one can be termed 'the psychological approach', and takes the individual's leisure motivations as the focus of its study. The second, termed 'the cultural approach', studies social aggregates and looks at the wider cultural and political dimensions of museum visiting. It is suggested that the latter potentially provides the most penetrative account of the social role of museum visiting, but that important elements from the first approach need to be incorporated to formulate a balanced explanation of the phenomenon.

The psychological approach

The use of a psychological paradigm is the dominant approach in the study of museum visiting, especially in the USA, which now boasts a number of organisations, publications and conferences devoted to the topic (Bitgood 1989, 1990). Much of this work, both in the USA and elsewhere is concerned with the investigation and improvement of the educational experience received by visitors once they are already at the museum, and takes its cue from work in educational psychology. In Britain, the work carried out at the Natural History Museum and the Science Museum has been pre-eminent in this field (McManus 1989; Miles et al. 1982).

Relatively little work using an explicitly psychological framework has, however, been carried out in the wider field of visiting and non-visiting. The most influential work so far has been conducted in the USA by Hood (1981, 1983) and in Britain by Prince (1982, 1983, 1985a, 1985b). Their approach is based on behavioural psychology, whereby museum visiting (or non-visiting) is argued to be most strongly influenced by the individual's attitudes to the museum. Hood terms these individual attitudes and perceptions 'psychographic variables' and argues that they are a much more powerful explanation of museum visiting than simple demographic variables (Hood 1981: 20-25). From an extensive literature search she isolates six major attributes underlying adult choices of leisure activities (Hood 1983: 51):

1. Being with people
2. Doing something worthwhile
3. Feeling comfortable and at ease in one's surroundings
4. Having a challenge of new experiences
5. Having an opportunity to learn
6. Participating actively

From the results of her telephone survey of 502 residents of Toledo, Ohio, she finds that frequent visitors highly value all six leisure attributes, especially those of learning, having new experiences and doing something worthwhile, and they perceive all six to be present in museums. Occasional visitors, on the other hand, find that some of the leisure attributes they value are present in museums, but not in sufficient strength to warrant regular attendance. Non-visitors most value participating actively, meeting people, and being in comfortable, casual surroundings. However, they do not perceive these attributes to be present in museums, which are on the contrary seen to be formal and formidable places. Hood concludes that 'museums generally offer or emphasize the very qualities that are least appealing to the occasional participants and non-participants, who are looking for significantly different leisure satisfactions' (Hood 1983: 56).

Hood's approach is helpful because of her insistence that attitudes towards museums should be the main focus of an explanation of museum visiting or non-visiting. However, her work, like much of the North American approach to visitor studies, is flawed by its avoidance of social analysis. Demographic factors are rather dismissed as not being predictors of museum visiting, although they are correlated with it (Hood 1981: 284). Such a dismissal substantially reduces the potential to explain why some people have positive views of museums and others have negative views, because the proffered explanation that it depends on people's leisure needs begs the question of where these needs come from. Hood recognises that they are influenced by socialization, but does not place museum visiting in any social context, and thus has to sidestep the political and ideological roots of museum visiting which lie at the heart of an understanding of it as a cultural phenomenon.

Prince similarly argues that attitudes to museums are derived from the individual's perceived leisure needs, which in turn result from past experience and general life needs (Prince 1983: 242): 'the choice to visit a museum would be governed by the potential visitor's attitudes to museums as social institutions, and by the belief in the opinions of valued others (the subjective norm) about visiting museums in general' (Prince 1985b: 87).

However, Prince allows a much greater role to the social and environmental factors that shape leisure needs and attitudes to museums. Just as we have found earlier that similar people tend to visit a whole range of high culture activities, he discovers that those who use country trails are also likely to visit museums, nature reserves and craft centres. He suggests that people tend to maintain a behavioural consistency in their leisure activities, and that this consistency 'is rooted in leisure needs and nurtured by cultural orientation and subgroup allegiance through socialization and the maintenance of self' (Prince 1983: 240).

In the interpretation of these patterns he is careful first to look at any structural factors which might influence visiting. An important factor in countryside visiting is found to be access to a car, though it is not as crucial a predictor of visiting behaviour as the individual's attitudes and self-image. Having explored structural explanations, Prince then examines behavioural explanations of visiting by suggesting the possible derivations of different leisure needs. Two of the most important influences are held to be the individual's position in the life-cycle and his or her social class. In the first case, drawing on the work of Rapoport and Rapoport (1975) it is suggested that leisure needs and motivations change over time and that certain stages of the life cycle will be accompanied by distinct leisure patterns. Museums are argued to appeal most to the 'establishment' phase which is characterised by a commitment to family-based leisure. In the second case, Prince notes examples of class-based leisure needs, such as the (supposed) tendency of working class individuals to prefer collectively organised and passive holidays, and the desire of middle class individuals to use their time constructively, for example by museum visiting and reading (Prince 1983: 243).

Prince's work convincingly confirms, then, that it is people's attitudes to museums that are the strongest influence on their visiting, and that cultural influences and social status are important factors in shaping these attitudes. His explanatory approach, and his distinction between structural and cultural factors, have been important influences on the research presented here. However, the adoption of the psychological approach only partially fulfils the aim of understanding museum visiting in its social context. This is because, although it identified socio-cultural factors as being important, it is unable to move beyond this observation to an understanding of how it is that these factors actually operate to bring about the patterns in cultural consumption continually detected by surveys. No explanation is offered, for example, why it is that these different 'leisure needs' occur. Under the psychological paradigm, these dispositions just seem to exist amongst members of different classes, as if they are inherent in membership of that class. To a large extent this is because the psychological approach focuses at the level of the individual or small group, which makes it difficult to deal with larger social groups which cannot be observed at the same level of detail. Psychology thus tends to ignore these larger groupings and the political and ideological concepts associated with them. The psychological approach to museum visiting is thus an apolitical one, and treats attitudes to museums as simply different rather than the product of a hierarchical culture. The dynamic element to these different attitudes is ignored because to explore it would involve stepping outside the scientific observables of psychology into the more speculative realms of history and cultural theory.

The cultural approach

To add this dimension we have to turn to the level of the social group, for it is only at this level that the historical derivation and contemporary operation of museum visiting as a cultural activity can fully be discerned. Central to such an enterprise must be a consideration of the work of Pierre Bourdieu, which, along with most other wider cultural theory, is only just beginning to have its impact in the world of museums (Shelton 1990).

Bourdieu's work is particularly important as he is the only major social theorist who has specifically worked on museums and integrated this work into his overall project, which has been to understand the reproduction of power and privilege. In order to understand the part that museums play in this, it is useful first to step back and review his general social theory, particularly that concerning 'code' and 'cultural capital'.

Bourdieu is particularly concerned to stress that all social life must be viewed as a unity, as a series of homologous 'fields', rather than conceived as separate, largely unrelated areas such as 'culture' and 'economy'. He sees the systematic unity of the various fields in terms of an economic analogy which he calls 'the economy of practices' (Bourdieu 1977: 183), based around two mutually convertible forms of power, the symbolic and the economic.

In common with the analyses of ideology discussed earlier, Bourdieu argues that the reproduction of hierarchical social relations relies on the 'misrecognition' of their essentially oppressive basis, and that symbolic power is the mechanism behind this misrecognition (*ibid*: 195-7). For example, deference to authority is misrecognized as being the natural and legitimate order of things, rather than a strategy by which hierarchy is reproduced. For social reproduction to occur, it is therefore not enough for dominant groups to possess economic power alone. Economic power has to be legitimated by an appropriate degree of symbolic power in order to be used and reproduced. It is symbolic power which produces a consensus that the dominant have a right to their position and in this way it produces a complicity amongst the dominated in their own domination. The symbolic or cultural aspects of the reproduction of social relations are therefore just as important as the economic aspects. In Bourdieu's analysis, museum-visiting acts in the realm of cultural reproduction and thus, ultimately, helps to ensure economic reproduction.

Symbolic power itself is derived from the possession and accumulation of 'cultural capital', which in turn has two components. The first kind of cultural capital is the taste, manners and style deriving from prolonged exposure to higher, or bourgeois, culture (Bourdieu 1984: 75). Aspects of this, such as connoisseurship and an aesthetic ethos, only come about through a long investment of time by parents and teachers. The second kind of cultural capital is the material manifestation of these cultivated 'dispositions', such as school and university certificates. These can act as an important medium of exchange between cultural and economic capital, because the investment of time and resources in the accumulation of cultural capital has an initial pay-off in the acquisition of educational qualifications, and, through these, an ultimate economic pay-off in the job market (Bourdieu 1977: 183-97). The specific ways in which this works is best shown by examining the role of the educational system in legitimating the reproduction of hierarchical society.

The educational system: codes and competence

Bourdieu argues that for both teachers and pupils, the schooling system acts through the 'ideology of the gift', or talent, whereby academic success is seen to be a result of natural virtues, or acquired through hard work and thus deserved (Bourdieu 1968: 608). Similarly, schools and universities *appear* to have absolute autonomy and freedom of thought and thus to be politically neutral. They are therefore seen to be inherently fair and democratic institutions (Bourdieu and Passeron 1977: 65). It is in opposition to this pervasive view that Bourdieu formulates his wide-ranging critique of education.

In contrast, Bourdieu argues that schooling imposes an arbitrary set of values (arbitrary in the sense that they are not fixed or resident in nature) which reflect the interests of the dominant class in the maintenance of hierarchical social relations. As the school puts forward an illusion of neutrality, it produces a 'culture of consensus' which (mis)recognises this arbitrary set of values as legitimate and natural for everyone in society. Schooling therefore inculcates a *recognition* both of the legitimacy of the dominant culture and of the illegitimacy of the culture of the dominated (Bourdieu and Passeron 1977: 35-41), and a *misrecognition* that the dominant culture is an arbitrary construction (*ibid*: 5).

At the same time, schooling produces a culture of distinction (Bourdieu 1971) which will separate out the cultivated and the non-cultivated. This process is set in motion from the child's earliest pre-school days when what Bourdieu terms a primary 'habitus' is formed by the family and its social environment. The habitus is defined as a 'system of internalized structures, schemes of perception, conception and action common to all members of the same group or class' (Bourdieu 1977: 86), or in short, a shared culture and way of approaching the world. The family habitus in which a child is reared is of great importance because it is this which will shape his or her performance in school. If a family develops a habitus in which books, learning, discussion and abstract concepts are highly valued, the child's 'linguistic capital' is likely to be greater than that of a child not exposed to these influences. The former child is consequently predisposed to achieve more in school, because he or she shares in the habitus of those who construct the syllabus and comprise the teaching staff, and is more likely to feel at home in the culture of the school.

School culture can be seen as a form of code which has to be correctly deciphered in order for its messages to be fully assimilated. The success of initial schooling will thus depend on the degree of congruence between the primary habitus of the child and the habitus of the school. Initial reaction to the schooling experience is crucial. It is during this period that the competence of the child in mastering the school code will be evident, and this competence will be strongly influenced, although not determined, by the child's initial habitus. In turn, the individual's habitus will be shaped and transformed by the school experience, but will still retain a firm imprint of the primary habitus.

While the concept of habitus has the flexibility to allow for underprivileged individuals to achieve well in the educational process, in a generalised statistical sense, those who are not predisposed to achieve well at school tend indeed to leave at the earliest opportunity, while those who are predisposed to achieve well generally do. As the habitus will influence what is felt to be reasonable behaviour, individuals possessing a certain habitus will adjust their expectations to the likely probability of them being satisfied. This is termed 'the causality of the probable', whereby 'inherited dispositions predispose individuals to occupy the positions towards which they orient them' (Bourdieu 1984: 365). In other words people will tend to exclude themselves from participation in a field in which they feel they have little competence, unless they are on an upwardly mobile social trajectory and wish to assume a more cultured lifestyle.

In summary, then, education produces both a common culture of consensus and an exclusive culture of distinction by inculcating all with a recognition of the legitimacy of the dominant taste culture while at the same time equipping only a portion fully to take part in it. The dominated, not possessing the competence in dominant culture, exclude themselves from it while recognizing its legitimacy and the illegitimacy of their own culture, condemning themselves to what Bourdieu calls 'cultural allodoxia' or 'misapprehension', which is the gap between 'recognition' and 'knowledge' ('*reconnaissance*' and '*connaissance*') (Bourdieu 1984: 323). This self-exclusion is essential for social reproduction because it is misperceived as a choice ('the choice of the necessary') and consequently is much more effective (Bourdieu and Passeron 1977: 41). It is thus a fundamental principle of Bourdieu's work on reproduction that the dominated tend to collaborate in their own domination, without the dominant usually needing to have recourse to overt means of coercion: 'Once a system of mechanisms has been constituted capable of objectively ensuring the reproduction of the established order by its own motion..., the dominant class have only to *let the system they dominate take its own course* in order to exercise their domination' (Bourdieu 1977: 190, emphasis in original).

Museums and art galleries

In addition to their formulation in an educational context, some of these ideas were developed in the course of a large-scale project carried out in the mid-1960s on museum visiting in France and the rest of Europe (Bourdieu and Darbel 1991). Although the main focus was on art galleries, many of the ideas discussed are applicable more generally. In common with other surveys reviewed here, they found that museum visiting was generally restricted to the better educated, and that the groups most represented in the general population were least represented in the museum public (Bourdieu and Darbel 1991: 15). In the analysis of this finding, the terms habitus, code and competence are used in a linked fashion as they are in the arguments concerning the education system, although now the experience of schooling has itself had a strong effect on people's habitus, and differences in cultural competence have been amplified.

The cornerstone of Bourdieu's interpretation is his rejection of the Kantian aesthetic whereby art can be appreciated for its own sake by the untutored eye. Instead, the works of art in art museums are seen as transmitting specialised messages, the deciphering of which is learned at school. Far from being innate, aesthetic appreciation is thus socially determined: 'the richness of 'reception' ... depends primarily on the competence of the 'receiver', in other words on the degree to which he or she can master the code of the 'message'" (Bourdieu and Darbel 1991: 38).

In contrast to adherents of the psychological approach, therefore, Bourdieu would see 'cultural needs' as being entirely socially constructed through education and family upbringing (*ibid*: 107). In his terms, the idea that leisure activities are selected according to a free choice shaped by the individual's wishes and needs is a misrecognition of their class-based derivation. Instead, museums are best understood by those who are in possession of the cipher with which to render their code meaningful; and a comprehension of the code is most likely to be prevalent amongst those whose habitus has predisposed them to do so. Confronted with works of art (or indeed other unfamiliar objects such as those produced by archaeology), those with little access to the appropriate cultural cipher feel 'overwhelmed' and can do little more than comment on the material qualities of the work such as size, colour, and the amount of time and labour used to produce it (*ibid*: 44-5).

Thus, museum visiting, like art and cultural practices in general, is emblematic of 'distinction', in that it is recognised as a cultured activity although only certain sections of the population participate in it, while others exclude themselves through their lack of familiarity with museum culture: 'In the tiniest details of their morphology and their organisation, museums betray their true function, which is to reinforce for some the feeling of belonging and for others the feeling of exclusion' (*ibid*: 112).

Borrowing heavily from Bourdieu's work, Dimaggio and Useem (1978) come to similar conclusions in a study of arts consumption in the U.S.A.. They argue that arts appreciation is trained rather than innate, that the setting of art displays favours the upper classes in its ambience, that arts consumption is a form of cultural capital, and finally that it serves to enhance class cohesion: 'The upper class can be expected to make efforts to exclude other classes from acquiring its artistic interests as a means of preserving elite boundaries and dominance from generation to generation' (Dimaggio and Useem 1978: 144).

Shortcomings

Despite its seeming comprehensiveness and attractiveness, Bourdieu's arguments have a number of shortcomings. In complete contrast to the criticisms put forward above in relation to the psychological approach, the cultural approach as outlined here has tended to play down individual variability and emphasised what are ultimately class distinctions to the exclusion of other explanatory factors. In their concentration on class and habitus, Bourdieu's arguments about museums have ultimately tended towards determinism[6], because together they are taken to explain all social behaviour: class determines habitus which in turn structures cultural behaviour in favour of economic and class reproduction. A contributory factor must be Bourdieu's concentration on art galleries where, as we have seen in the cases of the Tate Gallery and the Victoria and Albert Museum, visitors are much more highly educated and of higher status than in other more general museums, and where arguments about cultural and class divisions are easier to make.

The survey results presented here, together with those from other surveys, show that non-art museums are visited by a wider, though not representative, cross-section of the public than art galleries. Clearly class or status alone cannot explain these patterns, so we have to look to some of the factors suggested by the psychological approach to provide a fuller understanding. As a result of his concentration on art galleries, Bourdieu is purely concerned with the oppressive aspects of museums and their role in social reproduction, and his argument becomes a more sophisticated version of the dominant ideology thesis.

A further problem is that Bourdieu's arguments are directed towards the situation as it existed in France in the mid-1960s, arguments which may not be applicable to Britain twenty-five years later, after the 'heritage boom' has occurred and begun to decline. He is not easily able to explain the popularity of museums, which is a crucial factor in the understanding of museum visiting as a contemporary cultural phenomenon, and he studies visitors only and is therefore not able to take into account the deterrents experienced by non-visitors. Despite these shortcomings, Bourdieu's approach is sufficiently flexible to have provided us with a body of concepts that can be used to move beyond his own analysis towards a fuller explanation.

Synthesis

A review of the psychological and cultural approaches shows that both can provide useful insights into the phenomenon of museum visiting. Both, however, have limitations, but by combining elements from both, a comprehensive account can be formulated. From an examination of the psychological approach, it is clear that an important role has to be accorded to lifecycle position and structural factors, and from the cultural approach it is evident that museum visiting has to be considered in its historical and contemporary context. The broader perspective offered by this combination provides a fuller explanation of museum visiting by demonstrating the ultimately social determination of leisure choice. One element of this involves taking 'explanatory' factors such as age, class and structural constraints and examining their relationship with leisure patterns in their wider social context. The foundation for this approach lies in the work of certain leisure theorists such as Kelly (1982, 1983) who have attempted to reconcile the small-scale psychological approach exemplified by the work of Prince, with the large-scale sociological work exemplified by the work of Bourdieu.

Leisure theory

A crucial social factor in the explanation of museum visiting patterns is provided by the concept of 'leisure opportunity', used by Kelly (1982, 1983) in an attempt to integrate personal motivations with macro-scale sociology. The ideas behind this concept are just the same as those used by Bourdieu in explaining 'the choice of the necessary' (Bourdieu 1984: 372), or how an individual's habitus will tend in a statistical sense to structure his or her perception of what constitutes reasonable and appropriate expectations and behaviour.

The point of convergence is the insistence on uncovering the hidden social constraints on apparently free differences in individual leisure choices: 'Because of the 'free market' ideology, these differences appear as choices. In reality they depend on very different processes - the very real divisions of class, gender, race and age which structure choice' (Clarke and Critcher 1985: 119).

The crux of the argument is that a leisure activity is only undertaken if the 'opportunity' to undertake it is perceived as such. Every activity has various meanings associated with it, derived both from its history and from its contemporary role. It is each individual's relationship to these meanings that will most closely determine whether the opportunity to participate in the activity is perceived.

The effects of socialization

Kelly argues that social factors influence leisure not as direct determinants but through the opportunities that they provide. The sort of nominally independent variables used in surveys such as income, occupation, education level, age, sex, race and indices of social status he suggests are best understood as 'indicators of socialization probabilities'. For example, rather than being a direct determinant of leisure, status is an indication of the kind of interests and opportunities likely to be a part of a person's experience (Kelly 1983: 35).

The two main components of leisure socialization are the family (and other childhood influences), and the subsequent 'life career model' (Kelly 1982: 172) consisting notably of schooling and the influences of peers. The basic similarity with Bourdieu's theory becomes apparent here. Just as the primary habitus developed in the family will structure the reception of the school experience, so too will initial family socialization set the scene for the subsequent perception of leisure opportunities.

Opportunities are constrained by social factors in a dual way, because 'class' can be both economically and culturally defined: low income will be a constraint on certain activities which become part of the culture of the group, and an individual socialized into certain activities will develop a disposition which internalizes these cultural and material constraints as actual choices (Kelly 1983: 46). Thus, leisure can be seen to operate in the same way in which

Bourdieu notes that education works: to promote the self exclusion of those least equipped to participate in it, misrecognized as a *choice* not to participate.

The mutually re-inforcing effect of social position and socialization acts, according to Parker, to divide society into two classes, those who are privileged with respect to a unified and fulfilling work-leisure life, and those who are underprivileged in both areas (Parker 1983: 110). Although the simple division of society into two such classes may be over-exaggerated, the idea of a 'double effect' does seem at least to fit the pattern of participation in heritage activities, with their higher culture connotations. The ways in which this works will now be investigated in a concluding section which draws together a number of arguments into an interepretation of the social context of museum visiting.

The role of museum visiting in contemporary Britain

So far the survey has shown that museum and heritage visiting is part of a package of higher culture activities participated in by higher status individuals and those who are relatively young, out of proportion to their numbers in the total population. At the same time it has to be recognised that museums are in fact very popular institutions, being visited by 47-58 per cent of the population each year. The task then is to explain why museums are not visited by some groups but are visited by others. In other words it is not just the unpopularity of museums which has to be explained, but also their popularity; why for example nearly half of the museums in the country have been founded since 1971. Drawing on the vocabulary of both Bourdieu's work and of leisure studies, an interpretation will now be put forward which will attempt to do both.

The historical burden of the image of the museum

One of the most important factors in influencing whether museum visiting is undertaken or not is the image that an individual holds of the museum. In order to understand this it is necessary to look at the history of museums and how their social mission has shaped people's images of them.

The first public museums have their roots in the earlier cabinets of curiosities. In these, exhibits were arranged in encyclopaedic fashion in an attempt to encompass the known natural and artificial world (Impey and MacGregor 1985). As the contents were usually known intimately to the collector himself (and they were almost exclusively men), or were accumulated for purposes of prestige rather than didacticism, they required little supporting explanation. The earliest public museum collections in Europe were modelled on the same lines as the great private collections and housed in similar structures (Wittlin 1970: 71). Indeed, in many instances, such as that of the Louvre, a private collection was simply declared open to the public and remained in the same building, arranged in the same manner (Bazin 1967). Many of them continued to be administered as if they were still private, and their imposing nature and unhelpful layout were compounded by the difficulties of access which an interested public would have experienced. At the first public museum in Britain, the Ashmolean in Oxford (opened 1683), initially only one group was admitted at a time, with entrance fees proportional to the amount of time spent on the tours (Ovenell 1985: 88-9). Entry to the British Museum (opened 1759) was a long and complicated procedure in which it was necessary to make two or three enquiry visits and wait several weeks merely to obtain a ticket to pass the armed guards, who were not removed until 1863 (Crook 1972: 53-4). That access was not encouraged to the treasures has been admirably demonstrated by the diary of a Birmingham stationer in 1784, who, having gone through all the entrance procedures was 'hackneyed through the rooms with violence' in 30 minutes by an uncommunicative guide and 'came away completely disappointed' (quoted in Hudson 1975: 9). The motivation for opening museums to the public seems to have been more one of civic pride in possessing such an institution than a genuine desire to attract a public other than the antiquarians familiar with the collections and the aristocracy familiar with the palatial scale of the buildings. The messages given out by the buildings and the layout of the collections were ones emphasising the demonstration of the power of the state, region or institution: sometimes this was made directly through the exhibition of what was essentially plunder from less powerful countries.

The same criticisms can be levelled at many museums of the Victorian period, but by this time, in addition to civic pride, a much more explicit social purpose in opening them to the public can be discerned. It is particularly significant that the previously-defined 'breach with the past' coincides with the initial expansion of museums in Britain. This growth of museums has to be seen against the background of social reform in the first half of the nineteenth century. On the one hand this period saw the development of a genuine growth in desire for social justice and humanitarian reform, and there is little doubt that much of the general programme of improvement came about through Christian philanthropy and a desire to better the lot of the working classes, both physically and morally. Lewis (1984: 29) shows that reformers advocating the foundation of museums were quite clear about their social role, when he points out that a committee of MPs convened to investigate remedies to 'the vices of intoxication amongst the labouring classes' recommended the provision of open spaces, libraries and reading rooms in their report published in 1834. Another important factor in paving the way for museum legislation was a desire to improve knowledge of arts and design in order to maintain a competitive edge to Britain's industry, and, it was argued, increase the general level of wealth in society. From this perspective, museums were of moral and financial benefit to society, and their growth represented an important effort to give working people an additional chance for education and self-improvement, and they can thus be seen as an index of democracy (Adam 1939: 14-15, Crook 1972: 32).

On the other hand, as Raymond Williams has pointed out, the move towards cultural democratisation was very much a double-edged sword as it also worked in favour of the dominant classes, because: 'Respectable schemes of moral and domestic improvement became deeply entangled with the teaching and implication of particular social values, in the interests of the existing class society' (Williams 1961: 57).

By placing the early nineteenth century museum movement in the context of the social upheavals and reforms of the period, it is clear that those who advocated the development of museums believed that as well as alleviating drunkenness and promoting design they could also crucially contribute to the control of a potentially explosive population.

It has to be remembered that the experience of the French Revolution had made the propertied classes of Britain deeply fearful of a similar social upheaval caused by the grievances of a growing industrial workforce, and their fears were fuelled throughout the century by revolution abroad and workers' movements at home. It is no coincidence that the years which saw the crucial developments of the municipal museum movement and culminated in the Great Exhibition of 1851 have been described as 'the years of fluctuating discontent' (Briggs 1983: 198). Without in any way wishing to insinuate causal connections, it is interesting by way of background to place museum developments during this period alongside the wider political developments of which they were a product.

In the same year, 1824, as the first Mechanics' Institution was formed in Glasgow, and plans for the formation of the National Gallery were approved, the Combination Acts which had forbidden trades unions were repealed as a result of pressure from workers. While those who supported reform felt that such unions would disappear if restrictive laws were repealed, others felt that the unions presented a grave threat to society. The Metropolitan police was formed in 1829 in part to deal with such threats. The 1830s saw a succession of demands by an increasingly organised workforce and subsequent reforms by government. The first Reform Bill was passed in 1832, only to be followed by a peak of trade union organisation and the martyrdom of the Tolpuddle workers in 1834 (the same year the committee on alleviating drunkenness reported). 1835 saw both the Municipal Corporation Act and the establishment of another Select Committee on ways of improving design (Lewis 1984: 29).

Three years later the People's Charter was put forward outlining the Chartist political programme. This was followed by riots in Birmingham and Newport the next year and in 1842, the fourth year of bad harvests and heavy unemployment, the Chartists presented their second national petition. In 1845 the Museums Act was swiftly passed through Parliament and allowed local authorities to spend a half-penny rate for museum purposes. The year after the Corn Laws were repealed and in 1848 the 'year of revolutions' occurred, a huge meeting of Chartists on Kennington Common threatened to bring down the government, and the Communist Manifesto was produced by Marx and Engels. The effects of reform were thus not apparent to all: indeed many seemed to feel that to improve the education of the working classes would only to be fuel their demands. Thus, the public library legislation introduced by a museum campaigner, William Ewart, in 1850 encountered vigorous opposition as it 'was considered likely to cause civil agitation rather than public morals' (Lewis 1984: 29). Such was evidently not the view of Prince Albert, because only three years after the Chartist rallies nearly brought down the government, the Great Exhibition in Hyde Park opened, taken as a symbolic closure of the early Victorian period and an affirmation of the triumph of industrialisation.

Another influential figure who advocated museums as a direct means of keeping the workforce in check was Lieutenant General A. H. L. F. Pitt-Rivers. Aged twenty-one at the time of the Chartist demonstrations, he pursued a career in the army and amassed a large collection before retiring to his estate on Cranborne Chase where he excavated numerous archaeological monuments and built up his own typological museum at Farnham in Dorset. Towards the end of his life he expounded the rationale behind this museum (and the Pitt-Rivers Museum in Oxford) in a paper to the Society of Arts. In this he affirms his belief in the power of education in keeping the workforce placated by showing that change was brought by gradual evolution rather than revolution:

> We have thought proper to place power in the hands of the masses. The masses are ignorant, and knowledge is swamped by ignorance...The knowledge they lack is the knowledge of history. This lays them open to the designs of demagogues and agitators, who strive to make them break with the past, and seek the remedies for existing evils, or the means of future progress, in drastic changes that have not the sanction of history. It is by a knowledge of history only that such experience can be supplied...The law that Nature makes no jumps, can be taught by the history of mechanical contrivances, in such a way as at least to make men cautious how they listen to scatter-brained revolutionary suggestions. The knowledge of the facts of evolution, and of the processes of gradual development, is the one great knowledge that we have to inculcate, whether in natural history or in the arts and institutions of mankind; and this knowledge can be taught by museums, provided that they are arranged in such a manner that those who run may read. The working classes have but little time for study; their leisure hours are, and always must be, comparatively brief. (Pitt-Rivers 1891: 115-6).

Museums were also envisaged as promoting respect for the political and religious order. Aspects of this are expressed by Greenwood in his book *Museums and Art Galleries* (1888). He explicitly links museums (in approving terms) with political control by asserting that no municipality is complete without a museum, library, workhouse, prison, and 'the preservers of law and order' (*ibid*: 21). He also felt that museums should provide instruction 'in those measureless departments of nature which lie at our feet, and a knowledge of which should give an infinitely higher and more deeply reverential feeling of the Almighty' (*ibid*: 177).

Many museum buildings seem to have been particularly suited to some of these purposes. Pre-Victorian museums tended to be housed either in grand palace-like structures which directly associated control of power and knowledge with the aristocracy, or in classical 'Temples of Culture' promoting a religious reverence for the exhibits (Cameron 1971, Grana 1971: 104-5). With the development of the Victorian High Gothic style of architecture for public buildings a number of museums came to resemble Christian churches, more explicitly making the spiritual link suggested by Greenwood.

Whether Victorian museums were successful in maintaining the social status quo is uncertain. It seems that, by their intimidating surroundings they deterred those to whom the messages were aimed, because contemporary accounts show that visits to them were generally uncomfortable and alienating for the majority who were not used to such experiences. An article written in 1870 in the journal of the Bath and West Society is a good example:

> Local museums are, generally speaking, places so cold and repelling in their nature that, if a person have the hardihood to enter them, he cannot fail to be struck by the chilling nature of their contents, the unsatisfactory method of lighting, and the death-like stillness that reigns (quoted in Hudson 1975: 46).

Even fifty years later, the same attitude towards local museums is voiced by an eminent archaeologist:

> The word 'museum' is itself a byword for dulness, dust and general decrepitude. The very atmosphere reeks of decay, and the sight of a few skulls and stuffed birds completes the illusion of a charnel- house. Our local museums are too frequently the tombs of the dead past, and the wonder is that they attract any visitors at all (Crawford 1921: 215).

The image of the museum as being musty and dead is one that has been popularized by cartoonists from the Victorian period onwards, and this is the image that seems still to be uppermost in people's minds in the associations of the museum revealed in the survey. One reason for this could be that many of these early museum buildings are still in use (although approaches to display have changed greatly), and their grand structures could still intimidate certain groups of people. Another reason may be the historical association of the word 'museum' with high culture and dominant values. From its origins it derives an elitist image associated with the sort of conspicuous display of wealth and knowledge noted for the leisure class by Veblen in the last century (Veblen 1899: 95), and from its expansion in the Victorian period derives an image associated primarily with education and the almost forced imposition of 'correct' (ie. dominant) modes of thought and behaviour.

From their inception, museums have been removed from the everyday world as havens of knowledge and scholarship. This, together with the social mission of the museum and their architectural styles of temple and church, has led to the relationship between museums and the outside world being that of the sacred versus the profane. Modern museums may be suffering from the fossilisation of this outdated image, whereby, despite improvements in displays and facilities they are unfairly seen to be irrelevant to the concerns of the contemporary world and of interest only to those who are initiated into the mysteries of these silent cathedrals of learning. Perhaps too because the search for the meaning of existence has been transferred from orthodox religion to the cult of the past, museums and other sites of historical tourism have taken on the character of a pilgrims' shrines, re-emphasising the sacred associations of the institutions which might act as a great deterrent for some.

The deterrent 'double effect'

On the other hand the image may not just be a historical burden placed on the shoulders of modern museum directors, but it may still in fact be justified. As we have seen, half of the museums in Britain have opened since 1971, so the explanation cannot lie purely in historical legacy; negative images might be expressing something about the way in which museums still operate in contemporary society. In order for such an adverse image to survive, it must still fulfil some sort of useful role in articulating what certain social groups feel about museums. In other words, the persistence of negative images of museums deriving from their historical role shows that this divisive role is still one that they play today, and which thus deserves the negative images held amongst non-visitors. The way in which this contemporary adverse image of museums works is a product of social position and socialisation.

Age Table 4.3 has shown that age is one of the principal factors influencing museum visiting, and that the main effect of this is seen amongst the over 60s, 50 per cent of whom have either never visited a museum or last visited one more than five years ago. In the last chapter it was shown that only a relatively small part of this could be explained by structural factors such as ill-health and lack of money. Examination of the historical image of the museums, and of leisure opportunity, suggests that age has a double effect in either encouraging or discouraging museum visiting: the elderly are both less likely to have been socialized into museum visiting when young, and are also likely to be more 'disengaged' from society than other groups (and conversely, younger age groups are more likely to be socialized into museum visiting and to be more 'engaged').

The first reduction in opportunity is a 'period effect', i.e. the effect of the conditions of the period in which those who are now over 60 were initially brought up. Anyone over 60 at the time of the survey was born before 1925 and consequently brought up before the Second World War. In 1940 there were around only a third of the museums that are available today (calculations based on Prince and Higgins-McLoughlin 1987 Figure 2.3) which means that there would have been fewer opportunities to visit. In addition, crosstabulation of age by education shows that the over 60s are more likely than any other group to have left school at the minimum age (Table 6.1).

Table 6.1 Age by education

Age	Minumum education	Stayed on at school	Tertiary education	(%)	N
<35	60	21	19	100	291
35-59	74	15	11	100	372
>60	77	13	10	100	268

Furthermore, until 1932, the minimum school leaving age was fourteen, so that the elderly are not only more likely to have left school at the minimum age, but they are also more likely to have received a shorter education while they were there. At the same time, many museums tended to be the dull and musty places criticised by Crawford (1921) and thus less conducive to repeated visiting for those who were not schooled into seeing them as a worthwhile leisure choice. Finally, there may have been fewer school trips organised to them as well.

For those who are over 60 now, a number of factors would therefore have dictated that they were less exposed to museum visiting in their early years, and would have received less socialization into the museum code while at school. This lack of exposure would have been accompanied for those from a working class background, by a habitus that was not immediately disposed to making the most of museums, so that many might never have visited a museum during their childhood and would be unlikely even to visit one now, having learned from an early age to exclude themselves for lack of 'competence' in reading the museum code.

In addition to the 'period effect' making for a low incidence of museum visiting among the over 60s, there is also a 'biological effect' associated with being old. The work of Rapoport and Rapoport (1975) on leisure and the family lifecycle suggests that the likely expectations and motivations people have at different stages of their lives will strongly affect the kinds of leisure activities that are undertaken. They isolate four main phases of the lifecycle: young people, young adults, the establishment phase, and later years. When considering the relative lack of participation by the elderly in museum visiting, it is necessary to look at the ways in which old age is socially constructed as well as its biological effects. For example, although many elderly people are constrained in their leisure activities by deteriorating health, and by lack of income and transport (the latter two in fact social factors produced by the marginal position of the elderly in our society), there is considerable evidence that interest in out-of-home leisure activities actually subsides in this time (Roberts 1981: 79).

This has most concisely been expressed in the concept of 'disengagement', whereby 'Ageing is an inevitable mutual withdrawal or disengagement resulting in decreased interaction between the ageing (person) and others in the social system to which he belongs' (Cumming and Henry 1961: 14). Subsequent research has both confirmed and denied the theory of disengagement, but the general consensus seems to be that it is a more accurate explanation of the leisure of the elderly than the converse theory of re-engagement (Roberts 1981: 79).

Disengagement does however seem to be strongly class-based (Parker 1976: 61), so that those who are relatively well-educated and affluent may use their retirement to 're-engage' with activities made possible by the extra time available, while those who were not socialized into wide leisure opportunities will tend to withdraw into home-based activities. For many, retirement from work is a psychological blow accompanied by feelings of social uselessness and a disengagement from most areas of public activity. This is especially true for those who were not initially socialized into perceiving a wide range of leisure opportunities, i.e. those who are of low status.

Thus, those who are now of retirement age, especially those who are of low status, are doubly discouraged from museum visiting. In the first place, many would not have been socialized into seeing museum visiting as worthwhile and may have received a negative image of museums from early experiences of alienating local museums. In the second place, even those who did visit museums are less likely to do so now because of the structural and psychological factors associated with old age and especially with retirement which tend to be accompanied by withdrawal.

Status As with age, status has a similar double effect on the opportunity to visit museums, partly because of the interaction of age and status (especially amongst those of low status). Thus, those who are of high status are in a sense doubly advantaged compared with those of low status because they will have both a socialized competence in museum visiting and the structural advantages such as income and a vehicle which certainly play a part in encouraging general heritage visiting, if not specifically in museum visiting. The patterns of leisure visiting outlined above (Tables 5.18-22) show that higher status people have a greater opportunity (measured by socialization and structural factors) than other groups both to participate in a wider range of activities, and to participate more frequently.

Following on from the arguments presented above, the continued unpopularity of heritage presentations amongst certain sections of society can be variously ascribed to the alienating historical image of the museum as dusty and lifeless, to the effects of unfulfilling early museum experiences amongst those not competent in their decoding, and to the effect of 'leisure opportunity'. As far as the latter is concerned, those who have not been socialized into museum 'competence' will tend to exclude themselves from participation, justifying this as a deliberate choice ('the choice of the necessary'), and therefore not perceiving of museum visiting as a viable or worthwhile activity. The commonest way in which the justification of this 'choice' will be manifested will be in negative images of museums amongst non-visitors. The continued effect of museums, therefore, is to divide the population into those who possess the 'culture' or 'competence' to perceive them as a leisure opportunity and make sense of a visit, and those who do not. The latter, who tend to be those of low status, have a habitus whose initial (family-based) effects are so strong that schooling does little to alter it and they therefore exclude themselves at the earliest available opportunity both from school and heritage presentations and justify this by seeing them in an unfavourable light, as not being worthwhile.

It has also been shown (Chapter 5) that people with positive attitudes to the past were actually *less* likely to be museum visitors than those with negative attitudes. It was suggested that, because high status people tend to have less favourable images of the past, that they use the past to legitimate their current social position to themselves. It can consequently be argued that museum and heritage visiting is more about status affirmation in the present than it is about orientations to the past. Visiting museums and historic buildings is associated with being cultured and has, historically, aristocratic connotations which are enjoyed and emulated by some, and rejected by others. This is essentially the argument put forward by Bourdieu in claiming that such activities as museum-visiting are productive of 'distinction' between social classes: 'art and cultural consumption are predisposed, consciously and deliberately or not, to fulfil a social function of legitimating social differences' (Bourdieu 1984: 7).

As noted earlier, however, by concentrating on art, at the more esoteric end of culture, and by stressing class as an explanatory factor to the detriment of others, Bourdieu cannot however explain the popularity of museum-visiting. Although it is agreed that the basic role of heritage and museum visiting is to distinguish a 'cultured' group from other groups, his model lacks the dynamism to allow for the incorporation of the heritage boom that has occurred since his analyses were carried out.

Explaining the popularity of museums

The current popularity of museums and heritage attractions can be explained by the specific conjunction of numerous historical factors, which has led to an increase in the number of people who are advantaged with regard to the range of leisure activities they can undertake. In the first instance, long-term studies have noticed a steady increase of leisure time available to people (Central Statistical Office 1990: 152) and a generally steady increase in disposable income (*ibid*: 85). This has been accompanied by a general increase in many kinds of leisure outlets, from restaurants to holidays, and some of the expansion of the heritage market must be accounted for by the tourism boom predicated on this expansion of available leisure time and money (although this boom is now greatly dissipated by recession). However, as was discussed in Chapter 2, there seem to be particular reasons why the past and heritage are so popular. It was suggested that much of the past-orientation of contemporary society is a product of the changes consequent upon industrialization and post-war social and economic changes, and also of the uncertainty about the future which has accompanied Britain's decline as a world power and the advent of nuclear weapons. The 'turn to the past' seems a genuine phenomenon, and individuals' intrinsic interest in actually knowing more about the past should not be underplayed. Much of the specific popularity of museums and historic buildings must lie in a genuine wish to come to terms with the past.

However, the arguments presented above on the divisiveness of museums indicate that museum visiting is mainly about the demonstration of social position in the present. The explanatory vocabulary is flexible enough, however, to allow its consistent use also to explain the contemporary popularity of heritage visiting.

The expansion of secondary education, the increase in numbers of museums, and the improvement in museum presentations have accompanied the increase in leisure time and disposable income outlined above, so that more people than ever before have the structural and intellectual opportunity to take advantage of heritage presentations. Robert Hewison (1987) argues that the expansion of heritage presentations is an index of Britain's decline, and in the senses outlined above, a desire for the past may seem to be so. However, visiting of these presentations can conversely be seen as an index of affluence. This is because it tends not to be those who have experienced decline (the unemployed, for example), who visit museums and heritage presentations, but those who are relatively affluent. As education and the amount of disposable income has increased for all socio-economic groups, it is arguable that the traditional working class ethos has been gradually eroded by more middle class values. It is possible that more and more people are taking up museum visiting as part of a lifestyle that is appropriate to their changed status.

This can be seen as a version of the 'embourgeoisement thesis' formulated in the 1960s following a large-scale investigation of manual workers (Goldthorpe *et al.* 1969). The original thesis was that when certain manual workers gained higher wages and improved their living standards, they would gradually abandon working class attitudes to political and industrial advancement by collective action. The investigation by Goldthorpe and his colleagues into affluent workers did show that they were greatly concerned to improve the standard of living enjoyed by their family. In comparison with less affluent workers, these individuals displayed a more individualistic and family-focused social outlook. However, the embourgeoisement thesis itself was not supported, because it was shown that affluent workers still believed in collective action to achieve these ends, perhaps because 'people in jobs with little career potential will be hard pressed to use individualistic means to achieve the goals of a middle-class society' (Hirsch 1977: 172).

In the context of people's leisure, which was not studied in the original investigation, the embourgeoisement thesis still holds many attractions. While collective action may be appropriate for material advancement (and indeed attitudes to its effectiveness may anyway have changed in the last twenty years), it may be that individual leisure time may be used for social advancement. It has been suggested in the earlier discussion of cultural and economic capital that affluence needs to be legitimised and operationalised by the assumption of an appropriate lifestyle. In their leisure, then, it is to be expected that groups experiencing relative affluence would use something like museum-visiting with its higher cultural associations, to acquire a certain amount of cultural capital, or, for those denied advancement in the labour process, it may actually be the main means of advancement.

One of the reasons for the recent popularity of museums may therefore be because they are ideal institutions for those wishing to improve their cultural capital. They are associated, both historically and in the contemporary mind, with being cultured. There are currently more opportunities than ever before to visit them because people are educated for longer and go on more museum visits with the school than ever before, which makes them more familiar with the code of museums. In addition, there are greater numbers of museums available, and they are open institutions in the sense that they are free or relatively inexpensive to enter and people can wander freely about them and leave when they wish.

By their relative openness, museums can be used by those wishing to assume a more cultured lifestyle to achieve or demonstrate upward social mobility. Some confirmation of this is given when an approximate 'social mobility' variable is constructed (Table 6.2), which shows that museum-visiting is most likely to be undertaken by those who are upwardly mobile[7]. There do seem therefore to be two groups of people: the group who are still excluded from museum and heritage participation by its divisive operation, and the group (seemingly increasing) who take up visiting as emblematic of affiliation to a certain cultured lifestyle.

Table 6.2 Social mobility by annual museum visiting

| Social Mobility | Museum visits per year | | | | | |
	None	1-2	3-10	11+	(%)	N
Upward	35	48	17	1	100	256
Static	44	37	17	3	100	645
Downward	56	44	–	–	100	16

Conclusions

This investigation of the social context of museum visiting suggests that it should be separated out into two stages or processes. First, there has to be a conception that museum-visiting is a valid use of leisure time. The availability of this opportunity to visit museums immediately restricts substantial segments of the population from participation. Between a third and a fifth of the population exclude themselves from visiting museums because of their unwelcoming image and their associations with high culture. In addition, others who may once have visited museums, cease to be active visitors with the onset of old age.

At a broad level, therefore, the population can be divided into those who feel able to participate in the culture of museums, and those who find the cultural barriers too great and find their sense of the past in other areas. In this sense, museums are a symbol of social divisions.

Once this hurdle is overcome, however, the act of museum visiting is an expression of incorporation into the ranks of the cultured. A dynamic component to this has been added by educational improvements and greater efforts in museum display which have made museums easier to 'read', and by higher standards of living and greater leisure time, which have stimulated a concomitant wish amongst greater numbers of people to legitimate their higher status by assimilating themselves into the ranks of the cultured. These developments mean that probably more people than ever before have the opportunity to visit museums. The determination of which specific museums are visited will be influenced by particular factors beyond the scope of this survey. These will include things such as individual interests and structural factors such as the proximity of museums, admission charges and mobility, all of which come into play at this level.

This two-tier effect that museums have of exclusion and incorporation reinforces the argument that, at a group level, they maintain the ideological role they have always had. However, as has been noted earlier, this does not mean that they spoonfeed a dominant ideology to an unthinking mass. The cultural act of visiting a museum must be separated from visitors' reactions to the information presented in museums. It may be acceptable to argue that the former perpetuates social divisions, but the survey work shows that people vary greatly in their conceptualisation of the past, and those who visit museums regularly do not necessarily exhibit images of the past consistent with uncritical acceptance of a dominant ideology. The truth is that we do not know the effect that museum presentations have on the people who visit them, and it may well be that their impact is much less than is commonly thought.

It has been established that nearly all people are interested in the past, but that many are deterred from pursuing this interest by visiting museums because of cultural barriers. If we see museums not as nefarious ideological institutions but as enablers where people can harness their creative energies to construct a meaningful past of their own, then the existence of these cultural barriers is denying access to people's right to their past. A fundamental task for museums therefore becomes to dismantle these cultural barriers so that everyone can participate in the past they offer. In order to begin to do this, we need to look at ways in which the past is experienced in non-museum ways to see what they can teach us.

7 *Archaeology and alternatives – sanctioned and non-sanctioned approaches to the past*

In this chapter, archaeology has been chosen as a case study of an academically sanctioned activity, and metal-detecting and beliefs in 'alternative archaeology' have been chosen as non-sanctioned phenomena. The latter include beliefs in prehistoric visits from extra-terrestrials or mysterious forces at Stonehenge (associated with ley-line beliefs (Williamson and Bellamy 1983)), chosen because of their apparent popularity, and because there were suggestions in the literature that they would be embraced by the sort of people who do not visit museums. By understanding the attraction of these alternatives, our comprehension of the role of the past would be widened, and museum curators and archaeologists would be in a better position to understand the sorts of approach to public dissemination that might appeal to non-visitors.

The image of archaeology

Anecdotal evidence

There seems to be a consensus amongst most archaeological writers that, as far as the public are concerned, the words 'archaeology' and 'archaeologist' conjure up a range of distinct images. Archaeologists themselves are felt to fall into several categories. There is the distinction between 'the hairy-chested' and 'the hairy-chinned' noted by Kidder (quoted in Ascher 1960: 402), i.e. the macho cowboy and the absent-minded professor (Woodall and Perricone 1981: 506, Fowler 1977: 155). To these two basic images, popularised by Victorian illustrators, early film-makers and more recently by the Indiana Jones films, others are occasionally added. Bray (1981: 225-7) for example, adds 'the collector' to 'the explorer' and 'the antiquarian scholar'; Fritz (1973: 75) adds the archaeologist as 'intermediary between the worldly and the other worldly', a shadowy figure involved with mummies and spirits; and Ascher

(1960: 402) notes that the archaeologist is often portrayed as 'the expert', someone called in to take over when a discovery is made.

Intimately connected with the image of its practitioners is of course that of the discipline itself. The consensus here is that archaeology is about digging, and is especially associated with death and treasure (Fowler 1986: 10, Hudson 1981: 121). Ascher's (1960) review of ten years of archaeological articles in *Life* magazine isolated four themes in its presentation of archaeological work: the circumstances of the discovery, the reporting of the expert being called in, description of the technical methods used in archaeological work, and the emphasis on superlatives (oldest, first, largest, and so on). These images are all ones that have been put forward by professional archaeologists or historians as their own interpretation of how the public views archaeology.

Where systematic work has been done, in one case it only questioned archaeologists themselves (Woodall and Perricone 1981) and in another it restricted itself to looking at the position of women in the disciplinary hierarchy and in archaeological interpretations (Gero 1985). The only study which directly questioned the public was that carried out by Ian Hodder and various colleagues, already mentioned in Chapter 3. They found distinct variation in attitudes to archaeology and the past, with the better-educated and the more affluent placing a much higher value on both than the less privileged, some of whom thought archaeology 'generally useless' and a 'complete waste of money' (Hodder 1984a: 9). The latter groups tended to be more interested in their local past and in experiencing the past through objects rather than texts (Hodder 1986: 163).

In all of the studies cited, apart from this last one, the writers' failure to question the public directly has meant that there has been no way of assessing the validity of their suggestions as to the public's images of archaeology. The survey evidence does broadly confirm their interpretations, but shows that the range of images held is wider than is usually given credit for.

Survey results

General A random selection of answers given to the open-ended question 'Please write down what the word 'Archaeology' means to you' shows that, although the image of archaeology as digging persists, most people do not necessarily associate it with death or treasure, but do associate it with objects rather than processes:

- 'Study of Prehistoric Period'
- 'Old sites - digging for past relics'
- 'Research into the past in need of answers'
- 'Study of Past Civilisations'
- 'Searching into the past'
- 'The discovery of past life styles and habitations'
- 'Excavation in a very precise and careful way, then drawing conclusions'
- 'The discovery of artifacts and buildings from medieval and Roman times and before'

- 'Finding and unearthing places and items used by past civilisations'
- 'Learning about the people and happenings of long ago'
- 'Digging up ruins'
- 'Exploring physical features of the past'

As with the answers to other open-ended questions, the great variety shown in these responses can be reduced (at the loss of their detail and variability) to eight basic categories (Table 7.1). These show that most people connect archaeology primarily with the fairly distant past, and with old ruins and objects, which are dug up and then studied. The generalised image of archaeology seems to be that it is more interested in objects than people. Only 27 per cent of respondents see beyond this and give an indication that the aim of the research is to understand once-living *societies*. For the rest of the public, presumably, the activities of digging and studying objects must seem ends in themselves. No indication was given that archaeology might study social changes; all images of the subject were entirely static. This is no doubt a problem deriving from the way archaeological research is presented, especially in museums, where the decontextualized, object-centred approach still predominates.

Table 7.1 The image of archaeology

Frequencies of mention of words or phrases		
	(%)	N
Mentioned 'The Past'	62	538
Mentioned 'Ruins' or 'Objects'	53	463
Mentioned 'Digging'	45	388
Mentioned 'Study' or 'Research'	43	369
Noted aim of reconstruction of living societies	27	232
Mentioned 'Discovery'	10	86
Said archaeology meant 'Nothing'	6	51
Mentioned other categories	11	99

(Percentages add up to over 100 because many respondents gave more than one answer)

Perhaps because of the broadness of the categories, little significant variation in answers was apparent when crosstabulated by demographic variables, except that those to whom archaeology meant nothing were more likely to be elderly and of low status. Educational background produced the strongest differences in answers (Table 7.2). Those with the least formal education were most likely to associate archaeology with 'digging', 'the past', or 'nothing', and those with the most formal education were most likely to stress the element of discovery and of the reconstruction of whole societies.

Table 7.2 Image of archaeology, by education

	Percentage who mentioned various phrases (%)			
	Minimum	Stayed on at school	Tertiary education	N
★ 'The Past'	96	88	86	(507)
'Ruins' or 'Objects'	96	92	94	(446)
★ 'Digging'	92	89	79	(378)
'Study' or 'Research'	87	81	87	(361)
Living Societies	73	75	82	(231)
'Discovery'	41	39	48	(85)
★ 'Nothing'	35	16	5	(51)
(★ Statistically significant at 0.05 level)				

Knowledge of archaeology Although most individuals were capable of writing down the sort of generalised image they have of archaeology (perhaps being derived from magazines, films and television), when given the opportunity a great many show that they have little clear idea of what archaeology is really about. This was discovered as a by-product of a question about the teaching of archaeology in schools, where one of the answer categories was 'I don't know enough about archaeology to answer this question properly'. This was by far the most frequently chosen category (Table 7.3) and was most likely to be chosen by the elderly and those with the minimum education (Table 7.4). (Aside from this, most people expressing a preference wanted archaeology to be taught as a minor - non-examined - subject in secondary schools).

Table 7.3 Opinions about teaching of archaeology in schools

'Do you think archaeology should be taught in schools ?'	
Frequencies	(%)
Not at all	7
In Primary Schools only	2
Minor subject in Secondary Schools	27
Major subject in Secondary Schools	23
Don't know enough about it	41
	100
	(N = 938)

Table 7.4 Lack of knowledge about archaeology, by age and education

	Age			Education		
	35	35-59	60+	Minimum	Stayed on	Tertiary
(%)	37	40	47	45	43	26
(N)	108	149	127	291	43	44

Percentage choosing the response
'I don't know enough about archaeology to answer this question properly'

Answers to this question, and those to the open-ended question, suggest that archaeology has a general image associated with the excavation of material remains from the past, but that beyond that, a large number of people do not have a very clear idea of what the discipline involves. This may be because archaeologists and museum curators have not been successful in actually changing the long-held image of the subject. The responses suggest that it is in the area of education, especially in schools, that most effort should be expended. Drawing on the arguments used about the perceptions of museums, efforts to improve the image of archaeology should be concentrated particularly in schools, where children first come into contact with archaeology and history, and also in public dissemination work on television, archaeological sites, and in museums.

The relevance of archaeology Although 41 per cent do not seem very clear about what archaeology is, nevertheless the great majority of respondents fully endorse its value to contemporary society. This may be because archaeology is perceived to be part of legitimate culture and thus, in Bourdieu's terms, worthy of 'recognition' by the individual even though he or she may not possess 'knowledge' of it (Bourdieu 1984: 319). These answers may therefore be an index of the penetration of dominant values into wider society. However, certain groups tend significantly more than others to agree that archaeology is of little use to contemporary society, and these tend to be non-dominant social groups, such as those who left school at the minimum age, those of low status, the retired, the unemployed and homemakers. Those who do not visit any heritage presentations are also significantly more likely to agree that archaeology is of little use (Table 7.5). This again adds to the evidence that the dominant ideology does not permeate all levels of society, and that many consciously reject such values. In this specific case, significant proportions of the population question the relevance of archaeology; some even wrote on the questionnaire that they thought such a survey was a waste of money, mentioning issues that should be given priority, such as fighting the closure of hospital wards, educational cuts, and third world starvation. For some people, archaeology may have the image of being a luxury, a leisure pursuit for the cultivated (cf. Fowler 1986: 10).

Table 7.5 Attitudes to relevance of archaeology by age, status and type of heritage visitor

	'Archaeology has little of use to tell our own society'						
	Strongly agree	Agree	Neither	Disagree	Strongly disagree	(%)	N
Age (%)							
<35	5	8	16	49	22	100	293
35–59	3	7	10	55	25	100	367
>60	7	8	19	48	18	100	260
Status (%)							
High	2	7	9	54	28	100	145
Middle	4	7	14	52	23	100	595
Low <60	9	13	15	40	23	100	81
Low >60	12	10	24	46	8	100	86
Heritage Visitor (%)							
Visits none	6	14	32	41	8	100	202
Visits one	5	9	18	52	15	100	135
Visits two	4	7	10	55	24	100	188
Visits three	4	4	5	63	25	100	184
Visits all	3	3	9	47	38	100	183
All (%)	5	8	14	51	22	100	924

Archaeological museums Archaeological museums therefore face a double obstacle to the achievement of more widespread participation: the unfavourable image of museums in general amongst people who rarely or never visit heritage presentations, and the unfavourable or uninformed image of archaeology held by similar people. This double obstacle is reflected in two surveys which have gauged the public image of archaeological museums. In the first (Griggs and Hays-Jackson 1983), archaeological museums were associated with education and with a requirement of background knowledge and a particular interest before visiting, and were not felt to be particularly suitable for children. In the second (Prince and Schadla-Hall 1987), the archaeological collections of the museum in question (Kingston-upon-Hull) were poorly known by the local populace, and archaeology was given a low-interest rating. The authors suggest that the very word 'archaeology' discourages certain sections of the public (*ibid*: 70).

The image of prehistory Prehistory, as we have seen in Chapter 3 (Table 3.12) is perceived as being the least desirable period to live in; all groups in society agree on this without significant variation. One reason for this is doubtless the distance in time which separates the present from the prehistoric period. Indeed many people seem to feel that there is little connection between then and now. Most people (51 per cent) disagree that prehistoric people were basically the same as us, and only 38 per cent agree (Table 7.6).

Table 7.6 Comparison of prehistoric and contemporary people, by sex

	'Prehistoric people in Britain were basically the same as us'						
	Strongly agree	Agree	Neither	Disagree	Strongly disagree	(%)	N
Sex							
Male	3	28	12	42	14	100	473
Female	4	39	12	37	9	100	458
All	4	34	12	40	11	100	931

The most significant variation in answers is by gender, with women much more likely than men to agree that prehistoric people were like us (43 per cent compared with 32 per cent). This difference is difficult to interpret, but later in the chapter it is suggested that women may have a more sympathetic approach to the past than men, and have more time for non-sanctioned interpretations of the past.

Summary

The anecdotal evidence of public images of archaeology seems to be largely confirmed by the survey, except that it does not take into account the heterogeneity of the public and consequent variations in response. In particular, few people seem directly to associate it with death and treasure, although most see it as the simple recovery of objects and structures. A relatively small but significant proportion do realise that it has the ultimate purpose of trying to understand the development of past societies.

However, the fact that the majority of respondents see the subject as the mere excavation of objects confirms the concern felt by some writers that archaeology is still seen by the public as glorified treasure hunting. Some argue that many people are unsure of the difference between the two, and that this is one of the principal reasons why public opposition to metal-detecting has not been effectively marshalled (Clarke 1984: 70). Fowler (1986: 10) characterises this sort of perception of archaeology as a 'positive' perception, due largely to the fossilization of an old image, and contrasts it, rather confusingly, with a 'negative unperception', in which archaeology is not seen as useful or relevant. This 'negative unperception', like that of museums, may also stem from historical circumstances, because archaeology too has historically been associated with the more privileged elements in society. In the Victorian period, for example, 'it was not the British who were being given the opportunity to learn more about the antiquities of their county or country; it was, with rare exceptions, the upper and upper middle class British' (Hudson 1981: 47).

Archaeology today may be suffering from the persistence of this image, but, again as with museums, the image may still be to a certain extent true. Just as with museums, archaeology is least likely to be valued by those who have not been schooled into 'competence' in it, or who consciously reject it as being part of the dominant culture. It may even be that in the eyes of certain social groups archaeology is the study of a past that is not theirs. Certainly the animosity generated between treasure-hunters and archaeologists has raised the question of whose past archaeologists claim to study (Wright 1987). A comparison between participation in, and attitudes towards, sanctioned, archaeologically-related activities and non-sanctioned 'alternative' activities and beliefs can help us to understand the social connotations of both.

Participation in archaeologically-related activities

History and archaeology societies

Four per cent of respondents claim to have been a member of a local history or archaeology club at some time in their lives. The consequent small number of such people in the survey (37) means that statistical tests are not very reliable. However, members of such clubs seem very likely to be of high status, have had some tertiary education and to be 'culture vultures' (Table 7.7). There were no differences by age or sex. Regression analysis showed that education was the only significant variable in explaining participation (Table A2.7). The fact that there were no differences in participation by age seems to confirm Stebbins's suggestion (1979: 147-53) that archaeological societies, and amateur archaeology in general, lend themselves to participation by people of all ages.

Table 7.7 Membership of history or archaeological societies, by status, education, type of heritage visitor and activity status

'(Have you ever) been a member of a local history or archaeology club?' (%) and (N)					
Status	High	Middle	Low <60	Low >60	
Members %	6 (9)	5 (28)	0	0	
Education	Minimum		Stayed On		Tertiary
Members %	2 (13)		2 (2)		13 (22)
Heritage visitors	Visits None	Visits One	Visits Two	Visits Three	Visits All
Members %	1.5 (3)	1 (1)	2 (4)	6 (11)	9 (17)
Activity Status	Student	Retired	Full time	Part time	Unemployed	House-wives
Members %	20 (3)	5 (10)	4 (19)	4 (3)	1.5 (1)	0.5 (1)

When crosstabulated by activity status, students are more likely than others to have participated, presumably because of their educational level and the opportunities provided at college (Table 7.7). The retired are the group next most likely to have participated. This might indicate that archaeological and historical societies have a positive role to play in the leisure of the elderly, but it may also be an age effect: the elderly may just have been members in their youth. While such clubs may seem evenly balanced by age and sex (although the above discussion makes age balance impossible to assess using this data), the imbalances of status and education are strong.

Studies of Victorian archaeological societies (Brooks 1985, Dellheim 1983, Hudson 1981, Levine 1986) have shown that, although they may have been organisations which would allow people of different classes to mix, their emphasis was strongly on obeisance to dominant values, and the classes doing the mixing were almost exclusively the bourgeoisie and the aristocracy. As with museums, the working classes were effectively excluded (Levine 1986: 57). Cunliffe feels that, although society has moved on, county archaeological societies have essentially remained the same so that they are largely irrelevant for most people. He does, however, note the rise of a substratum of smaller, less formal, locally based groups, more active in fieldwork (Cunliffe 1982: 60). This survey would not pick up the difference in participation between the two groups, but the overall figures confirm the persistence of a socially restricted membership of archaeological and historical societies in general. This no doubt arises from the combination of several factors: the historical image of archaeology and archaeological societies, and the fact that through education and background only fairly restricted social groups perceive the 'opportunity' and desire to join such clubs. This in turn emphasises the image and creates a cycle which is difficult to break out of.

Participation in archaeological fieldwork

As the subjective experience of most archaeologists might have suggested, archaeological fieldwork is participated in by a wider range of people than are archaeological societies. 10 per cent of respondents claim to have 'gone on an archaeological dig or gone looking for pottery'. This may be a correct figure, reflecting the wide participation of amateurs before, say, the 1970s and the subsequent use of labour through the MSC programmes. On the other hand it might be an overestimation because there is an ambiguity in the question, such that it would be possible for someone who had merely visited an excavation or walked across a field to answer affirmatively.

Of all the demographic variables, age is the only significant predictor of involvement in fieldwork (Table 7.8). Being under 60 is almost a precondition for participation, but beyond that participation is fairly evenly spread amongst the two other age groups. Although the strong age effect makes most statistics significant, participation under the age of 60 is not as socially uneven as membership of archaeological societies. For example, middle-aged people of low status seem about as likely to participate as young people of intermediate status, and middle-aged people of high status as likely to participate as middle-aged people of intermediate status (Table A2.8).

Students are easily the most likely to have participated, although their small number in this sample may be misleading. Interestingly, the next highest category of respondents to participate are the unemployed (Table 7.9). This

Table 7.8 Participation in archaeology, by age

	Participation (%)	N
Age		
<35	15.5	45
35–39	12	44
>60	3	7

may either reflect the precarious nature of archaeological work (in that archaeologists on short term contracts may often find themselves unemployed), or it may reflect the impact of MSC and similar labour in archaeology, whose trainees may also end up unemployed after the end of the scheme, or again it may suggest that archaeological fieldwork is an activity that unemployed people enjoy as a hobby. Finally, those who participate, or have participated, in archaeological fieldwork are most likely to visit all heritage presentations, compared with those who have not participated, who are most likely not to visit any presentations at all (Table 7.10).

Table 7.9 Participation in archaeology, by activity status

Activity Status	Participation (%)	N
Student	31	5
Unemployed	17	11
In full-time work	12.5	54
In part-time work	11.5	10
Housewives	7	8
Retired	4	8

Table 7.10 Participation in archaeology, by type of heritage visitor

	Type of Heritage Visitor						
	Visits none	Visits one	Visits two	Visits three	Visits all	(%)	N
Participated in fieldwork?							
Yes	12	6	27	25	31	100	67
No	25	16	20	20	19	100	849

Cumulatively these statistics suggest, first, that age again has a double effect on participation. Those who are now retired are less likely than those who were born more recently to have had the opportunity to participate in excavations when they were young, and now they are less likely to take it up because of the disengagement effects noted in the previous chapter. After the age effect is taken into account, it is clear that participation in archaeological fieldwork is relatively democratic, possibly because it offers many different things to different people. Indeed, the fact that those of high status are least likely to participate in it adds greater weight to the proposition in a previous chapter that higher status people who tend to do 'cultured' activities such as museum-visiting do so because they have been socialized into a particular lifestyle, and their commitment does not extend to the discomforts of fieldwork. Those who participate in archaeology no doubt do so because of genuine interest and desire to be involved, and their visiting of heritage presentations may be a similar manifestation of this interest. These differences would seem to be a good indication of the differences between diggers and the more genteel archaeological society members, although of course there is considerable overlap between the two.

It is tempting to suggest that museums and archaeological societies are linked by their fossilized image, their academic connotations, and their tendency to operate at one remove from the context of archaeological fieldwork, which is still for most people the basis of archaeology. At the other end of the scale, in some ways archaeological fieldwork has greater links with treasure hunting because of their mutual emphasis on original research and discovery carried on out of doors, and their recovery of primary evidence, although one is an academically sanctioned activity and the other is not.

A systematic analysis of participation in the two activities tends to confirm the validity of the comparison. Comparison between the two suggests that what contemporary professional archaeology lacks is an allowance for the widespread participation of interested amateurs, for whom the main attractions of archaeology are the excitement of discovery and the stimulation of the imagination caused by excavating evidence of past people. Metal-detecting and 'alternative archaeology' have at least partly arisen in response to these missing factors.

Participation in treasure hunting

Participation in treasure hunting with a metal detector is claimed by 7 per cent of respondents. It is difficult to know how accurate this figure is, as it could cover both the professional treasure hunter and anyone who has just used a friend's detector once in their garden. However, if we believe the editor of *Treasure Hunting* magazine (quoted in Pearce 1990: 139) that there are up to 100,000 people actively involved at any one time in networks of treasure hunting clubs, the figure may well be an accurate one. This participation seems to be about the same as that for more conventional archaeology. In a detailed survey in 1985-7 the Council for British Archaeology suggested that up to 100,000 people were represented in amateur archaeological societies across the country (BTA/ETB 1989: 24). It is worth bearing in mind, too, that metal detectors have only been available on a large scale for about fifteen or twenty years (Gregory 1986: 25), and there is thus a very strong age effect on participation. The elderly are the group least likely to have used a metal detector, perhaps as a result of this lack of opportunity combined with the general effects of disengagement and reduced mobility (Table 7.11).

Table 7.11 Participation in metal detecting, by age

	Participation (%)	N
Age		
<35	12	36
35–59	7	25
>60	3	8

Crosstabulations with the simple status variable (high — middle — low) seem to show that metal detecting is most likely to be participated in by those of low status, but when age and status are combined, it is evident that age has the strongest effect: young people of low status are most likely to use metal detectors, followed equally by young people of intermediate status, young people of high status, and middle-aged people of low status (Table A2.9). Regression analysis confirms that age is the strongest predictor of

Table 7.12 Participation in metal-detecting, by sex, education, type of heritage visitor and activity status

	Participation (%)	N
Sex		
Male	9	42
Female	6	27
Education		
Minimum	8	52
Stayed on at school	7.5	8
Tertiary	5	9
Heritage visitor		
Visits none	3.5	8
Visits one	3	4
Visits two	9	18
Visits three	9	17
Visits all	11	21
Activity status		
Unemployed	12.5	8
Student	10.5	2
In full-time work	10	42
Housewives	6.5	8
In part-time work	5	4
Retired	2.5	6

participation, the only other significant factor being status (Table A2.10). Interestingly, metal detecting is the only past-related activity that is more likely to be participated in by unemployed people than any other occupation group (Table 7.12).

This may reflect the attraction of the possible financial rewards which may come with treasure hunting, but it is just as likely to be explained by the isolation frequently associated with unemployment. Metal detecting is something that can be done by a lone individual, with the minimum of organisation and cost (after the initial purchase of the detector). In addition, and crucially, it does not seem to have any of the elitist connotations of archaeological societies and does not require any specific 'competence', lack of which might lead to self exclusion.

As we have seen already, metal detector users tend mainly to be under 35 and, in addition, though secondarily, tend to be of low status. They are also significantly more likely to be male rather than female, and slightly more likely to have left school at the minimum age, though this difference is not significant. They are, however, much more likely to visit all of the heritage attractions studied here at least once a year (Table 7.12). It might be possible to suggest that this is because such people go to museums to have their finds identified, and visit historic houses, castles and ancient monuments to use their detectors clandestinely. This would be a rather uncharitable interpretation, because metal detector users tend to have a positive view of archaeology and of the past, as 71 per cent of them disagree that archaeology is

Table 7.13 Participation in metal detecting by feelings about the relevance of archaeology

	'Archaeology has little of use to tell our own society'						
	Strongly agree	Agree	Neither	Disagree	Strongly disagree	(%)	N
Detector User	3	9	17	48	23	100	67
Detector Non-user	5	7	14	51	22	100	844

Table 7.14 Participation in metal detecting by feelings about knowing about the past

	'Do you think it is worth knowing about the past?'					
	Definitely	Probably	Perhaps	No	(%)	N
Detector User	81	16	1	2	100	68
Detector Non-user	79	12	6	4	100	857
			[p = .2306]			

of little use to today's society, and 97 per cent believe the past is worth knowing about (Tables 7.13-14). In addition, several commentators have noted that financial gain is only of secondary consideration to all but a tiny minority of ruthless 'cowboy' treasure hunters: most do it for interest and relaxation (Crowther 1983: 15, Gregory 1986: 26, Wright 1987: 17). The majority of the public seem to see metal-detecting as a relatively harmless pursuit, possibly because archaeologists have not alerted people to the dangers of disturbing archaeological layers. 63 per cent agreed with the phrase 'Metal detecting is just a harmless way for ordinary people to discover the past', and 65 per cent agreed that 'People owning a metal detector should have the right to try to find relics from the past' (Table 7.15). The strongest support came from those of low status, while those of high status were less likely to agree. These answers could reflect the depth of the commonly-held view amongst treasure hunters that any curbing of their activities is an infringement of personal liberties by the establishment.

Table 7.15 Attitudes to metal-detecting, by status

'Metal detecting is just a harmless way for ordinary people to discover the past'				
Status (%)	Strongly agree	Agree	Neither	Disagree	Strongly disagree
High	3	51	10	24	13
Intermediate	12	51	11	20	6
Low <60	19	55	15	6	4
Low >60	12	58	14	12	4
All (%)	11	52	12	19	7

'People owning a metal detector should have the right to try to find relics from the past'				
Status (%)	Strongly agree	Agree	Neither	Disagree	Strongly disagree
High	6	50	12	19	13
Intermediate	14	51	12	18	5
Low <60	13	60	15	9	4
Low >60	19	56	17	8	–
All (%)	13	53	13	16	6

Archaeology and treasure-hunting compared

Comparison of the various characteristics of those who have participated in archaeological fieldwork and treasure-hunting with a metal detector shows little difference between the two groups: they are both most likely to consist of males under the age of 35 who are students or unemployed, and who visit all heritage presentations, and who are least likely to be of high status. These similarities hold implications for the interpretation of the role of treasure hunting. They suggest first that metal detecting is not simply a working class phenomenon arising in opposition to middle class archaeology (as Gregory (1983, 1986) would have it), something that is in fact denied by metal detector users themselves (Wright 1987: 17). It does on the other hand add considerable weight to the arguments of those who blame the large-scale exclusion of amateurs from participation in excavations consequent upon the professionalization of archaeology in the 1970s and 1980s (Cleere 1986: 24, Cunliffe 1982: 61). In the words of archaeologist David Baker, 'Many of those who turn to treasure hunting might have had their spare time energies diverted to amateur archaeology if it had not become less involved in field activity in recent years' (Baker 1983: 76).

This interpretation may be confirmed by the fact that people who have done archaeological fieldwork are more likely also to have used a metal detector for treasure hunting than those who have not (Table 7.16). This statistic may indicate that many of those who used to do fieldwork have now turned to metal detecting, or that some young people have graduated from metal-detecting to fieldwork, or that some people do both. Whichever is the correct interpretation, the effect is strongly significant and confirms that at the general level, treasure hunters are indistinguishable from amateur archaeologists, at least in terms of their background and interests.

Table 7.16 Participation in archaeological fieldwork by participation in metal detecting

	Participated in metal detecting			
	Yes	No	(%)	N
Participated in fieldwork				
Yes	21	79	100	97
No	6	94	100	844

Studies of metal detector users, as noted above, have shown that the greatest satisfaction of the activity is the thrill of discovering something. As archaeology has become more professional and academic, and attempted to shake off the historical image associated with treasure hunting outlined above, it has tended to disparage objects in themselves, the thrill of discovery, and to play down the more romantic and enjoyable aspects of the subject in an attempt to gain academic respectability. Instead in the field it has concentrated on structures (or the voids left by their decay), and in the universities it has often concentrated on drawing up the boundaries of the discipline as a rigorous academic subject by adapting various grand theories (systems theory, structuralism, Marxism, for example) to archaeological purposes.

Part of this process has also involved attempting to unify archaeology into a corporate profession. The net effect has been that the non-specialised public, increasingly individualistic, and the archaeological profession, increasingly corporate, have been moving in opposite directions (Cunliffe 1982: 60). As archaeology has expanded, jobs have been created for university-trained professional archaeologists who have tended, in their attempt to weld a professional ethos, to exclude amateurs from excavations, disparaging their abilities and relegating them to more mundane activities (Burt 1983: 34, Williamson and Bellamy 1983: 202). It seems, then, that, excluded from the basic excitement of discovering objects from the past through excavation, many people have turned to metal-detecting, being an activity that can be done cheaply and easily with rapid results. The vehemence with which they have been attacked by many archaeologists is an indication that their activities are very similar to those which archaeologists used to do, or were thought to do by the public.

In a perceptive article, Patrick Wright has highlighted these similarities (Wright 1987). In their concentration on the decontextualised object, their detailed knowledge of certain classes of material culture, and the meetings where they display their finds, treasure hunters very closely resemble the antiquarians of the nineteenth century (cf. Dellheim 1983: 55); in their collections of finds they have even re-invented the cabinet of curiosities. In many ways 'the metal detector confronts the profession with its own strictly repressed unconscious' (Wright 1987: 17).

At a deeper level, no doubt the passions raised over metal detecting can also be partly explained by the fact that treasure hunting and its more vociferous practitioners have fundamentally challenged the right of archaeologists to discover and formulate 'our' common past. As Burt (1983: 35) has noted, treasure hunting is not a misunderstanding of the 'true' role of archaeology; it is actually contesting this 'true' role. Thus a columnist named 'Boudicca' calls metal detector users 'people's archaeologists' (Boudicca 1982: 9), denigrates archaeologists as self-seeking careerists, and archaeology as 'a hobby which has managed to con the establishment into paying its expenses' (Wright 1987: 15).

The challenging of archaeologists' right to excavate sites and write about the past from a position of credibility is clearly a serious threat to them, because the alternative would be a chaotic free for all; as Hudson (1981: 151) notes, 'metal detectors are disturbingly democratic'. If the arguments of 'Boudicca' were accepted, then everyone would construct their own past by digging up objects at will all over the country. Hence the virulence of the image put forward by archaeologists of the treasure hunter 'as vandal and land pirate' and of the image put forward by treasure hunters of archaeologists 'as communists who seek to elevate their own definition of the public interest over private property and the traditional freedoms of the people' (Wright 1987: 16).

However, it is clear from the survey and from other commentators that most metal detector users are quite responsible and co-operate, or are willing to co-operate, with archaeologists and museum curators (Crowther 1983: 17, Selkirk 1982: 36). They value the past and archaeology, and as Table 7.17 shows, they especially value finding things above reading about them in a book.

Cumulatively this does seem to confirm that metal detector users are essentially the same sort of people as those who participate, or have

Table 7.17 Attraction of finding old objects, by participation in metal detecting

'It is much more interesting to find a piece of old pottery yourself than to read a book about ancient civilisations'

	Strongly agree	Agree	Neither	Disagree	Strongly disagree	(%)	N
Detector							
User	31	35	16	16	1	100	68
Non-User	14	45	17	21	3	100	854
All	16	44	17	21	3	100	935

participated, in archaeological fieldwork, and that metal-detecting owes a great deal of its popularity to the fact that it allows the thrill of discovery that professional archaeology now less frequently allows the non-specialist.

Metal detector users seem to be enthusiastic in their interest in the past, if, in archaeologists' eyes, rather undiscriminating. Some of this might be accounted for by their youthfulness: Stebbins (1979: 165) finds that many archaeological society members had been pothunters in their youth, and it is possible that some metal detector users will move on to being archaeologists. This might suggest that many young people find an outlet for their interest in the past through metal detecting either because there is no local club for young archaeologists, or because they find such clubs too formal, constricting and not sufficiently involved in fieldwork.

Taken together these results suggest that, as a phenomenon, the popularity of metal detecting, if not directly the fault of archaeologists, is a by-product of recent changes in the discipline. If archaeologists wish to remove the destructive threat of metal detecting, it is clear that, as well as ensuring that the necessary legislation is passed, they must attempt to win back the support of the interested non-specialist who used to constitute the backbone of archaeological practice. More people, especially the young, must be actively encouraged to participate in archaeological fieldwork.

If the absence of one quality in contemporary archaeology has stimulated the popularity of metal detecting, the absence of another quality in contemporary society in general, that of the romantic imagination, has contributed to the popularity of beliefs in 'alternative' archaeology.

Beliefs in 'alternative archaeology'

Convictions that extra-terrestrials helped shape early civilisations and that Stonehenge has mysterious forces associated with it were taken as examples of non-sanctioned beliefs which are contrary to accepted archaeological interpretations. Beliefs in the Loch Ness Monster were also gauged as an additional paranormal phenomenon. Each belief was crosstabulated with demographic variables and then subjected to a regression analysis which included demographic variables and attitudes to the past and present.

7 per cent of all respondents agreed that 'spacemen from another planet

helped create our early civilisations', a suggestion put forward by numerous writers, such as von Daniken (1970, 1972). The only demographic variable that produced any significant variation was that of education, with those having had the minimum formal education most likely to believe in the statement (Table 7.18).

Table 7.18 Belief in astro-archaeology, by education

	'Spacemen from another planet helped create our early civilisations'						
	Strongly agree	Agree	Neither	Disagree	Strongly disagree	(%)	N
Education (%)							
Minimum	2	6	30	34	28	100	635
Stayed on at school	2	5	37	31	26	100	103
Tertiary	–	4	26	25	45	100	171

There was a far wider belief that 'there are mysterious forces connected with places like Stonehenge'. This was agreed by 40 per cent of respondents. The strongest variation was found with age, with 50 per cent of those under 35 agreeing, compared with 33 per cent of those over 60. Significant variations were also found with status and gender, with those of low status who are under 60 years old most likely to agree, and women more likely to agree than men. The unemployed were also more likely to agree than any other activity group, as were 'culture vultures', although these last two were not statistically significant (Table 7.19). Given the recent clashes over the ownership of Stonehenge, both physical and literary (Chippendale 1990), the existence of these beliefs clearly shows both that archaeologists are not getting their message across very effectively, and that Stonehenge does act as a very important arena for the negotiation of different approaches to the past.

In addition, a quarter of respondents agreed that the Loch Ness Monster probably exists. Significant variations were found by gender and by type of heritage visitor, with women more likely to believe than men, and, interestingly, 'culture vultures' more likely to believe than those who visit no heritage presentations (Table 7.20).

Although the three belief types have different agreement levels, and slightly different demographic associations, they are all united by one factor, which is attitude to the present. Regression analysis performed on each belief showed that the less favourable an individual's attitude is to the present, the more likely he or she is to accept the belief (Table A2.11). This seems to show that these alternative beliefs are expressions different in kind from involvement in archaeology or metal-detecting, neither of which is affected by people's attitude to the present.

Table 7.19 Belief in mysterious forces at Stonehenge, by age, sex, status, activity status and type of heritage visitor

	'There are mysterious forces connected with places like Stonehenge'						
	Strongly agree	Agree	Neither	Disagree	Strongly disagree	(%)	N
Age							
<35	10	40	28	15	8	100	297
35–60	5	31	32	21	10	100	365
>60	4	29	34	24	9	100	269
Sex							
Male	8	29	33	19	12	100	472
Female	5	38	30	21	6	100	463
Status							
High	2	30	27	25	16	100	147
Middle	7	36	30	20	8	100	601
Low <60	17	30	30	15	7	100	80
Low >60	2	25	46	21	6	100	90
Activity Status							
Housewives	4	36	32	16	12	100	113
Retired	4	31	32	24	9	100	219
Student	11	34	21	21	13	100	16
Unemployed	18	35	33	8	7	100	66
Part-time work	6	39	32	16	8	100	88
Full-time work	6	32	31	22	9	100	429
Heritage Visitor							
Visits none	5	31	37	20	7	100	212
Visits one	7	31	37	15	10	100	138
Visits two	6	33	28	23	10	100	189
Visits three	4	35	33	22	7	100	185
Visits all	10	35	24	22	10	100	180

These alternative beliefs are most likely to be espoused by young people and/or those of low status. In addition, as we have seen from the crosstabulations, they are more likely, except in the first case, to be espoused by women and by keen heritage visitors. This suggests that certain people are going regularly to museums but interpreting them in their own way or ignoring conventional interpretation and preferring alternative ones.

Those who claim to have participated in some form of archaeological fieldwork are no more likely to believe in extra-terrestrials or the Loch Ness Monster than anyone else. However, with regard to 'ley beliefs' such as the

Table 7.20 Belief in Loch Ness Monster, by sex and type of heritage visitor

	'The Loch Ness Monster probably does exist'						
	Strongly agree	Agree	Neither	Disagree	Strongly disagree	(%)	N
Sex							
Male	4	20	29	24	22	100	472
Female	4	21	34	30	10	100	467
Heritage Visitor							
Visits none	–	18	40	25	16	100	210
Visits one	2	23	32	23	20	100	138
Visits two	5	20	27	30	18	100	189
Visits three	8	24	29	26	13	100	183

existence of mysterious forces at places like Stonehenge (cf. Michell 1969), they fall into two groups: the larger group (52 per cent) who believe in them and a smaller group (33 per cent) who do not (Table 7.21). We can suggest, then, that those who have participated actively in fieldwork (on their own or more officially organised) can be divided into those who accept the ethos of professional archaeology and firmly reject the paranormal, and those whose participation in conventional archaeology does not shake their credence of unusual phenomena; indeed archaeology may be taken up precisely because it provides an avenue to 'the mysterious past'. Such people may be finding in their mysterious and romantic interpretations values and emotions that they feel are not present in contemporary society. For the young and unemployed who espouse these beliefs they may offer an alternative to the apparently bleak future.

Table 7.21 Participation in archaeological fieldwork, by belief in mysterious forces at Stonehenge

	'There are are mysterious forces connected with places like Stonehenge'						
Participated in fieldwork?	Strongly agree	Agree	Neither	Disagree	Strongly disagree	(%)	N
Yes	17	35	15	22	11	100	95
No	5	33	33	20	8	100	825

Just as metal detecting offers something that has been played down by archaeology in recent years, which is the thrill of finding things, in a similar way 'alternative archaeology' allows full rein to the romantic imagination, something disparaged by archaeology and, arguably, by a rationalist society in general. The existence of this phenomenon must in part be an indication of the failure of contemporary archaeology to convince large sections of the population of its version of the past. Modern archaeology has been particularly blamed for deterring the interested lay public by its over-technicality and complexity, and for giving the impression that it is only for 'clever' people (Baker 1983: 77). In addition, archaeologists have been blamed for not refuting the claims of para-archaeology, with the result that they can easily take hold of the public consciousness (Bainbridge 1978: 39, Feder 1984: 534). Fowler sums this up well when he suggests: 'Scratch a 'Guardian' reader and she is more likely to be swinging a pendulum over a plan of the Cerne Giant than poring through the *Proceedings of the Prehistoric Society*' (Fowler 1981: 65).

Such misgivings have led some archaeologists to question the validity of their work. Demoule asks himself if *Gallia* sells several hundred copies a year and von Daniken sells millions, who is serving the needs of society ? (Demoule 1982: 753). However, this is really to misunderstand the nature of the problem. Although some of the uncritical acceptance of beliefs in spacemen and monsters might be accounted for by the relative lack of response from the archaeological community, the phenomenon, more so than metal detecting, largely stems from wider concerns outside the sphere of archaeology.

Alternative beliefs about the past seem to be manifestations of an approach to the past which is non-scientific, stressing the role of the emotions and the imagination in gaining a sense of the past. In many ways, then, beliefs which are anathema to archaeology are a problem beyond archaeology's control, occupying the space once occupied by more orthodox religious beliefs. In a study of what he terms 'cult archaeology', Cole (1980) argues that beliefs in prehistoric extra-terrestrials and the like are united by their non-acceptance of science. Rather like religious cults, these beliefs provide identity and new 'ways of knowing' which are not provided in a rational world, and that 'like more traditional cults, some cult archaeologies do attempt to give meaning, not just explanation, to being human' (*ibid*: 34)

The attractiveness to many people of this approach to the past can be seen as symptomatic of the wider social phenomenon of alienation and disillusionment with science. Loss of confidence in science has for many years been linked to the rise of mysticism and the cults of witchcraft, astrology and other 'New Age' phenomena (Toffler 1970: 450). This reversion to pre-scientific attitudes, he notes, is accompanied by a great surge of nostalgia for less turbulent times. In this way, as hinted earlier, the phenomenon of these alternative beliefs, rather than resulting from a dissatisfaction with archaeology, may be an expression of similar things to belief in ghosts and contemporary UFOs. Interest in pagan religion, the occult, and nostalgia for old times therefore form a network of interests for those disillusioned with the values of the late twentieth century.

Even if everyone were clear as to the established archaeological interpretation of Stonehenge or the Pyramids, this would not necessarily prevent many people from believing in spacemen and power fields, simply because these are more exciting explanations than the prosaic arguments put forward by archaeologists. Again, the need for excitement and imagination may outweigh the importance of the evidence. For certain people, particularly the young, the unemployed, and for women more than men, the present is apparently less attractive than the past: the rate of change is seen as too fast, and progress is no longer believed in. In an increasingly rational and materialistic society the past, especially prehistory, may offer a refuge for the creative use of emotion and imagination in the construction of a non-rational and non-materialistic past. This aspect of these alternative beliefs has been noted by Williamson and Bellamy in their study of ley lines. They conclude that 'ley writings combine a love of the countryside, a suggestion of the former existence of a Golden Age, criticisms of the decadence of contemporary society, and the presentation of the ideal society for the future' (Williamson and Bellamy 1983: 180).

The fact that people who believe in these alternative beliefs are also keen visitors to heritage presentations suggests they are enthusiastic about the past but that they reject or ignore the conventional interpretations given, yet again showing the redundancy of the dominant ideology thesis. Instead, as Hodder (1986: 162, 167) found, they create their own pasts, not necessarily by consciously rejecting the conventional media as he suggests but by using the material available for their own ends. Grimshaw and Lester (1976: 30) have noted how the endurance of the Loch Ness Monster idea is a result of its ability to mean many different things to different people. Museums and other presentations of the past can thus truly be 'dreamlands', not in the sense that Horne (1984: 1) intended as repressive fictions, but as arenas for individuals to create their own pasts.

Conclusions

The image of archaeology and participation in archaeological societies shows that the subject is still emblematic of 'distinction', with the less privileged elements of society least likely to value it or participate in it because they have not been socialized into perceiving it as a realistic 'opportunity'. Just as the earlier notion that we might expect increased numbers of museum visitors because there are greater numbers of unemployed people and greater leisure time was criticised as being based on a misunderstanding of the nature of leisure and unemployment, similar sentiments expressed concerning archaeology by Rahtz (1985: 174) are also misguided. There is no reason why increased leisure time and unemployment would bring an increased interest in archaeology; first it has to be perceived as a worthwhile activity.

There is no doubt that archaeologists could do more to make their subject better-understood and more widely enjoyed. This would involve a change of emphasis in the relationship between archaeology and the public. A critical and socially responsible archaeology would help people gain their own sense of the past by allowing their enthusiasm full rein, and allowing people where possible to participate in fieldwork. Part of the problem is that popularization has never been seen as an integral part of the archaeological process (Shanks and Tilley 1987), as it should be for a discipline which aims to study a past belonging to all. If archaeology were to see its public role as an integral part of the discipline rather than the icing on the cake, the subject would be transformed, and would be found more relevant by the public. This too has been admirably summarised by Fowler when he writes: 'Time may well show that the major archaeological change, and I would hope conceptual advance, of the last decade has been not so much the impact of applied science nor the advent of the 'new' archaeology but the emergence of archaeology as a socially-involved and socially-responsible field of activity *in addition* to its normal and essential academic obligations' (Fowler 1977: 155).

8 Gaining a sense of the past

Contrary to expectations, in the last chapter it was found that those who participate in treasure hunting or subscribe to beliefs in mysterious forces associated with ancient sites and in prehistoric extra-terrestrials are just as likely to be museum visitors as people who participate in more conventional activities. So far, then, we have isolated a constellation of activities and beliefs associated with the past, but they all seem to be participated in by people who visit museums. Parker's division of society into two leisure classes, privileged and underprivileged, seems to ring increasingly true (Parker 1983: 110), as it seems that a broad division can be made between those people who actively pursue their interest in the past, and those who do not. If we wish to broaden the range of people who use presentations of the past and the other services offered by museums, we must look in more detail at those people who tend not to visit heritage presentations and discover how such people approach the past.

Ways of finding out about the past

Unfortunately, it seems that museums are one of the least enjoyable means of finding out about local history (Table 8.1). In a question which asked respondents to name the most enjoyable way of finding out about local history, the three most popular means were visiting the site or area alone, having a guided tour, and watching a television programme about it. These are all united by the fact that they provide more of a feeling of context than museums do. Lack of context has been a problem long recognised by museum personnel, and strenuous efforts have been made to alleviate it by using reconstructions or models, or by developing living museums or eco-museums. Nevertheless as far as the public are concerned, these can still not compete with getting out in the field, or sitting at home in front of the television.

Strong differences are shown when preferences are crosstabulated with type of museum visitor (Table 8.2). Even frequent visitors place a visit to a museum second from last in enjoyment, showing that even those who have been

Table 8.1 Most enjoyable way of finding out about local history

'If you wanted to find out about local history or some old local place, what would be the most enjoyable way of doing it?'	
	(%)
Visiting the local area or site by yourself	20
Having a guided tour of the local area or site	19
Watching a television programme about it	16
Reading a book about it	14
Listening to an expert talk about it	12
Visiting a museum	7
Asking in your local library	7
Going to evening classes in local history	6
	100
	N = 904

brought up to participate in museums in fact prefer other ways of finding out about the past. The more frequently people visit a museum, the more confident they are likely to feel in their ability to experience the past on their own, in the context of the site. With decreasing frequency of visits, they are more likely to rely on additional help, such as a guided tour, while still wishing to experience history *in situ*. This is consistent with the findings of Bourdieu and Darbel that the more cultivated and competent art museum visitors prefer to visit alone and disdain the use of guidebooks and signs while the less cultivated are keen to use them. For the former, undertaking a visit without such aids is yet another affirmation of distinction (Bourdieu and Darbel 1991: 53-4).

For those who rarely or never go to museums, the most enjoyable way of finding out about local history is by watching television, though rare visitors are almost as likely to want to read a book about the subject. The factor that distinguishes them from all other types of museum visitor is that their preferred ways of finding out about the past are home-based, whereas those of the other groups are conducted in public, out of doors. This pattern is again perfectly consistent with the leisure patterns of those with least 'leisure opportunity' discussed in Chapter 6.

It might be tempting to conclude that people who do not visit museums have little sense of the past and little interest in gaining one, because they also consistently do not visit other historic buildings, participate in neither sanctioned nor non-sanctioned archaeology, and prefer to sit at home watching television. Experiencing the past by watching television can be seen

Table 8.2 Most enjoyable way of finding out about local history, by type of museum visitor

	Type of Visitor				
	Frequent	Regular	Occasional	Rare	Non visitor
Visiting local area alone	30	21	20	10	14
Guided tour of area	16	22	20	15	18
Watching TV programme	11	10	20	25	23
Reading a book	8	13	12	21	16
Listening to an expert	14	11	13	13	10
Visiting a museum	7	10	7	3	5
Asking in local library	3	6	5	10	12
Going to evening classes	11	7	4	3	2
(%)	100	100	100	100	100
N	154	334	129	126	155

as a much more passive form of consumption than visiting museums, and the public images of archaeology demonstrated by the survey suggest that the desired messages about the subject are not being assimilated. However, this viewpoint would be a misunderstanding of the way in which people use the past. It does not mean that they do not appreciate and enjoy the presentations that are given on television. Chapter 3 has shown that, whatever their derivation, people's images of the past show that they use the past in their own ways. For many people, excluded by lack of 'opportunity' from participation in conventional heritage, the television offers a convenient means of experiencing the past.

In addition, there is evidence that people excluded from conventional heritage presentations do have a strong sense of the past, but gain it in a different way. Their approach is often intangible, being based on the family, the home, and the locality. Material culture, such as treasured possessions, sometimes have an important role to play in making this sense of the past tangible, but many rely purely on memory, imagination and conversation, in which history is passed on verbally.

The role of material culture

Much has been written of the potential role of material culture in enabling people to construct their own sense of the past. Material remains from the past have been seen as providing an opportunity to encounter the past at first hand, and to handle objects used by people in the past (Prown 1982: 3, Hindle 1978: 5). Material culture's existence independent of the observer means that it can be open to any number of different interpretations by different people (Miller 1982: 21). In particular, several writers have suggested that experiencing the past directly through objects is a powerful vehicle for one thing that has been missing in many approaches to the past: the imagination (Fritz 1973: 79; Pallottino 1968: 323). In contemporary use, material culture has been seen to have a liberating potential, allowing different groups, especially the mute subordinate groups denied access to the normal channels of communications, to express their contemporary concerns (Hodder 1984b: 349, Moore 1982: 79). Material culture has been seen to operate in a similar fashion with regard to the construction of a sense of the past. Its imaginative potential allows it to be a vehicle for almost any experience of the past, constructed by the individual and possibly only meaningful in his or her terms. The tangibility of material culture and the plasticity of its meanings might be one way in which those who are frustrated by the glass cases inside museums find their sense of the past. However, the survey shows that different groups of people have different approaches to the possession of objects from the past, and that none of them are predominantly associated with those who tend not to visit museums. The activities surveyed included research into one's family tree, the formal collection of specific objects and membership of collector's clubs, to the saving of family souvenirs and relics.

Genealogy

Fifteen per cent of respondents claimed to have undertaken some research into their family tree, although the survey did not permit further details of how this was conducted. The relative popularity of this method of research no doubt demonstrates its potential to provide for the individual a keen sense of a personal past populated by real people, and one that makes a direct link between past and present in personal terms.

However, it too is far more likely to be participated in by frequent museum visitors, and those of higher status (Table 8.3). The reason for this may well be that, rather like collecting antiques, genealogy was a pursuit initially confined to the aristocracy, subsequently spread in the Victorian period to a bourgeoisie eager to legitimate itself (Dellheim 1983: 29-30), and has now become a common middle class pastime. Unlike the preservation of family mementoes (see below), it is a relatively formal activity that involves leaving the home and familiarising oneself with the procedures of libraries and records offices and being at home in an academic culture. Because of this, genealogy remains firmly within the constellation of cultured activities and retains the imprint of its aristocratic origins.

Table 8.3 Participation in family tree research, by status and type of museum visitor

	Overall Total : 15%		
Status (%)		**Type of Museum Visitor** (%)	
High	20	Frequent	22
Middle	15	Regular	16
Low <60	15	Occasional	12
Low >60	6	Rare	12
		Non-visitor	9

Table 8.4 Active collecting of objects, by age, status and type of museum visitor

'Do you actively collect any objects "					
		Overall Total : 32%			
Age	(%)	**Status**	(%)	**Type of Museum Visitor**	(%)
<35	37	High	37	Frequent	50
35–59	37	Middle	24	Regular	35
>60	19	Low <60	24	Occasional	27
		Low >60	20	Rare	16
				Non-visitor	11

Formal collections

The active acquisition of objects specifically to add to a collection is a widespread phenomenon in Britain, being practised by around a third of the population. The elderly are significantly less likely to indulge in it than other age groups, as are those of low status. In addition, the more assiduous museum visitors are more likely to collect things than other types of museum visitor (Table 8.4). This suggests that the creation of formal collections belongs with other conventional heritage pursuits, such as heritage sightseeing or , research into the family tree. Items that are collected tend to be those things that can be displayed as traditional decorations to a room (china, glass, silver, old books, pictures), as curios (rocks, fossils, brass), or used practically (furniture) (Table 8.5). In a separate category are those items that are less often collected as part of a general interior design plan. These tend to be objects such as coins, stamps, and other small items of ephemera or memorabilia that are collected in sets and stored away in albums (cigarette cards, postcards, football programmes). This is perhaps a different form of collecting; one that is not intended primarily for display as part of an overall room setting, but rather for the pleasure of the individual in the comprehensiveness and variety of the collection.

Table 8.5 Types of objects actively collected by respondents

Type of Object	(%)
Coins	18
China	17
Pottery/ceramics	8
Glass bottles	8
Books	7
Furniture	7
Stamps	6
Ephemera (cigarette cards, postcards, football programmes, matchboxes)	6
'Memorabilia' (Americana, material relating to railways, cars, ships, etc)	5
Models and toys	5
Rocks, fossils, shells	5
Old wooden objects (treen, old tools, etc)	4
Brass	3
Glass	3
Pictures	3
Pewter	3
Spoons	2
'Nick-nacks'	2
Records	2

(Percentages total more than 100 because many respondents collect more than one
type of object)

Notes: In addition, the following types of object were mentioned once: silver,
jewellery, clay pipes, plants, beer towels, old cameras, oil lamps, watches, family
memorabilia, fans, badges, thimbles, bronzes, bobbins, and bells.

Table 8.6 Membership of collectors' clubs, by type of museum visitor

Type of visitor	3% Membership overall		
	Member of club	Not a member	N
Frequent	5	95	161
Regular	5	95	345
Occasional	2	98	134
Rare	3	97	130
Non-visitor	1	99	165

Note: The figures are not statistically significant at the .05 level (p = .0597)

Few people, however, actually join formal collectors' clubs (only 3 per cent).
Frequent and regular museum visitors are more likely to belong to them than
those who visit museums less often, though the differences are not statistically
significant (Table 8.6). The formal collection of objects tends not, therefore, to
be a means used by those less interested in heritage to gain a sense of the past.

The same is also true, contrary to the hopes of material culture theory, with regard to the simple possession of old objects.

Possession of old objects

Over half of respondents claimed to possess something over fifty years old, but again it was those of higher status and the more frequent museum visitors who were likely to do so. Unsurprisingly, those in the youngest age group were least likely to own something over fifty years old (Table 8.7). The range of objects owned is enormous, ranging from items whose significance resides principally in the associations they evoke (photographs, family heirlooms), to antiques bought for the home which are valued for their beauty and craft.

Table 8.7 Possession of objects over fifty years old, by age, status and type of museum visitor

'Do you own any objects that are over 50 years old?'

Overall Total : 56%

Age	(%)	Status	(%)	Type of Museum Visitor	(%)
<35	48	High	73	Frequent	78
35–59	61	Middle	59	Regular	62
>60	59	Low <60	31	Occasional	50
		Low >60	38	Rare	45
				Non-Visitor	38

Table 8.8 Why an old object is attractive, by type of museum visitor

	Type of Museum Visitor (%)				
	Frequent	Regular	Occasional	Rare	Non-visitor
Possibly valuable	1	6	10	3	5
Family links	32	46	52	46	67
Direct link to the Past	14	13	10	11	6
Well made	6	5	8	15	7
Beautiful	43	28	19	14	11
Don't know	–	1	1	3	2
Other	4	2	2	9	3
%	100	100	100	100	100
N	121	215	64	58	61

Analysis of those who do possess old objects shows that frequent and regular museum visitors tend to value their favourite old object because it is beautiful (Table 8.8). This suggests that it is the aesthetic disposition which characterises their response to objects both in museums and in their own possession. They tend to see objects *as* objects, distancing them from their own experiences. This aesthetic stance can be seen as another badge of distinction, a demonstration of mastery of the correct codes, and of distance from necessity (Bourdieu 1984: 55-6).

The predominance of frequent museum visitors and those of higher status in collecting and owning old objects, and in demonstrating an aesthetic appreciation of them, is a telling instance of a phenomenon pointed out by several writers: that the dominant social groups tend not only to wish to control the past but also physically to own it. As Plumb has noted, 'the personal ownership of the past has always been a vital strand in the ideology of all ruling classes' (Plumb 1969: 31).

For example, the collections of Victorian antiquarians were an expression of the importance accorded to property during this period and expressed in concrete form the desire of the age to appropriate the past in the service of the future (Levine 1986: 60). The fact that now a third of the population collect things and over half own old things shows that this phenomenon has become widely democratized, but, as with genealogy, the statistics show that it still retains its original status connotations.

With the finding that even the ownership of old objects tends to be concentrated amongst those who are active museum visitors, strength seems to be added to the argument that there is an important sub-group in society largely dispossessed of any past of their own. This would be a superficial impression, however, because we have not yet considered the fundamentally different attitudes to old objects which characterise the dispossessed. Such groups (who tend to be the elderly, those of low status, and people who do not visit conventional heritage presentations) certainly do have their own sense of the past but it is a far less tangible one and therefore less easy to pin down with a questionnaire survey. A clue is provided by the responses presented in Table 8.2, where it is shown that those who tend not to go to museums would most prefer finding out about the past at home, by watching television or reading a book. It is this home-based approach which distinguishes them from other groups and which is the key to understanding how they experience the past.

'Dispossessed' approaches to the past

While frequent museum visitors value their favourite old object for aesthetic reasons, those who could be described as deprived or dispossessed, in the sense that their leisure activities are very restricted, value it for its family links, demonstrating the close personal way in which they gain access to the past. They are most likely to conduct their leisure at home because this is the main locus of their opportunities for leisure, a situation brought about by a combination of socialization, disengagement, and structural factors such as limited money or the presence of young children to look after. They are most likely to interact with family and relatives, and gain their sense of the past through them and through contact with family heirlooms of sentimental significance. Typical objects mentioned are as follows:

- Dolls House
- Silver Locket
- Medals
- Grandmother's Wedding Ring
- Family Photographs
- Silver Fob Watch
- Tea Service
- Child's Rocking Chair
- Antique Furniture
- Painting

Unlike the objects in a museum which have no direct personal link to the individual and are kept beyond touch by glass cases, for these people, these particular objects resonate with personal significance and no doubt give a real sense of communion with the person who used them, or with the individual's childhood. This sense of family history is quite different from that given by actual research into the family tree, which, as already noted, is a much more academic exercise involving frequent visits to libraries and archives. It can easily be characterised as an activity, genealogy, while 'thinking about the family' is not an easily classifiable activity. What perhaps characterises the approach of the dispossessed to the past is this lack of differentiation, and the difficulty of pinning it down and separating it out from other activities. In this way it is truly a 'sense' of the past which may be difficult to articulate and provide few manifestations other than family heirlooms and souvenirs.

The importance of different kinds of history

The idea that there are two different approaches to the past receives additional support in the answers to a question which presented respondents with a list of five different types of history: British history, world history, family tree, history of homeland (eg. Wales, Ireland, India, West Indies), history of local area, and asked them to rank them in order of importance as far as they personally were concerned. In order to crosstabulate these by status and by type of museum visitor, the mean ranking of each item for each group was computed, giving an estimate of the rank order distance of each group from each item (Table 8.9).

The first aspect to draw out is attitudes towards British history. High and intermediate status groups put it as the most important kind of history to know about, while the low status groups put it second. This could be seen as an example of the successful penetration of an ideology of patriotism, which inculcates a recognition by most that the history of the nation is the most important for the individual to know about. However, it is noteworthy that it is

Table 8.9 Rank order of different types of history, by status

High status	Middle status	Low status
1. British history	1. British history	1. Family history
2. World history	2. Family history/Local history	2. British history
3. History of homeland		3. Local history
4. Local history	4. History of homeland	4. Local history homeland
5. Family history	5. World history	5. World history

only those of low status who do not put British history as their first priority, preferring to put the history of their family above that, which suggests they are less enthusiastic about the idea of a national past than the higher status groups. This pattern is repeated when we look at the preferences of different types of museum visitor (Table 8.10). Here there is a sliding scale of choices, from the frequent and regular visitors who put British history, on average, as their second most important kind of history, to the non-visitors, who put it fourth in importance. This is a clear indication that dominant values (in this case, the recruitment of the past for purposes of enhancing national pride) do not necessarily penetrate all areas of society, and that dominated groups can resist and subvert dominant values.

Table 8.10 Rank order of different types of history, by type of museum visitor

Frequent	Regular	Occasional	Rare	Non-visitor
World	Family	Family	Family	Family
British	British/ Local	Homeland	Local	Local
Homeland	–	British/ Local	British	Homeland
Local	Homeland	–	Homeland	British
Family	World	World	World	World

The second, and more important, conclusion to arise from these statistics is that, once the effect created by attitudes to British history is removed, quite different ways of valuing the past emerge between different groups. High status individuals are more likely to put world history as the most important, while middle and low status groups are more likely to put family history as most important. Although the pattern is less clear amongst the different types of museum visitor, there does seem to be a sliding scale of preferences from the frequent visitors who are more likely to put world history as the most important kind of history, followed by British history, history of the homeland, local history, and family history as the least important, to the non-visitors who put family history as the most important, followed by local history, history of homeland, British history and world history. This adds weight to the idea that the approach to the past of higher status, more frequent museum visitors is intellectual, distanced, and impersonal, and the approach of the lower status, non-visitors is more personal, local and family-based.

From the cumulative evidence it can be suggested (although it would need to be confirmed by further work) that those who prefer to gain their sense of past at home and do not own any old objects as tangible memorials, do so by their personal memories, through the living history of their extended family, and through attachment to place. This attachment to the past may have no permanent tangible manifestations because it can take the form purely of memory, conversations with people, and walks in the local area. For these people, this may be a more vivid experience of the past than any number of museum visits, and probably best represents the concept of a 'personal past' as opposed to that of an 'impersonal heritage'.

The personal past and the impersonal heritage

'The personal past', then, is a sense of the past which is experienced in personal terms, of which the best examples are personal memories and family histories. Nostalgia is derived from this personal sense of the past, and can be contrasted with the impersonal sense of the past that Davis (1979) terms 'antiquarian feeling'[8]. This personal sense of the past seems to constitute the principal way in which the past is experienced by certain groups, apart from the passive consumption offered by television-viewing. For the reasons outlined in earlier chapters, people who do not have the competence to decipher the code of museum visiting exclude themselves from it as an inappropriate activity. Their leisure tends to be centred around their family, and the family focus of their sense of the past is the most appropriate and relevant one for them; they do not experience the need for anything else.

It is not suggested, of course, that people of high status, 'culture vultures' and so on, have no such sense of the past of their own. It is inevitable that everyone who has a memory has at least some sense of the past, just as it is intuitively clear that people from all areas of society derive a sense of belonging from the roots provided by their family and, often, a certain locality. For those of higher status, however, this past is overlain by another phenomenon which largely masks it: the sense of the past as an impersonal heritage. The existence of these two senses of the past amongst the same group of people can be seen in the ranking of different kinds of pasts. For example, 32 per cent of frequent museum visitors put world history as first choice, but the same percentage also put it fifth choice. Although 32 per cent of high status individuals put world history as their first choice, the next most frequent choice (28 per cent) was fifth. Similar, but less marked, disparities exist with those of lower status and those who visit museums less frequently. This strongly suggests that two competing senses of the past are coexisting here, and that in the case of higher status individuals, the impersonal global approach masks or coexists with the personal sense of the past because their upbringing and their consequent leisure expectations and opportunities prime them, when confronted with such a questionnaire, to stress their 'high' approach to the past.

The recognition that there are two basically different approaches to gaining a sense of the past has important implications for the future development of museums and related institutions. So far in their existence, museums have concentrated almost exclusively on presenting an impersonal history seen through the detached view of the academically-trained historian. Issues have been discussed thematically, with little real sense of living individuals behind these processes. The introduction of the results of oral history projects into museum exhibitions has been one of the first significant attempts to weave personal visions of the past into the official history presented by the museum. This dual experience of the past represents an important challenge to museums, and an acute moral dilemma. Should museums invade individuals' own experiences of the past and document them for others, or will this destroy their very essence? The next chapter considers this issue in an attempt to use the survey results to inform a critically aware museum practice.

9 Opening up museums

One of the principal conclusions to emerge from the survey and discussion presented in this book is that people use the past in many varied and creative ways to suit their own needs and their own feelings about their position in the world. This simple observation has important and wide-ranging implications for the development of a critical theory and practice of museology.

In one way, the acknowledgement of individual creativity in gaining a sense of the past can offer an attractive route out of the curatorial dilemma outlined in the introduction to the book, because if everybody constructs their own vision of the past then curators can hardly be accused of being conspirators in a massive plot to inculcate a dominant ideology. However, this argument can also lead to a dangerous relativism whereby anyone's view of the past is as good as anyone else's, and academic anarchy reigns. It is important therefore to examine closely the ways in which interpretation of the role of museums is affected by acknowledgement of the creative role of the individual.

For example, it does not imply that museums are no longer ideological institutions. Rather than being purely agents of an overarching dominant ideology, they are incorporative of the dominant themselves (ie. the affluent and the educated who form the backbone of the visiting public), and they are exclusive of non-visitors. As a contemporary phenomenon, museum visiting is still associated with the establishment, with high culture, and with the social status quo, as is the ideology encapsulated within the displays. The open nature of museums means that they can very effectively incorporate new and rising members of the educated and the affluent, who are joining the ranks of the empowered. However, although these criticisms can be levelled at museums, the survey shows, first, that many people exclude themselves from participation in museum culture, and second, that those exposed to the messages of museums are not empty vessels waiting to be filled, but interpret the messages in line with their own preconceived ideas and therefore only assimilate the dominant ideology incompletely.

If ideology is only partially consumed, and people create their own versions of the past, does this therefore mean that the content of museum displays is irrelevant? If museum visiting is essentially an expression of cultural belonging, then surely a visit is just an act of consumption: going to one museum is much the same as going to another. This kind of argument, however, arises from a confusion of different levels of analysis. It is quite possible at a general level to argue that museum visiting, just like attendance at the theatre, classical concerts or ballet, is an elite cultural phenomenonon,

131

at the same time as arguing that, at a specific level, the content of each visit or performance is extremely different and important. Once the cultural barrier of *being* a museum visitor (perceiving the opportunity to visit) is overcome, then the survey has shown that the majority of people visit specific museums because they are interested in their contents. To argue that the content of museums is meaningless would be analagous to arguing that it does not matter which plays are put on in theatres or which films are shown in cinemas because people will go, sheep-like, to them anyway.

The content of museum presentations is therefore important, as subjective observation of visitors' reactions to them confirm. What must be accepted, though, is that visitors will not necessarily interpret the displays in the way intended by the curator. This, too, has extremely widespread ramifications for the way in which we conceive the role of the museum.

Cultural empowerment

With the recognition of the plurality of interpretations of museum displays, the curatorial dilemma can be resolved, and resolved without descent into total relativism. One of the principal tasks of a critical museology has to be the removal of cultural barriers to widespread participation in museums. Opening up museums in this way means more, however, than achieving a visitor profile representative of the overall population. In order for widespread participation to continue, the overall philosophy of what museums do has to be transformed, by representing, in all aspects of museum work, those groups whose pasts and whose interests have hitherto not been represented.

This process has been termed 'cultural empowerment', and has been defined as 'transferring skills to others and providing opportunities for them to present their own points of view within the institutional context' (Ames 1990: 161). So far, much of the work in this area has occurred in relation to First Nation groups in the Americas and Oceania, but it can equally be applied to groups excluded from museums on other grounds. At Springburn Museum in Glasgow, for example, several projects have been undertaken where local people take their own photographs and mount their own exhibitions about themselves (O'Neill 1990). Perhaps the most striking Western example of empowerment has been in Berlin, where, in the face of official indifference, in 1985 a group of campaigners conducted an unofficial excavation to reveal the remains of the former Gestapo headquarters and establish a memorial to the victims of fascism. The Active Museum of Fascism and Resistance now consists of the remains of cells where prisoners were held, and a temporary exhibition area showing the extent of the Nazi terror and linking it with post-war collective amnesia about the Nazi past, and the rise of neo-Nazi groups today (Baker 1988).

The process of empowerment itself can, however, be fraught with problems, especially if efforts to enable cultural empowerment take place within an institutional framework normally associated with the dominant. We have already seen that two separate senses of the past exist, the personal and the impersonal. Those who feel excluded from museums are most interested in the personal and the local. However, this places museum authorities in yet another dilemma. If they simply decide that museums should represent 'the personal' more in their exhibitions in order to attract, in theory at least, a wider audience, they run the danger of destroying the very precious qualities of a personal sense of the past by appropriating it for public consumption in an institution, where it is scrutinised by others for whom it is not a personal past.

It would be wrong therefore of museums to make a simple linkage between the desire to empower culturally excluded groups and the finding that these groups respond most to the personal elements of the past. To colonise it in this way would be to destroy it: curators must be sensitive to the institutional authority of the museums they work in and how this can work against some of their best efforts. However, museums can attempt to provide a means whereby this personal past can both become more meaningful for the individuals concerned, and where it can sensitively be used to illuminate, in a personal way, aspects of impersonal history.

One way in which people's personal sense of the past can be enhanced, where an interest already exists, is by museum workers offering advice on ways of following up this interest. For example, a museum bus or trailer might tour non-museum venues offering advice on how to find out more about your family tree, offer an 'Antiques Roadshow' information on family heirlooms and mementoes, or offer advice on how best to look after and mount family photographs or other ephemera.

A further, and important, way in which the personal sense of the past can be encouraged without destroying its unique qualities is through its sympathetic weaving into overall historical processes. This is already common practice in oral history work where, when it is handled well, it can enhance a general historical narrative by illuminating previously undocumented aspects and by adding the immediacy of personal experience, and it can also return something to the communities and individuals who are the source of this history by showing them that their stories are important, interesting, and can actually constitute history rather then being relegated to the sidelines. The best examples of this sort of work have recently begun to have their impact in museums in exhibitions such as The Miles Tae Dundee (Dundee) and The People's Story (Edinburgh).

The issues thrown up by a brief consideration of oral history argue that if presently unrepresented or unempowered groups are truly to 'see themselves' in museums, museums will have to cease to be associated predominantly with a main building which is a repository of Truth validated by the interests of their staff, who look mainly to their peers for approval. Instead, museums should be seen as services which respond to the community they serve. Museum workers should see themselves as enablers, providing people with the materials and opportunities to pursue their need for, and interest in, the past and to construct their own 'truths' using source materials provided by museum staff. This new conception of museums is one that is slowly gaining acceptance in various circles, although there remains a long way to go before it becomes accepted practice. The remaining sections suggest, based on the results of the survey, some practical ways in which museums can begin to be opened up to the communities they serve.

The only way the cultural barriers will be removed is by long term and consistent policy and its implementation in good practice to remove the adverse images of museums. In this way, museums will eventually become associated with positive rather than negative things.

Museums as enablers: some suggestions

Recruitment

Most museums have equal opportunities policies of some sort, but rarely abide by them in their recruitment because, it is argued, there is a shortage of graduates trained in museum work from, for example, the ethnic minorities and disabled (eg. Ollerearnshaw 1990). It is vital, however, for the future health of museums that their staff reflect the broad composition of the community. Crucially, this does not just mean the warding staff, but also the curatorial and education staff who formulate displays and other programmes, and the trustees, Friends and volunteers. Programmes of active recruitment and positive discrimination therefore should be followed at the pre-entry stage. This will entail, first, drawing the attention of school pupils to the possibility of a career in museums, and in providing open days and work experience for appropriate schools and individuals. Museums might provide training and internships as has occurred in the USA (Dickerson 1990), and might recruit more imaginatively from graduates with good potential and train them for specific jobs within the museum. Recruitment of trustees (or their equivalent) from a broad community base will be important in gaining the support and confidence of the various groups in an area.

Community involvement

As organisations which are community-focused and wish to enable all to have the opportunity to participate in them, community involvement will have to be an increasingly important element of museum work. Active recruitment policies within different communities will help to foster closer links between them and the museum, but these links must be forged to the extent that the theoretical community ownership of museums becomes a reality. Most museums should appoint, as a few have done already, community liaison officers who can build up close relations with communities, and carry out collecting programmes in which a tangible end result is returned to the groups.

Collecting

If museums now become cultural centres with a historical theme, aimed at recruiting the active participation of all their constitutent groups in their own past, present and future, then it is clear that this will have a fundamental impact on their collecting. Traditionally museums have been associated with material culture and associated supporting information, and, as this is a vital role not being duplicated by any other bodies, it is one that must continue. In order fully to reflect cultural diversity, however, they must (as many museums already do) expand their definition of material culture to include all cultural representation, including those that are less tangible or collectable, such as food, dance, and music. These may of course best be recorded in storage media such as video or photographs. Where, as is usually the case, museums cannot collect representative samples of all the areas of culture they would wish to, they should make steps to draw up agreement with other bodies that do collect relevant material, such as libraries, archives, film companies and photographic agencies. The results of some of this work, such as videos exploring local history, could be hired to schools or sold in the museum shop and other outlets. For those people who prefer to find out about the past without leaving their home, videos and magazine articles might be one way of stimulating this interest.

Oral and visual history

Active contemporary collecting, especially from groups unassociated with the traditional museum public, raises in acute form one of the crucial issues surrounding cultural empowerment, which is that of appropriation. This is particularly apposite because the very issue of the appropriation of history by curators is one that prompted the move towards cultural empowerment by beginning to represent disenfranchised groups in museums. In order to do this, material deriving from these groups must be presented in the museum, and in practical terms at present this is usually done by middle class white curators pending a more representative recruitment into the profession.

In collecting this material these curators therefore have to be extremely careful that they are not simply replicating the appropriation of culture at one remove from the museum. This is an issue that has been of great concern to those undertaking oral history work, and by and large has been tackled by seeing collecting as a two-way process. Extensive consultation with community groups is undertaken and a great deal of time is expended on building up contacts in different areas. When oral history or video work is undertaken, it is done with permission, sensitively, and the results of the collecting are returned to the community in some way. This usually means that copies of the tapes, with transcripts and translations if necessary, are given to the individuals concerned, they are invited to the exhibitions in which they are portrayed, the curator goes to speak to community groups to summarise the results of the work, and ideally elements of any exhibition work are loaned to community centres.

Devolution to the local

One of the critical findings of the survey was that people who feel culturally excluded from museums tend to gain their sense of the past in terms of the local, as well as the personal. This emphasis on the local offers a possible route to enabling people who are interested in the past to exploit this interest in a fruitful way. It suggests that museums should devolve to as local a scale as possible where they can become an accepted part of the everyday community rather than perceived as irrelevant institutions separate from daily life. Their programmes can then be geared much more specifically to the small-scale local interests of local residents.

For example, even in a multicultural urban centre where much of the population is relatively transient and may have few roots in the area, great numbers of people will have a passing curiosity about the area they live in. This natural local interest provides an excellent avenue for exploring the history of the area. Every patch of land will have a geological and natural history, an archaeology (even if it is of fields and not structures), a more recent social history, and of course a present and future. By concentrating on presenting a cross-disciplinary history of particular, familiar patches of ground, and the relationship between people and this environment through time, museums can stimulate a latent local interest into an active one and place the circumstances of contemporary communities into a long term perspective.

These more local scale museums or exhibition centres can then be opened up to the community by inviting individuals and groups to use the display space to mount exhibitions of their own using the museum's technical advice but retaining editorial control themselves. In this way people come to create their own history as they see it, and it would soon become clear that there is no one view of the past. The role of the curator would be then to ensure that a range of views could be expressed over time, and that propaganda is eschewed. The way forward in this area has been shown in 'The Miles Tae Dundee' exhibition where different communities mounted displays about their own history in Dundee (Murray and Stockdale 1990). Community involvement can take other forms as well. In 'The People's Show' staged by Walsall Museum and Art Gallery, exhibition space was made available to show, instead of the museum's objects, collections made by local enthusiasts. The range of collections shown was enormous, and the attendant publicity brought the museum a new lively and humorous image (Suggitt 1990).

If it is not possible to devolve the museum to a very local level in a permanent building, much can still be done to take the museum outside its cloistered walls to meet the people it is supposed to serve. A tried and successful formula is the touring bus or trailer, which is a method of decentralising the museum which has still not been widely used enough to realise its full potential. Displays set up in touring buses which visit places where people congregate in informal surroundings, such as shopping centres or parks will attract a much more representative audience than the main museum building. Again, topics of directly local interest can be displayed, objects can be handled, and curators or educators can be present to answer questions and identify objects. As well as being a good advertisement for the main museum they can come to consitute the museum's main exhibition programme, because they provide an excellent opportunity for the museum service and its staff to interact in a local area, in a face-to-face way, with local inhabitants. In this way community links can be built up, and gradually opportunities for collecting and oral and visual history work will present themselves. Pre-publicity in a mobile trailer of an exhibition project, for example, may result in offers of help with information, objects and reminiscences.

In particular, mobile museums provide an excellent opportunity for museum education staff to visit schools in the area and introduce pupils to the idea of the museum being a lively and interesting service at an early age. Interpretation of the survey results suggests that the key to whether or not museum visiting is perceived as a worthwhile use of leisure time is the kind of socialization the individual has received from family and school. If more children can be introduced to the code of museums, and their experience of museums is remembered as one that was good fun rather than intimidating, then with time an increasing range of people will come to see a museum visit as a natural thing to do. With increased emphasis on evidence-based learning consequent upon the GCSE and the National Curriculum, and the attendant possibility that fewer schools will be able to visit museums, it is more important than ever before that museums start to go out to visit schools with appropriate teaching materials.

Opening up collections

One of the great challenges facing a community-focused museum is truly to become open and responsive to its diverse publics, and accountable to them. Recent critical attention has been focused on the often vast reserve collections held by museums that are rarely consulted, even by scholars (National Audit Office 1988). While not for an instant denigrating the role that museums play in preserving material for the future, the climate of accountability is such that museums also have to make strenuous efforts to make these collections known and used by people.

Fundamental to this enterprise is knowing what is in the collections and advertising their contents. The key to this has to be a flexible computer database. Once full computerisation of collections records has been achieved, museum workers are provided with an excellent opportunity to publicise the contents of their collections by producing indices of types of objects, localities, chronological periods, and themes. Publicity of the existence of the collections can be circulated in academic journals, local newspapers, and in the galleries themselves. With a well-planned system it should be possible to arrange for terminals with simple interactive programs to be available in the museum galleries for those who wish for further information and to know what else is available in the study collections. By pressing a keyword for their local area, for example, people should be able to discover what sort of material the museum holds for that locality, and how they can go about finding more about it.

Clearly, if this facility is to work, it will be necessary to devise storage and retrieval systems to cope with the anticipated increased demand. The ideal situation would be one where all museum stores were centralised into a Study Centre where material could be stored behind glass in supplementary galleries. If, as seems likely, most non-specialists are more interested in their locality than individual types of object, strong efforts could be made to store objects by area rather than by type (which reflects traditional curatorial preoccupations with classification), bearing in mind the usual conservation requirements. A Study Room would also be provided, with basic reference books and equipment where enquirers could undertake research of their own. Curators in the study centre might act rather as librarians in a book stack, fetching objects that are required for insepection, and supervising enquirers where necessary.

A further, and rather labour-intensive, step is to provide a Discovery Centre, where people can have full access to objects and information with museum staff on hand to assist them in activities relating to the collection. At the National Museums and Galleries on Merseyside, a consistent policy has been followed for over a decade to make collections open to the public, and has led to the establishment of a Natural History Centre with an activities room and collections room; a Ceramics Study Centre, a Maritime Records Centre and (until recently) a Large Objects Collection (Fewster 1990). At the Archaeological Resource Centre in York visitors help to wash and mark genuine archaeological finds, make Roman shoes, use a weaving loom, and have access to an interactive video which places finds in their context. The archaeological staff on the premises themselves work in glass-sided offices where visitors can see the sort of work they do. This process of demystifying the museum and of showing the great amount of work that goes on, usually unseen by the public, is one that can go a long way to help people understand the role of the museum. An orientation gallery in the main museum can also play a useful role in explaining the behind-the-scenes work and dispel the myth that all people who work in museums wear uniforms and patrol the galleries.

Main site exhibition and interpretation

We know from the survey data that main museum sites can be intimidating places for those who do not feel at home with the institutional code of museums, and that one way of dealing with this is to devolve the museum beyond its walls. This might suggest that we no longer need a main site other than to house staff and central services. However, it is very useful indeed for museums to have a main focus for a disparate service, which people can identify with and which can provide visitors with a number of services, such as film showings, workshops, collections, and more extensive exhibitions, that cannot easily be devolved. The main way in which people come into contact with museums is through their displays and it is in this area that most can be done to dispel the cultural barriers associated with museum visiting.

As a basis for operation, the themes for exhibitions should be those that are of interest (perhaps shown by survey work) to the public (or identifiable sections of the public) and not primarily to the curators. The survey showed that the perceived lack of relevance of museum displays was one deterrent to non-visitors, and there is no reason for curators to follow traditional exhibition topics. Exhibitions should be on themes that are likely to be of interest, whether or not material is available in the collections. Topical subjects can also be raised, including those concerning local issues such as housing, employment and the environment.

Just as with collecting, communities can and should be consulted about exhibitions that deal with their history. Empowerment can be achieved and appropriation avoided if involvement is extensive at an early stage. Simple efforts, such as translation of labels into the languages spoken by local groups can make a huge difference to the way in which museums are perceived. If museums are really felt to be owned by all of the community, they will begin to fulfil their potential.

Interactive video

As with many areas of museum work, it is simply the employment of good practice in display techniques that will help make museums more accessible to all. The use of sound, video, and reconstructions will provide a context for objects where site museums are not available. An extremely important development in this area is the interactive video. The combination of moving film, stills, text, and a computer program allowing a number of different pathways to be followed, offers exciting possibilities in answering some of the display dilemmas outlined earlier (Walsh forthcoming).

Interactive video offers first the opportunity that any video does, which is to allow interpretation to move beyond the museum's confines and show film of the countryside and the town, both historic and contemporary, and thus provide a context for the material displayed by the museum. Human interaction with the environment can much more easily be dealt with in this way. Most importantly, it allows the visitor to choose the level and type of information that he or she is interested in. This ability to discover things for oneself has been shown by the survey to be something that is enjoyed by large numbers of people. Using interactive video, some areas can be ignored, and others can be explored in ever-increasing detail. Different interpretations can be offered of the same material, as has been attempted at the Gallery 33 project at Birmingham Museum and Art Gallery, where four key artifacts can be discussed by four different collectors, a missionary, a collector, a tourist and a native museum curator, and questions posed of them (Peirson Jones 1990). The visitor, then, has some control over the interpretative experience rather than relying on the single view that the curator has selected to present. It might be possible too to link up the interactive video programme with the computer database of objects in the museum's study collections so that visitors interested in certain aspects of history can then obtain information concerning all of the museum's holdings in their area of interest. While its flexibility is great, however, it cannot be a substitute for the experience of real objects or of getting out into the land- or townscape itself. Nevertheless, for museums with fixed sites it offers great potential in opening up interpretation.

Conclusion

In order to fulfil their basic duty to the public, museums must become community-focused and open themselves up for use by the people they serve. Opening up access to museums is important because they are one of the principal means whereby people can gain access to their history.

We need to enable all people, in all their complexity, to participate in museums, and we need to return people as sentient individuals into our analysis of heritage because, in the words of one of the survey respondents, 'After all, it is people that create history'.

Notes

1. See Appendix 1 for a general discussion of this problem in cultural surveys.

2. Factors are best thought of as underlying constructs that structure similar attitudes, and the identification of such factors greatly simplifies the description and understanding of complex phenomena. The analysis itself observes the degree of correlation between all of the variables and groups them together according to a small number of common factors.

Analysis was performed on all of the closed questions concerning the past, present and future, and the results are shown in Table A2.12. Five factors were extracted, explaining just over 50 per cent of the variance. This leaves much of the variance still unexplained, but a large degree of 'noise' is not unusual in such analyses. The first factor explained almost twice as much of the variance as any other factor. This was taken as a factor representing 'attitudes to the past'. The variables comprising another factor suggested its interpretation as 'attitudes to the present'.

3. In order to avoid greater complexity to the questionnaire, a 'visitor' was defined here as someone who had visited within the twelve months prior to the survey.

4. The items on the list were combined to give a balance between two associations deemed to be negative ('monument to the dead' and 'church or temple'), two that could be either positive or negative, depending on the respondent's attitude to formal learning ('school' and 'library'), and two deemed to be positive in that the associations are communal, and informal or everyday ('community centre' and 'department store'). The particular reason for the latter two choices is that some museum commentators have felt that the museum should become more like a community centre, or that it should borrow some of the display techniques of department stores in order to become more accessible. There is however another school of thought which would argue that associations with a department store adds to the 'commodification' of the past, e.g. Shanks and Tilley 1987.

5. Attitudes to ancient monuments were not surveyed as it was felt that their

great diversity would make it difficult for an individual to hold an overall attitude to them.

6. This is a characteristic that has been noted elsewhere in Bourdieu's work (Jenkins 1982).

7. Those who left school at the minimum age and own their own homes and one or more vehicles were classified as upwardly mobile; those over 50 who had received further education but did not own their own homes or a car, were classified as downwardly mobile. The remainder were classified as static.

8. The distinction between a personal and impersonal sense of the past has already been noted in Chapter 3 for people's images of what life in the past was like.

Appendix 1: The survey method

Requirements and constraints of the survey

In formulating the survey, the priorities were to achieve a representative sample of the whole of the British public. In other words, the sample had to include individuals who were not museum or heritage visitors as well as those who were. In addition, a good response rate to the survey was crucial for the work to be representative of the total population. Finally, the method had to be one which would allow quite a large number of questions to be asked, including a series of demographic questions to enable different sub-groups of respondents to be isolated.

The two major constraints on the project were cost and organisational resources. As it was being carried out with limited funds raised from external sources, the project had to run at the minimum budget, and had to be manageable by one person. Postal survey was chosen as the most appropriate method, for the reasons outlined below.

Advantages of postal surveys

The two main advantages of postal surveys over interview research are low cost and uncomplicated administration. It is possible to conduct a large-scale survey by post which would not be affordable by the interview method. For example, the present survey of 1500 people cost in the region of £1,500 to implement, most of which was taken up by postage. The research organisation, Marplan, quoted a figure of £8,750 to do the same sort of survey by interview on a sample of 1000.

The organisation and execution of a postal survey can be done centrally by one person, whereas an interview survey by its very nature has to be carried out by a number of different people in different places. To obtain a random sample of 1500 half-hour interviews on this topic would have taken a single researcher about 375 days of fieldwork, and would have incurred very high travelling costs. The opportunity for centralised control of the survey by one person afforded by the postal method ensures the uniformity of the approach and avoids the problem of varying quality of interview data (Erdos 1970: 5-11).

Unlike personal interviews, postal surveys can be carried out anywhere in Britain that has a postal address. In this way it is possible to achieve a truly random sample across the whole country which avoids the clustering necessary for interview surveys. By sending the questionnaire by post, it is possible to get at those elusive people who are rarely at home between 9 am and 9 pm when interviewing is usually conducted (Hoinville, Jowell, *et al.* 1978: 124).

Although the lack of an interviewer can in some ways be seen as a limitation on postal surveys because of the consequent inability to clarify questions and probe further (see below), it can also be an advantage, because the presence of an interviewer can introduce a certain bias into the research. In an interview, respondents are more likely to answer positively to the subject in question in order to gain the approval of the interviewer, or exaggerate their answers to behavioural questions by claiming, for example, that they visit museums more often than they do. They are less likely to be severe in their criticism and more likely, given the lack of anonymity, to be reticent about divulging personal details (Sudman and Bradburn 1979: 51-63). This bias is lessened in the postal questionnaire. The respondent is assured anonymity, and feels less of a need to gain the research organisation's approval. It was particularly important in the survey to collect accurate information about visits to heritage presentations and accurate assessments of attitudes towards them.

As a further consequence of the absence of an interviewer, the quality of response also increases because the respondent has more time to consider his or her replies. This is particularly valuable in a questionnaire of this nature where questions are elicited concerning behaviour and attitudes to subjects which are not part of the everyday experience of the respondent. The respondent can set his or her own pace in replying to the questions, and having time to reflect on the subject means that replies are likely to be more accurate than those from a time-pressured personal interview. Comments on some of the returned questionnaires, and the fact that some people had altered their replies after further consideration, are further evidence of this.

Limitations of postal surveys

Until relatively recently, the limitations on postal surveys were thought to be too great for them to be used effectively for the collection of data on behaviour and attitudes (Moser and Kalton 1971: 256). The standard complaint against the method was that it registered low response rates, which made the information gathered of little statistical value. However, recent studies (especially Dillman 1978) have demonstrated that with careful preparation, postal surveys can achieve response rates of up to 76 per cent for general population samples and 95 per cent for samples of specialised groups. When compared with the average 70-80 per cent rate of successfully completed survey interviews (Hoinville, Jowell *et al.* 1978, Hough and Mayhew 1983, Jowell *et al.* 1987), postal surveys are potentially as valuable as interview surveys as a research method. However, some limitations do still exist and should be noted when considering the kind of information which is required by the survey.

Absence of interviewer

The absence of a human presence in the postal survey process means that any misunderstanding on the part of the respondent cannot be corrected; probing for further information is impossible; screen questions cannot easily be employed, and the characteristics of non-respondents (especially age, sex, ethnic group and type of housing) cannot be determined as easily as they could from the personal observation of an interviewer (Moser and Kalton 1971: 259). The lack of control of the answering process in a postal survey means that a different person might respond from the one who was requested to do so, consultation with other individuals can take place, and recourse to works of reference can be made. For this reason, questions of 'fact' cannot easily be asked. In particular, the questions about visits to different attractions in the last twelve months might be unreliable, as people's memories and estimation of time vary. However, this is a problem with all research questioning concerned with past behaviour. The only way to reduce the chances of a different person answering the questionnaire is to stress the importance of the named individual in the cover letter. The lack of personal contact can also mean there is less of an incentive to reply (although this incentive can be increased by other means), and there is no guarantee that respondents will not skip questions which they feel to be too long or tedious.

In addition, the inability to explain or probe means that it is much more difficult to ask open-ended questions successfully. Consequently most questions have to consist of multiple-choice answers to statements of propositions arranged in a Likert scale (eg. 'Strongly Agree–Agree–Neither Agree nor Disagree–Disagree–Strongly Disagree'). However, open-ended questions are a problem in all kinds of survey research. The difficulty of coding and comparing answers to open-ended questions, and the fact that answering can be influenced just as much by the powers of expression of the respondent as by his or her beliefs, has led to their sparing use even in interviews, so their scarcity in a postal survey should not necessarily be seen as a disadvantage inherent in the postal method in particular. Questions asking reasons for behaviour are similarly difficult to ask, because many people cannot articulate conscious reasons for doing something (Henry 1953), and again answers may only reflect an individual's literary skills.

Length and complexity of questionnaire

Heberlein and Baumgartner (1978), in a review article of postal survey methodology, show that one of the crucial factors in response is the 'cost' to the potential respondent in terms of physical and mental effort. Self-completion questionnaires thus often have to be briefer than many interview surveys, in order for them to be completed at all, and very easy to answer. In practice this means that explicit instructions have to be provided for each question (thus taking up more space), questions requiring sequential response cannot easily be asked, and complex filters cannot be used. In a postal survey, determining a respondent's occupation would be such a process, because many people do not know their full job title and some are too vague for useful analysis (Berdie and Anderson 1974: 145).

Limits on attitudinal data

One common criticism of surveys, such as the one in this project, which collect attitudinal information by means of answers to closed questions, is that the questions themselves create attitudes which were not held (because never thought about), and that forcing respondents to choose between predetermined answers cannot possibly capture the range of attitudes present (Schuman and Presser 1981: 289-96). This criticism might be justified to a certain extent if, for example, the survey were conducted throughout with a tone favourable to Britain's heritage. However, the attitudinal statements used have largely been collected from members of the public during initial test interviews, and roughly balance positive and negative attitudes to the heritage. In addition, the use of the Likert scale enables respondents some degree of choice in the expression of their level of agreement or disagreement with the statement, and, importantly includes the category 'Neither agree nor disagree', which ensures that respondents are not forced into making a choice against their will (Andrews 1984). The fact that the majority of respondents do make some definite non-random choice in the selection of their answers suggests that individuals find that, on reflection, they do have a definite point of view on a certain subject, even though it may not be part of their everyday consciousness.

A related problem is that of the literary skills of the potential respondent. Unlike a verbal interview, the postal questionnaire requires a certain degree of literary competence, such that an individual feeling ill-equipped with such skills is unlikely to reply. Goyder (1982: 552) has shown that non-respondents to mailed questionnaires are likely to be people with the minimum formal education. Similarly, answers to open-ended questions are likely to reflect the degree of fluency of the respondent. These problems are ones that cannot be completely eradicated; they can only be reduced by ensuring that there is a minimum 'cost' to the respondent in completing the questionnaire.

Relevance

Goyder and Leiper (1985) have clearly demonstrated that the relevance of the study to the individual is another crucial factor in response. Whereas in an interview survey, the presence of an interviewer at the doorstep might make refusal less likely even for esoteric subjects, the self-completion questionnaire must be seen to be relevant by the person completing it. The project in question – heritage visiting and images of the past – must have low relevance for most potential respondents, and thus required a correspondingly greater effort in producing a 'low cost' format and in persuading the potential respondent of its actual relevance.

The total design method

One of the reasons that postal surveys have gained in academic respectability in recent years has been the formulation of methods designed to overcome previous deficiencies in response rates and quality of information. These have been the result of at least twenty years of experimental work which has tested the effects of different methods, such as the number of reminders, the addition of incentives (such as gifts), the effect of different lengths of questionnaire, and the effect of including postage stamps compared with Business Reply envelopes. Summaries of experimental work are contained in Erdos (1970), Goyder (1982), Heberlein and Baumgartner (1978), Linsky (1975), Scott (1961) and in a special issue of the *Journal of the Market Research Society* (27/1, 1985).

The method

The most comprehensive synthesis of such experimental work into an effective postal survey method has been carried out by Dillman (1972, 1978, 1983) in his formulation of the 'Total Design Method' (TDM). 'The Total Design Method (TDM) consists of two parts (a) identifying and designing each aspect of the survey process that may affect response in a way that maximises response rates; and (b) organizing the survey effort in a way that assures that the design intentions are carried out in complete detail' (Dillman 1983: 360). In his work, Dillman claims that the 28 studies conducted by 1983 which used the TDM in full achieved an average response rate of 78 per cent, while the 22 using the TDM to a large degree, but not completely, have achieved an average rate of 67 per cent (*ibid*).

The TDM is described most fully in Dillman (1978), and it is this which was used as a basis for designing and implementing this survey. Where Dillman's guidelines were not fully followed, this was for reasons of cost or because the recommendations were felt to be superfluous. The major deviations from Dillman's scheme are noted below, and may account for a certain degree of non-response. Above all, the organising principle was adhered to: the survey, consisting of questionnaire, cover letter, mail-out envelope, return envelope, postcard reminder, replacement questionnaire with envelope and different cover letter, should be viewed as a unity, in which attention had to be paid to seemingly trivial details in order that the 'Total Design' should elicit maximum response. In particular the basic principles propounded by Dillman were adhered to. An example of the survey package is included at the end of this Appendix.

Booklet Design The questionnaire was typed in A4 format, photoreduced, and produced as an A5 booklet with illustrated front cover and blank back cover, to reduce its imposing appearance. For financial reasons the questionnaires could not be printed, as was suggested by Dillman, and high quality photocopies were used instead. Copying was done in monochrome on white paper to avoid resemblance to advertising material.

Question Design and Layout The most relevant and interesting topics were dealt with first, because these initial questions were the most crucial in capturing the interest of the potential respondent. The demographic questions were asked last, when it was hoped they would seem less offensive or prying. Great care was taken on unambiguous wording and clear layout of questions. Each question had clear instructions as to how it should be completed. Only major blocks of questions were numbered, so that there appeared to be fewer questions than there actually were.

The Cover Letter The appearance and content of the cover letter was vital to the success of the survey, and so particular care was taken on this. It had to be contained on one side of an A4 page and headed by the letterhead of an official but disinterested body. Goyder (1982) shows that surveys conducted by government organisations have an average 13 per cent higher response rate than that of other (commercial) organisations, so the letterhead of a University body was chosen on the basis that this would give the project some sort of official status. In this case, 'St. John's College, Cambridge' was selected, as 'Department of Archaeology' might have influenced respondents to answer more positively about the heritage than they might otherwise have done. Personalisation was an equally important factor in encouraging response (Dillman 1978: 172), so the greeting and signature on each letter was done by hand in blue ballpoint pen.

The cover letter had to stress the relevance of the study to the individual respondent, the value of the study in general terms, the importance (due to sampling procedure) of the named individual alone completing the questionnaire, the way it should be completed and returned, and assurances of confidentiality. Particular stress was laid on the importance of replies from non-museum visitors.

Reminders The first postcard reminder and the second letter were similarly constructed to stress the importance of each individual's reply in being representative of a large section of the population.

The Envelope The envelope had to be white, to avoid the connotations of cheapness and disposability that a brown envelope might have, and had to be personalised as much as possible. This was done by printing names and addresses directly onto the envelope in the first wave of 1500 mail-outs. This was felt to be more personal than using computer-generated sticky labels. Such labels were used for the first and second reminders, as it was not felt that the extra effort involved in printing these on directly would have resulted in significantly increased returns. Finally, both mail-out envelopes and return envelopes had first-class postage stamps affixed to them in preference to metered mail or Business Reply envelopes. This was done for three reasons: first, the use of real postage stamps makes the survey seem less like sales literature; second, it emphasises the importance of the project and the urgency of prompt reply; and third, it increases the likelihood of reply because of the 'guilt factor' of a first-class stamp being enclosed for the return postage.

The Total Design Method, by its careful attention to all design details, appeared to offer a powerful method of implementing postal research, in which the response rates of good quality data could reach those normally obtained for interview surveys. Given the somewhat esoteric nature of the research project, the achievement of a high response rate was of crucial concern, and the final rate of 66 per cent shows that the time and effort involved in following the TDM was well justified.

Formulation and testing of questionnaires

Interviews

Initial qualitative work in the summer of 1984 took the form of ten interviews of 30-60 minutes' duration with Cambridge residents selected from three different areas of the city. No formal sampling strategy was followed, but the three areas were known to be broadly working class, lower middle class and upper middle class respectively. The interviews were structured around a 34-question schedule which covered all of the main themes in the project as it then stood. Respondents were asked about their visits to different heritage presentations, their likes and dislikes about them, their images of life in the past, their image of archaeology and archaeologists, their feelings about 'alternative' approaches to the past, and their possession of old objects. They were encouraged to talk freely and not confine themselves to the actual questions asked, and were asked also to comment on the questions themselves. This process was extremely useful in gauging the sort of questions that might profitably be asked.

Qualitative testing and formulation of pilot survey

The questionnaire was then formulated on the basis of the research priorities of the project, on reading of previous surveys, on discussion with colleagues, and on the interviews. By this stage it contained mostly closed category questions formulated as far as possible on the basis of actual comments made in the interviews. The importance of testing questionnaires with qualitative pre-testing and a quantitative pilot survey is continually stressed in survey research textbooks (eg. Moser and Kalton 1971: 48), but has often been ignored in surveys undertaken, for example, by museum personnel. It is essential that all of the techniques used in a full-scale survey, especially in a once-and-for-all operation such as postal research, are tested at a small scale level before full implementation. In this way, any important errors can be detected which might have had otherwise disastrous consequences. For example, in this case it was important to test the likely response rate (too low a return would jeopardise the validity of the whole project), the effectiveness of the organisation of mail-outs and reminders, and check for problems in question phrasing. Initially, therefore, the survey was tested on ten colleagues and eight non-academics and revisions were made in question phrasing and layout. These revisions then formed the basis of a larger scale pilot survey.

The pilot survey

The pilot survey used all of the techniques which the full scale survey would involve, except that it was conducted in Cambridge rather than at a national level. This was because it had been initially intended to follow up both respondents and non-respondents for their comments on the questionnaire. However, the response rate was sufficiently high for this not to be considered necessary. A sample of 100 Cambridge residents was selected randomly from the electoral register. The survey was mailed to them on 14th February 1985 and the last returns were received by 20th March. Of the 78 replies received, 64 were usable. The other 14 were returned unanswered due to death or severe illness (2), lack of interest (8), and unknown reasons (4).

On the evidence of the pilot survey, the questionnaire was reduced in length. The questions discarded were ones which the pilot survey showed did not produce useful enough information in relation to the amount of space they occupied, or produced little variation in their answers. The questionnaire was eventually reduced to its minimum of 14 pages containing a possible maximum of 111 responses. Layout of boxes and spacing of words was also changed to produce a more attractive appearance.

The pilot survey was also analysed using the full range of techniques available in the SPSS-X package which was to be used in the analysis of the full-scale survey. This enabled coding problems to be anticipated, the command files to be prepared, experience in SPSS-X to be gained, and estimates to be made of the amount of time that data-entry would take. This latter experience was invaluable in planning the timetabling of the project.

The full scale survey

Sampling

For a postal survey aiming at a representative coverage for the whole country, the electoral registers for Great Britain were chosen as the most suitable sampling frame. Unfortunately, no suitable sampling frame exists for individuals under the age of eighteen, making it extremely difficult to select a representative sample of this group, and impossible using the postal survey technique. The survey is therefore restricted to adults on the electoral register, and the absence of the under-18s is its largest bias. A further consequence of the selection of the postal survey method was that non-response was likely to be the next greatest biasing factor, far outweighing sampling bias (Butcher and Todd 1981). It was therefore not necessary to choose a sampling strategy where the probability of a constituency being selected was proportionate to its size. Instead, a simpler method was used and experiments were subsequently carried out to determine whether these discrepancies had any effect on the results.

The main determinant of sample size was the number of subgroup analyses that would have to be performed (i.e. the size of the crosstabulation cells). Hoinville, Jowell *et al.* (1978: 61) recommend that the smallest subgroup should have between 50 and 100 members, and Sudman (1983) recommends that where the number of subgroup analyses are 'None or Few', sample size should be 1000 - 1500, and where they are 'Average', sample size should be 1500 - 2500. In this survey, a typical number of crosstabulation cells would be twelve (a three by four table). Bearing this in mind, and the increased costs of increased sample size, a sample of 1500 would be predicted by the pilot survey to achieve around a 64 per cent response rate, which would yield an actual sample of 960, or an average of 80 responses for a 12-cell table. This was deemed to be sufficient for purposes of analysis.

Sampling was carried out in the library of electoral registers held by the Office of Population and Census Surveys in London. The 623 constituencies in the sampling frame are grouped by county in alphabetical order, with the English counties first and the Scottish last. A strategy of systematic sampling was followed. This gives every member of the sampling population (ie. every constituency) a statistically equal chance of selection. A random number (6) was selected from tables, yielding Wansdyke, Avon as the first constituency, and a selection procedure based on a fixed interval of 7 yielded 89 constituencies. The remaining 11 were then selected entirely randomly from the 623 using random number tables.

Within each of the 100 selected constituencies, 15 polling districts were selected. The number of polling districts in each constituency was divided by 15 to gain the sampling interval (rounded up to the nearest whole number). A random number was chosen, and 15 districts were selected by fixed interval. In this case as well, probability of selection was not proportionate to size of electorate. Finally, one address was selected from each polling district by choosing a random number from tables. All voters in the polling district thus had an equal chance of selection.

These 1500 names and addresses then had to be converted into true postal addresses because there is no national standardisation of the format of electoral registers. While some do include a postcode, many streets are just associated with the name of a constituency, ward or polling district, which do not have any necessary correspondence with geographical entities recognised by the post office (Wansdyke, for example, is not a recognised postal address in Avon). The lengthy process of conversion into true addresses had to be carried out by consulting a combination of telephone directories, street atlases and postcode indexes.

Implementation

The first wave of 1500 questionnaires was sent out by first class post on 14th October 1985. This was followed by a postcard to all addresses ten days later, thanking those who had responded, and asking those who had not to reply as soon as possible. Finally, a replacement questionnaire and different letter were sent on 7th November 1985 to the 706 people who had not responded in any form by that date. By 20th December 1985, 1076 total replies had been made, of which 965 were usable, a response rate of 66 per cent.

Table A1.1 Survey response rate

Sampling Population: All persons eligible to vote in private households in Great Britain (excluding Northern Ireland)		
Sampling Frame: Electoral Registers		
	No	(%)
Addresses selected from register:	1500	
Found to be out of scope:	18	
Assumed to be out of scope:	13	
In-scope addresses:	1469	100
Response rate	965	66
Non-respondents	504	34
Of which:		
No. of individuals from whom no response at all obtained	393	27
Individuals replying but not completing questionnaire	111	7
	504	

Of these 111, the following reasons for non-completion were given:	
Refusal/not interested	26
Moved house	25
Incomplete address	4
Too old/survey too complicated	18
Questionnaire too confidential	3
Other	4
Not known	31
	111

Response rate (See Table A1.1)

The response rate to a survey is calculated according to fixed guidelines, summarised by Hedges (1977). From the 1500 selected in the original sample, 'out-of-frame' individuals are deducted. These include vacant, demolished or non-residential addresses, and people who have moved out of the country (Hedges 1977: 5). For the purposes of this survey, those whose questionnaire was returned because they were too ill or disabled to complete it were also categorised as out of scope. This was because they would also be unlikely to visit any heritage presentations. Those who returned the questionnaire uncompleted because they were 'too old' were deemed to be in scope because there was no evidence that they physically could not complete the questionnaire or visit heritage presentations.

The final percentage of usable replies (66 per cent) falls within Dillman's (1983) predictions for response rates to surveys partially implementing the Total Design Method. It is also very close to the rate predicted by the pilot survey (64 per cent), which again demonstrates the value of such tests in planning the outcome of the full survey. Bearing in mind that the survey is longer than the maximum length recommended by Dillman and Erdos, and of a considerably more esoteric nature than most of the examples given in their manuals, the achievement of a 66 per cent response rate is most respectable. It is close to the highest figure (67.6 per cent) given in Nederhof's (1985) comparison between European and North American response patterns where the mean response rate was 59 per cent, and it is higher than Dillman's mean response rate of 62 per cent for questionnaires of 14 pages (Dillman 1978: 56).

Comparison with response rates to interview surveys of the general population shows that the response rate to this survey is not dissimilar to that normally achieved by personal interviews. The 1987 Social Attitudes Survey, for example, achieved a 70 per cent rate of successful interviews (Jowell *et al.* 1987), while the 1982 museum visiting interview survey carried out for the English Tourist Board achieved a 65 per cent completion rate (NOP 1982). The postal survey, far from being an inadequate method of data-gathering, can thus reasonably claim to be a rigorous alternative to the interview. In the case of the current survey, although the response rate is 5-10 per cent below that which might have been achieved by interviews, comparison with the characteristics of the full general population can show where the non-response biases lie, and answers can be weighted accordingly.

Sources of bias

Sampling bias

As noted earlier, the greatest bias in the survey is its lack of coverage of people under the age of eighteen. However, in addition to this there are a number of smaller biases that must be taken into account. The electoral register consists of a list of the names and addresses of those registered for the vote. In theory, all British subjects, Commonwealth citizens and citizens of the Irish Republic resident in Britain, who are aged 18 or over during the 12-month period of the currency of the register, should be included on the list. However, as Butcher and Todd (1981) have shown, around 4 per cent of eligible people will be excluded by mistake or misunderstanding, and these exclusions will mainly be concentrated among Commonwealth citizens or those about to attain voting age.

A further bias is caused by population mobility and the length of time the register has been in operation. When they come into force on February 16th each year, the registers list the addresses of electors as they stood at October 10th of the previous year. Gray and Gee (1967) have estimated that an average of 0.66 per cent of the electorate move house each month. By the time the registers come into use, about 3 per cent of electors will therefore have moved, and by the end of their currency (February 15th the following year), about 12 per cent will have moved (Hoinville, Jowell *et al.* 1978). This survey was conducted from October to December, when the information on the electoral register was a year old, during which time a significant percentage (estimated at 8 per cent) of electors may have moved house. 2 per cent of these are accounted for by returned postal packets, so it is reasonable to assume that 6 per cent of the 34 per cent non-response can be explained by change of address.

Another bias was caused by the limitation of the sample to those living in private households, which excludes those living in institutions such as hospitals, nursing homes and prisons, and those working in the armed forces or merchant navy. These latter two groups include 278,400 persons of voting age (OPCS 1984).

As described above, sampling was carried out on a three stage basis. The first two stages, those of selection of constituencies and polling districts, were not carried out on the basis of probability proportionate to size but by a simpler fixed interval method. This method ignores the differences in size between different constituencies and polling districts. This meant that individuals in smaller constituencies and districts had a greater chance of selection than those in larger ones. In order to check the degree of sampling bias caused by this, an experiment was performed whereby the values of respondents' answers were weighted according to their constituency's probability of selection. The effect of doing this was negligible as the different weights cancelled each other out. Weighting the polling districts was also unlikely to make a great difference to the results, so compensation of size of constituency and district was not carried out. Instead effort was concentrated on understanding response bias and compensating for that.

Response bias

In a general population sample, it is always desirable to determine to what extent the answers given by respondents are representative of those of the general population as a whole. By comparing the two populations, weighting factors can be formulated for the survey population which enable it to emulate the full population (See Table A1.2).

Non-Respondents From the comparison laid out in Table A1.2 between the characteristics of those completing the survey and those in the total population, it can be deduced that non-respondents have the following characteristics: they are slightly more likely to be female, more likely to be over 65, more likely to be council house or private tenants, much less likely to have access to a vehicle, and much more likely to have left school at the earliest opportunity. This profile of non-respondents is that which might have been expected from the results of other work. Hoinville, Jowell *et al.* (1978: 137) argue that non-respondents to postal surveys are likely to be elderly, disengaged or withdrawn, likely to live in urban rather than suburban or rural areas, and likely to feel that they will be judged by the responses that they make. In a wide-ranging review, Goyder (1982) has added to this by showing

Table A1.2 Comparison of survey demographic profiles with those of the general population

Variable	Survey (%)	General population (%)
Sex		
Male	51	48
Female	49	52
	100	100
Age		
20-24	11	11
25-34	20	19
35-49	28	26
50-59	16	15
60-64	9	8
65 +	17	20
	100	100
Vehicle access		
None	23	39
One	48	44
Two or more	30	17
	100	100
Housing tenure		
Owner Occupier	65	59
Council House	22	29
Other	14	11
	100	100
Finished education		
16 or less	70	79
17-20	19	13
21 or more	11	8
	100	100

that males are more likely to return questionnaires than females, that occupation and education have strong effects on response rate, and that response is about 13 per cent lower in urban areas than in rural or mixed populations. This latter point is borne out in the breakdown of response rates for different areas of Britain, with Greater London providing the lowest number of returns (Table A1.3).

Table A1.3 Response rates for different areas of Great Britain

Area	Response rate (%)
1. Northern England	64
2. Yorkshire and Humberside	61
3. East Midlands	49
4. East Anglia	76
5. South-East	75
6. South-West	57
7. West Midlands	70
8. North West	70
9. Wales	62
10. Scotland	58
11. Greater London	46

Coping with non-response

One way of gaining an indication of the likely characteristics of non-respondents to the survey (apart from attempting to interview them, which was beyond the means of the project) was to telephone a sample of them. This was carried out for nine of those returning their questionnaires uncompleted but offering no explanation (Table A1.4). The telephone follow-ups demonstrated that one of the nine was out of scope and seven would be classified as no longer active museum visitors, the majority of them being elderly. The selection of a greater sample of non-respondents was prohibited

Table A1.4 Analysis of nine telephone follow-ups of persons returning a blank questionnaire with no explanation

1. Explained he had not received the questionnaire because someone else had returned it while he was away. Visits museums two or three times a year.

2. Mother answered for someone who is deaf, has difficulty reading, and tears up circulars. Does not visit museums.

3. Too old (aged 75) and not interested. Last went to a museum about 20 years ago.

4. 75 years old, not interested, has no money. Last went to a museum about ten years ago.

5. Not interested, doesn't like forms. Never been to a museum.

6. Wife explained the individual was in hospital and too ill to answer the questionnaire.

7. Aged 81. Last went to a museum when at school.

8. No time to visit museums. Last went over 20 years ago.

9. Individual had moved away from that address.

by the cost of telephoning and a feeling that it might be intrusive. Generalising from this extremely small sample, it is thus possible that up to 88 per cent of non-respondents were also non-visitors.

Weighting to emulate a representative sample

The best way to account for non-respondents in the analysis of the survey is to weight the sample so that it emulates the characteristics of the general population. Experiments were performed to determine the most appropriate weighting factor. Weights were calculated by comparing the proportion of a certain characteristic of the general population (eg. housing tenure) with its proportions in the survey, using the formula

$$\text{Weight} = \frac{\text{percentage of characteristic in general population}}{\text{percentage of characteristic in sample population}}$$

Different weights based on housing tenure, vehicle access, education, and date of return (on the assumption that the later ones were more like the non-respondents) were constructed and the results of each weighting system were compared in order to find the one most accurately emulating the characteristics of the full population. It is not possible to use weighting systems together, as they affect each other differently. Weighting by Housing and Education, for example, will not produce a sample where both the educational characteristics and the housing tenure patterns will be the same as they are in the general population, because the two weights will work on each other. The weights thus have to be tested separately and a single one chosen which is most appropriate to the purposes of the survey. The effects of different weighting systems on the sample are shown in Table A1.5, where the results are compared with the characteristics of the general population. From this can be seen that, of the demographic weighting factors, weighting by access to a vehicle produces a demographic profile closest to that of the general population. Weighting by date of return might make the sample more representative in terms of non-respondents, but it produces demographic profiles quite different from those of the general population. In addition, it has to be borne in mind that a weighting system does not truly compensate for non-response, because, for example, the characteristics of those who replied late to the questionnaire might be completely different from those who did not reply at all. They can thus never be a true substitute. In view of this, the system of weighting by access to a vehicle was chosen as the one which produces a sample profile most nearly representative of the whole population. All tables presented in the book are weighted by this factor.

Table A1.5 Comparison of the effect of different weights on the survey demographic profiles

	Full population (%)	Vehicle weight (%)	Housing weight (%)	Education weight (%)	Date of return weight (%)
Vehicle access					
None	39	39	26	23	23
One	44	44	47	48	47
Two +	17	17	27	29	30
	100	100	100	100	100
Housing tenure					
Owner-occupier	59	58	59	64	62
Council tenant	29	28	29	23	24
Other	11	13	11	13	14
	100	100	100	100	100
Finished education					
16 or less	79	73	71	79	71
17-20	13	17	19	13	18
21 or more	8	10	10	8	11
	100	100	100	100	100

Acquiescence bias

In survey analysis it is important to be able to distinguish between answers that are the result of a considered opinion, and ones that are the result of other factors, such as the tendency of certain people to agree to statements more than others (acquiescence) (Schuman and Presser 1981: 224-30). This was checked by isolating groups of positive and negative statements and comparing the number of times different groups agreed with them. It was found that those who left school at the minimum age were significantly more likely than more educated groups to agree to positively-worded statements about the heritage, and also more likely to agree to negatively-worded ones (Table A1.6). This is clear evidence of a tendency amongst this group to agree to all statements. This is an effect that should be borne in mind when examining the survey results; it seems that around 7 per cent of the agreement of the least educated group may be accounted for by acquiescence.

Table A1.6: Tendency to agree to statements, by education

	Agreement to 11 Positive Statements (%)			
Education (%)	Up to 6 times	7 and over	(%)	N
Minimum	41	59	100	655
Stayed on at school	47	52	100	153
Tertiary	62	38	100	123
All (%)	45	55	100	931
	Agreement to 17 Negative Statements (%)			
Education (%)	Up to 5 times	6 and over	%	N
Minimum	53	47	100	655
Stayed on at school	60	40	100	153
Tertiary	60	40	100	123
All (%)	55	45	100	931

Explanatory variables

Demographic variables

The principal demographic variables used have been age, sex, activity status (working, retired, etc) and educational background. The latter is a three-fold variable dividing respondents into those who left school at the earliest opportunity, and those who stayed on at school only, and those who went on to tertiary education. Class or socio-economic group is also a useful demographic variable, but in survey terms its operational definition is difficult (this is even more the case with Bourdieu's concept of 'habitus'). In interview surveys, the occupation of the respondent is the most frequently used means of socio-economic classification. However, to ascertain this correctly needs around eight sequentially-asked questions which are difficult to control in a self-completion questionnaire, and take up a large amount of space. In addition, occupational classifications have become extremely complex and difficult to use (OPCS 1980). Fox and Goldblatt (1982: 205-212) have shown that occupational classifications have concentrated on the occupation of the head of the household, and with a growth in interest in women, children and the elderly, this has become less appropriate. They suggest that a more realistic classification is based on the household, because characteristics such as type of housing tenure or access to a vehicle apply to all members. Accordingly, in this survey differences in these two variables (housing tenure and access to a vehicle) were used as indications of socio-economic group. These were combined with educational background into a three-tier 'status' variable in the following way:

High status: Home owners, access to a vehicle, above minimum education.

Low status: Tenants, no access to a vehicle, left school at earliest opportunity.

Middle status: The remainder, i.e. a combination of the above.

Some of the demographic variables were found to have greater explanatory power than others. Gender, vehicle access and housing tenure, for example, were not as useful as the variables of age, education and status and they are therefore not cited so frequently. Education is a more useful explanatory variable, but generally not as powerful as status, of which it forms a component.

Intercorrelation of demographic variables

Although the main explanatory variables of age and status are used independently here, it is important to bear in mind that they are intercorrelated to a significant degree. Table A1.7 shows the extent of this intercorrelation. One way of overcoming this problem would be to present a combined age and status variable showing young people of high status, middle-aged people of low status, and so on. However, this produces a nine-fold variable that is not only difficult to use and read, but in which the numbers of cases in the crosstabulation cells are too small for analysis to be statistically reliable. It can be seen that the main effect of the intercorrelation is amongst the over-60s, who are much more likely to be of low status than those of other age groups. Accordingly, whenever the status variable is presented, age is controlled for amongst those of low status. In other words, high status, middle status, low status under 60 and low status over 60 are presented.

Table A1.7 Age by status

		Status			
Age	High	Middle	Low	(%)	N
<35	17	71	12	100	294
35-59	19	68	13	100	373
>60	11	56	34	100	270

Non-demographic variables

Although the demographic variables are treated as the primary explanatory devices, it has been useful to construct some non-demographic typologies as an aid to clarification of patterns of heritage participation and images of the past. The two principal ones used are a museum-visiting variable and a heritage-visiting variable. These are both fully described in the relevant chapters.

St John's College　　　Cambridge CB2 1 TP　　　Telephone (0223) 61621

At the moment £116 million is spent each year on studying the past and presenting it to the public. No-one really knows what people think of things like museums and historic buildings, so the government doesn't know whether it should be increasing or cutting back spending on them. This survey is designed to find out what people like yourself think of the usefulness of preserving the heritage and knowing about the past.

You are one of a small number of people chosen to give their opinion on these matters. Your name was drawn from the electoral register in a random sample of the whole of the adult population of Great Britain. This is the first such survey ever carried out in Britain, and you will play an important part in its success if you could take the trouble to fill in the enclosed questionnaire and return it in the envelope provided. No stamp is necessary.

In order that the results will truly represent the thinking of the people of Britain, we would be very grateful if the questionnaire could be completed and returned by you alone, and not a different member of your family. We are particularly interested in finding out the opinion of people who do not go to museums and other heritage presentations very often, so please do not throw the survey away because you think it does not apply to you.

The questionnaire is entirely confidential. It has an identification number for postal purposes only. This is so that we can cross your name off the mailing list when the questionnaire is returned. Your name will never be placed on the questionnaire.

The results of this research will be made available to government representatives, tourist boards, museum organisations and all interested members of the public.

I would be happy to answer any questions you might have. Please write or telephone. The telephone number is 0223-359714, extension 33.

Finally, I would just like to repeat that we are interested in hearing from everyone, not just those people who regularly go to museums.

Thank you very much for your help.

Yours sincerely,

Nicholas Merriman, Project Director.

St John's College   Cambridge CB2 1 TP   Telephone (0223) 61621

About three weeks ago I wrote to you asking your opinion about the way our heritage is presented to the public and asking you general questions about the past. As yet we do not seem to have received your completed questionnaire.

Our research unit has undertaken this study because we believe that in planning government spending on public amenities, the opinions of ordinary people should be taken into account.

I am writing to you again because of the significance each questionnaire has to the usefulness of this study. Your name was drawn through a scientific sampling process from the electoral register, in which every adult in Britain had an equal chance of being selected. This means that only about one in every 20,000 people in Britain are being asked to complete this questionnaire. In order for the results of this study to be truly representative of the opinions of all people it is important to have your views on this matter.

I appreciate that it might not be easy to find time to fill in the questionnaire. However, it should only take about half an hour, and would help us a very gret deal in our work. We are trying to collect the opinions of ordinary people on the heritage, in an effort to improve the service that is provided for the public.

I would stress that we are particularly interested in hearing from people who do not go to museums and who do not make use of heritage presentations. If you think that government money spent on such things is a waste, then we believe your opinion is an important one and should be heard by the government.

We would therefore be very grateful indeed if you could find the time to complete the questionnaire and return it to us. In case it has been misplaced, a replacement is enclosed.

Your co-operation is greatly appreciated.

Yours sincerely,

Nicholas Merriman
Project Director

Ten days ago a questionnaire asking your opinion about the use of museums and our heritage was sent to you. Your name was drawn in a random sample from the electoral registers of Great Britain.

If you have already completed and returned it to us please accept our sincere thanks. If not, please could you try to complete it today and send it to us? Because it has only been sent to a small, but representative, sample of British people, it is extremely important that yours also be included in the study if the results are to accurately represent the opinion of British people.

Yours sincerely

Nicholas Merriman (Project Director)

HERITAGE SPENDING

1. At the moment, £116 million is spent each year on studying the heritage, preserving it and presenting it to the public. What are your feelings about this level of spending? **(Tick one box)**

- IT SHOULD BE GREATLY INCREASED
- IT SHOULD BE SLIGHTLY INCREASED
- IT SHOULD STAY THE SAME
- IT SHOULD BE SLIGHTLY DECREASED
- IT SHOULD BE GREATLY DECREASED

2. There has been a lot of discussion recently about charging admission for museums that are supported by ratepayers' taxes, because it is the best way for them to gain enough income to carry out their services.

a. Do you support this policy?

YES ☐   NO ☐   DON'T KNOW ☐

b. Would you be prepared to pay, say £1.00, to go into a museum?

YES ☐   NO ☐   DON'T KNOW ☐

KNOWING ABOUT THE PAST

3. Do you think it is worth knowing about the past? **(Tick one box only)**

- DEFINITELY
- PROBABLY
- PERHAPS
- NO

4. What do you think is the main reason for studying the past?

....

....

1

5. These are some of the things people have said who believe studying Britain's past is not of much use. How far do you agree or disagree?

	STRONGLY AGREE	AGREE	NEITHER	DISAGREE	STRONGLY DISAGREE
I don't feel my history is part of British history	☐	☐	☐	☐	☐
It can't help us with today's problems	☐	☐	☐	☐	☐
Studying the past is usually rather boring	☐	☐	☐	☐	☐

6. How many times, roughly, have you visited any of these in the last year?

(Place one tick in each column)

	MUSEUM OR GALLERY	CASTLE	HISTORIC HOUSE	ANCIENT MONUMENT
NOT AT ALL				
1 OR 2 TIMES				
3 – 10 TIMES				
MORE THAN 10 TIMES				

7. How many times have you gone to any of these things in the last year?

	THEATRE	CLASSICAL CONCERT	BALLET	OPERA
NOT AT ALL				
1 OR 2 TIMES				
3–10 TIMES				
MORE THAN 10 TIMES				

2

MUSEUMS

8. Which of these things do museums remind you of most?

   (Tick one box)

   A monument to the dead

   Community centre

   Church or temple

   School

   Library

   Department store

   Other (Specify) ....

Please answer these questions even if you have not been to a museum recently. If you have never been, please go to question 10.

9a Which museum did you visit last?

   ....

b When did you go? (Give the year) ....

c Who did you go with? ....

d Were you away on holiday or a day trip?

   YES [ ]   NO [ ]

e. Who organised the trip?

   Myself

   Friends

   Family or Relatives

   School

   Other organisation

f. Why did you go to that particular place?

   ....

10. These are some of the things people have said they like about museums in general. How far do you agree or disagree with them? (Please answer these questions even if you have not been to a museum recently)

    (Tick one box on each line)

	STRONGLY AGREE	AGREE	NOT SURE	DISAGREE	STRONGLY DISAGREE
They have a pleasant atmosphere	[ ]	[ ]	[ ]	[ ]	[ ]
You learn a lot in them	[ ]	[ ]	[ ]	[ ]	[ ]
They provide plenty for children to do	[ ]	[ ]	[ ]	[ ]	[ ]

11. These are some of the things that people have said they dislike about museums in general. How far do you agree or disagree with them?

    (Tick one box for each line)

	STRONGLY AGREE	AGREE	NEITHER	DISAGREE	STRONGLY DISAGREE
The presentation can be dull	[ ]	[ ]	[ ]	[ ]	[ ]
Museums have nothing to do with our daily lives	[ ]	[ ]	[ ]	[ ]	[ ]
The attendants are like guards	[ ]	[ ]	[ ]	[ ]	[ ]
They are too middle class	[ ]	[ ]	[ ]	[ ]	[ ]
There are too many words to read	[ ]	[ ]	[ ]	[ ]	[ ]

12. Do you prefer to visit places on a guided tour or to wander on your own?

    GUIDED TOUR [ ]

    WANDER ON OWN [ ]

3

CASTLES AND HISTORIC HOUSES

(Please answer these questions even if you have not been to a castle or a historic house recently)

13. Here are some of the things that visitors have said about **castles**. To what extent do you agree or disagree? **(Tick one box for each line)**

	STRONGLY AGREE	AGREE	NEITHER	DISAGREE	STRONGLY DISAGREE
You can imagine how people lived in castles	☐	☐	☐	☐	☐
Castles provide good facilities (cafe, toilets, shop, etc)	☐	☐	☐	☐	☐

14. Do you prefer ruined castles or ones with furniture in them?

RUINED	☐
WITH FURNITURE	☐

15. These are some of the things people have said about **historic houses** (stately homes). How far do you agree or disagree with them?

	STRONGLY AGREE	AGREE	NEITHER	DISAGREE	STRONGLY DISAGREE
You can imagine how people lived in stately homes	☐	☐	☐	☐	☐
Stately homes provide good facilities (cafe, toilets, shop)	☐	☐	☐	☐	☐
Stately homes get too crowded	☐	☐	☐	☐	☐
The attendants are like guards	☐	☐	☐	☐	☐

16. Now some questions about both castles and historic houses together. Do you agree or disagree with these things that people have said?

	STRONGLY AGREE	AGREE	DON'T KNOW	DISAGREE	STRONGLY DISAGREE
They bring the past to life better than museums	☐	☐	☐	☐	☐
One of their main attractions are the other things there (eg fair, zoo, park)	☐	☐	☐	☐	☐
They only show the life of the rich	☐	☐	☐	☐	☐
Not enough information is provided about their history	☐	☐	☐	☐	☐

INTEREST IN THE PAST

17. If you wanted to find out about local history or some old local place, what would be the most enjoyable way of doing it? **(Tick one box only)**

- Visiting a museum ☐
- Reading a book about it ☐
- Visiting the local area or site by yourself ☐
- Having a guided tour of the local area or site ☐
- Asking in your local library ☐
- Going to evening classes in local history ☐
- Watching a television programme about it ☐
- Listening to an expert talk about it ☐

18. Have you ever done any of the following things? **(Tick which ones)**

- Been a member of a local history or archaeology club ☐
- Been a member of a collectors' club ☐
- Used a metal detector for 'treasure-hunting' ☐
- Gone on an archaeological dig or gone looking for pottery ☐
- Researched your family tree ☐
- Attended an adult education class ☐

LIFE IN THE PAST

In this section I want to ask you what you think life was like in the past compared with today. I'm not interested in whether you know the facts, but I'd like to know what your opinion is.

For these questions, 'the past' is any time from before your grandparents were alive, as far back as the first people.

19. Please describe what you think life in the past was like for the ordinary person

....

....

20. What would you say were the single best and worst things about living in the past (any time before your grandparents)?

(Please write down your answer in words)

"The best thing about life in the past was that...."

....

"The worst thing about life in the past was that...."

....

21. To what extent do you think these statements about life in the past (any time before your grandparents) are true or false?

(Tick which point along the row is nearest to your opinion)

TRUE ◄————————————————► FALSE

The family was closer
Life was more peaceful
There was less crime
People were more religious
There was no unemployment
People were generally happier
People had to work harder
Life was shorter

7

---

22. How far do you think life was better or worse in the past (before your grandparents) because of the following things?

(Tick one box for each line)

LIFE WAS...

	A LOT BETTER	A LITTLE BETTER	A LITTLE WORSE	A LOT WORSE	NOT SURE
Because there was less industry	☐	☐	☐	☐	☐
Because there were no computers	☐	☐	☐	☐	☐
Because women were much less free than today	☐	☐	☐	☐	☐
Because people lived closer to nature	☐	☐	☐	☐	☐

23. Please put these periods in order, depending on how much you would like to live in them. (Put a 1 by the one you would most like to live in, a 2 by your next choice, and so on till you put 6 by the one you least like).

Victorian

Elizabethan

Middle Ages

Roman

Prehistory

The present

24. How far do you agree or disagree with these sentences?

(Put a tick in one box for each line)

	STRONGLY AGREE	AGREE	NEITHER	DISAGREE	STRONGLY DISAGREE
Mankind is always progressing to better things	☐	☐	☐	☐	☐
Prehistoric people in Britain were basically the same as us	☐	☐	☐	☐	☐
Money spent on the past would be better spent on the future	☐	☐	☐	☐	☐

8

25. Please tick your level of agreement or disagreement with these.

	STRONGLY AGREE	AGREE	DON'T KNOW	DISAGREE	STRONGLY DISAGREE
God created the earth	☐	☐	☐	☐	☐
Spacemen from another planet helped create our early civilisations	☐	☐	☐	☐	☐
There are mysterious forces connected with places like Stonehenge	☐	☐	☐	☐	☐
The Loch Ness Monster probably does exist	☐	☐	☐	☐	☐

26. Which of these is most important for you to know about?

(**Please rank them in order of importance by putting '1' in the box opposite the most important one, '2' opposite the next most important one, and so on.**)

- British history
- World history
- My family tree
- The history of my homeland (e.g. England, Wales, India, Jamaica)
- The history of the local area I live in

☐	☐	☐	☐	☐

27. Where do you feel your historical roots lie? (**Tick one box only**)

Britain in general ☐	Europe in general ☐
England ☐	Asia ☐
Scotland ☐	Africa ☐
Wales ☐	West Indies ☐
Ireland ☐	Elsewhere (indicate) ....
A particular European country ☐	

9

ARCHAEOLOGY QUESTIONS

28. Please write down what the word 'Archaeology' means to you

....

....

29. How far do you agree or disagree with these sentences? (A metal detector is a machine which can detect metal (such as coins) buried in the ground).

	STRONGLY AGREE	AGREE	DON'T KNOW	DISAGREE	STRONGLY DISAGREE
People owning a metal detector should have the right to try to find relics from the past	☐	☐	☐	☐	☐
Metal detecting is just a harmless way for ordinary people to discover the past	☐	☐	☐	☐	☐
Archaeology has little of use to tell our own society	☐	☐	☐	☐	☐

30. Some people say archaeology should be taught in schools. Others say this is not realistic when subjects such as history are being cut. Do you think archaeology should be taught in schools?

(**Tick One Box**)

Not at all	☐
In primary schools only	☐
In secondary schools as a minor subject (no state exams taken in the subject)	☐
In secondary schools as a major subject (With C.S.E.'s O- and A-levels in it)	☐
I don't know enough about archaeology to answer this question properly	☐

10

31. How far do you agree or disagree with these sentences?

(Put a tick in one box for each line)

	STRONGLY AGREE	AGREE	NEITHER	DISAGREE	STRONGLY DISAGREE
It is much more interesting to find a piece of old pottery yourself than to read a book about ancient civilisations	☐	☐	☐	☐	☐
Museums, castles and historic houses are mainly aimed at educated and wealthy people	☐	☐	☐	☐	☐
It is time now to preserve the countryside before it is destroyed forever	☐	☐	☐	☐	☐
At some time in the past everyone was equal	☐	☐	☐	☐	☐
Historians ignore the past of recent British immigrants	☐	☐	☐	☐	☐
The National Trust should save more things belonging to the mass of less wealthy people	☐	☐	☐	☐	☐
The past shows us that change is best achieved by calm argument rather than revolution	☐	☐	☐	☐	☐
In spite of what people say, the lot of the average person is getting worse, not better	☐	☐	☐	☐	☐
The rate of change in society is too fast these days	☐	☐	☐	☐	☐

12a. Do you own any objects that are over 50 years old? (Tick your response)

YES ☐   NO ☐   DON'T KNOW ☐

(If 'NO' or 'DON'T KNOW', go on to question 33 on page 13.)

b. If 'YES': Write down your favourite object in the box.

FAVOURITE OBJECT ☐

c. How did it come into your possession?

Inherited ☐

Given as present ☐

Bought for home ☐

Obtained for a collection ☐

Other (Specify).............

d. What attracts you most about the object? (Put one tick only)

It might be valuable ☐

Family links (sentimental value) ☐

It gives you a direct sense of life in the past ☐

It is better made than modern things ☐

It is beautiful in itself ☐

Don't know ☐

Other (specify)............. ☐

e. Do you actively collect any objects?

YES ☐   NO ☐

f. IF 'YES', WHAT SORT OF THINGS DO YOU COLLECT?

....

QUESTIONS ABOUT YOURSELF

Finally, I'd just like to ask a few questions about yourself, so that we can compare your answers with those of other people. Please remember that this is entirely confidential

33. How old are you?

☐ YEARS OLD

34. What sex are you?

Male ☐

Female ☐

35. At what age did you finish your full time education?

(Write age in box provided. If you are still in full-time education, put a cross 'X' in the box)

☐ YEARS OLD

36. How many cars and vans are normally available for use by you or members of your household?

NONE ☐

ONE ☐

TWO ☐

3 OR MORE ☐

37. How do you occupy your accommodation?   **(Tick one box)**

Owner-Occupied
(including purchase by mortgage) ☐

Renting from Local Authority
(Council or New Town) ☐

Privately rented ☐

Other (Specify)..............................
....

13

38. How long have you lived in the area you are now living in?

Less than a year ☐

1 - 3 years ☐

4 - 10 years ☐

More than 10 years ☐

39. Which one of these work categories do you fall into?   **(Tick one box)**

Looking after the house ☐

Retired ☐

Student or at school ☐

Unemployed ☐

Working part time ☐

Working full time ☐

Other (Specify) ....

40. What sort of secondary school did you go to?

(Tick box or boxes)

Comprehensive ☐

Secondary Modern ☐

Independent School ☐

Direct grant or Assisted school ☐

Grammar School (or Scottish equivalent) ☐

Overseas School ☐

Technical College ☐

Other (specify)...............

That is the end of the survey. Thank you very much indeed for taking the time and trouble to answer these questions. Could you please now put this in the envelope provided and post it as soon as possible. If you have any comments on the questionnaire, please feel free to use the remaining blank space to air your views. Thank you once again for your help

14

Appendix 2: Additional tables

Table A2.1 Worst thing about life in the past

'The worst thing about life in the past was that...'		
Frequencies	(%)	N
Illness and death more frequent due to lack of medicine	32	262
General poverty and lack of food	28	226
Absence of modern amenities such as electricity and sanitation	25	201
Social division and exploitation	24	194
General harshness of life	8	62
Other	13	105

(Percentages add up to over 100 because many respondents gave more than one answer)

Table A2.2 Regression analysis of attitudes to the past with age and status

Stepwise regression analysis			
Dependent variable = Attitudes to the past			
Variable	**Beta Values**	**F**	**Sig F**
Age	.349939	129.762	.0000
Status	−.146170	22.640	.0000

Table A2.3 Regression analysis of attitudes to present with age and sex

	Stepwise Regression Analysis		
	Dependent variable = Attitudes to the present		
Variable	**Beta Values**	**F**	**Sig F**
Status	.276320	78.129	.0000
Sex	.139213	19.831	.0000

Table A2.4 Regression analysis of attitudes to the past with attitudes to the present

	Stepwise regression analysis		
	Dependent variable = Attitudes to the past		
Variable	**Beta Values**	**F**	**Sig F**
Attitude to the present	-.267971	71.948	.0000

Table A2.5 A model of historic building visiting

	Stepwise regression analysis		
	Dependent variable = Type of historic building visitor		
Variable	**Beta Values**	**F**	**Sig.F**
Attitude to Historic Buildings	.225795	45.885	.0000
Access to Vehicle	.165127	25.333	.0000
Level of Education	.078563	5.606	.0181

Table A2.6 Regression analysis of museum visitor type with attitudes to the past, age and education

	Stepwise regression analysis		
	Dependent variable = Type of museum visitor		
Variable	**Beta Values**	**F**	**Sig F**
Attitude to the past	−.149559	18.770	.0000
Education	.146587	20.515	.0000
Age	.140969	17.008	.0000

Table A2.7 Regression analysis of membership of history or archaeology clubs with demographic variables

Stepwise regression analysis
Dependent variable = Membership of history/archaeology club

Variable	Beta Value	F	Sig. F
Education	.173436	28.253	.0000

Table A2.8 Participation in archaeological fieldwork by sex and age/status combined

	Participation (%)	N
Sex (%)		
Male*	12.2	57
Female	8.5	40
Age/status combined (%)		
Young, High Status	8.4	4
Young, Middle Status	17.6	36
Young, Low Status	15.0	5
Middle-Aged, High Status	11.1	8
Middle-Aged, Middle Status	10.8	27
Middle-Aged, Low Status	17.9	9
Elderly, High Status	–	–
Elderly, Middle Status	3.9	6
Elderly, Low Status	2.0	2

Note: not statistically significant

Table A2.9 Particpation in metal detecting, by combined age/status variable

	Metal detector user	Non-user	N
Age/Status (%)			
Young, high status	11	89	49
Young, middle status	11	89	206
Young, low status	20	80	35
Middle aged, high status	5	95	71
Middle aged, middle status	7	93	252
Middle aged, low status	11	89	48
Elderly, high status	—	100	27
Elderly, middle status	2	98	146
Elderly, low status	6	94	88

Table A2.10 Regression analysis of participation in metal-detecting

Dependent = Participation in metal detecting			
Variables	**Beta**	**F**	**Sig. F**
Age	.156157	21.679	.0000
Status	−.081151	5.855	.0157

Table A2.11 Regression analyses of beliefs in 'alternative archaeology'

1. Dependent = Belief in extra terrestrials			
Variables	**Beta**	**F**	**Sig.F**
Attitudes to the present	−.090237	6.924	.0087
Status	−.089067	6.740	.0096

2. Dependent = Belief in Loch Ness Monster			
Variables	**Beta**	**F**	**Sig.F**
Attitudes to the present	−.150624	20.772	.0000
Age	−.077640	5.519	.0190

3. Dependent = Belief in forces at Stonehenge			
Variables	**Beta**	**F**	**Sig.F**
Attitudes to the present	−.169170	25.458	.0000
Age	−.163258	24.501	.0000
Status	−.092399	7.379	.0062

Table A2.12 Rotated factor matrix of attitudes to past and present

Attitudes in Factor 1	Attitudes in Factor 2
Life more peaceful?	Life better because less industry?
Less crime?	Life better because women less free?
People more happy?	Life better because no computers?
People more religious?	Life better because people closer to nature?

Families closer?

Attitudes in Factor 3	Attitudes in Factor 4
People's lot worse?	People had to work harder?
Everyone once equal?	Life was shorter?
Rate of change too fast?	

Attitudes in Factor 5

Mankind always progressing?

Money best spent on future?

Percentage of Variance

Factor 1	17.5
Factor 2	10.2
Factor 3	9.6
Factor 4	7.2
Factor 5	6.8

Bibliography

Abercrombie, N., Hill, S. and Turner, B. 1980. *The Dominant Ideology Thesis*. Allen and Unwin, London.

Adorno, T.W. 1975. Culture industry re-considered. *New German Critique* 6: 13-19

Adam, T.R. 1939. *The Museum and Popular Culture*. American Association for Adult Education, New York.

Althusser, L. 1971. Ideology and Ideological State Apparatuses. In *Lenin and Philosophy and Other Essays*. New Left Books, London: 121-173.

American Association of Museums, 1972. *Museums: Their New Audience*. A.A.M., Washington

Ames, M. M. 1990. Cultural empowerment and museums: opening up anthropology through collaboration. *New Research in Museum Studies* 1: 158-173

Andrews, F. 1984. Construct validity and error components of survey measures. *Public Opinion Quarterly* 48(2): 409-42.

Arnold, B. 1990. The past as propaganda: totalitarian archaeology in Nazi Germany. *Antiquity* 64: 464-78.

Ascher, R. 1960. Archaeology and the public image. *American Antiquity* 25: 402-3.

Bainbridge, W.S. 1978. Chariots of the gullible. *The Skeptical Inquirer* 3(2): 33-48.

Baker, D. 1983. *Living with the Past*. David Baker, Bedford.

Baker, F. 1988. History that hurts: excavating 1933-45. *Archaeological Review from Cambridge* 7(1): 93-109.

Bazin, G. 1967. *The Museum Age*. Dessor, Brussels.

Berdie, D.R. and Anderson, J.F. 1974. *Questionnaires: design and use*. Scarecrow Press, Metuchen, New Jersey.

Bitgood, S. 1989. *Visitor Studies – 1988: Theory, Research and Practice*. Center for Social Design, Jacksonville, Alabama.

1990. *Visitor Studies: Theory, Research and Practice, Vol 2*. Center for Social Design, Jacksonville, Alabama.

Bommes, M. and Wright, P. 1982. 'Charms of residence': the public and the past. In Centre for Contemporary Cultural Studies (Ed.) *Making Histories*. Hutchinson, London: 253-301.

'Boudicca' 1982. Professional archaeology versus people's archaeology. *Treasure Hunting*, November 1982: 9-10.

Boulton, W.N.D. *The Romance of the British Museum*. Sampson, Low, Marston and Co Ltd, London.

Bourdieu, P. 1968. Outline of a sociological theory of art perception. *International Social Science Journal* 20(4): 589-612

1971. Systems of education and systems of thought. In Young, M.F.D. (Ed.) *Knowledge and Control*. Collier-Macmillan, London: 189-207.

1977. *Outline of a Theory of Practice*. Cambridge University Press, Cambridge.

1984. *Distinction*. Routledge and Kegan Paul, London.

and Darbel, A. 1991. *The Love of Art. European Art Museums and Their Public*. Polity Press, Cambridge

and Passeron, J-C. 1977. *Reproduction in Education, Society and Culture*. Sage, London.

Bowler, P. J. 1989. *The Invention of Progress: The Victorians and the Past*. Basil Blackwell, Oxford.

Bray, W. 1981. Archaeological humour: the private joke and the public image. In Evans, J.D., Cunliffe, B., and Renfrew, C. (Eds.) *Antiquity and Man. Essays in honour of Glyn Daniel*. Thames and Hudson, London: 221-229.

Briggs, A. 1983. *A Social History of England*. Penguin Books, Harmondsworth.

British Association. 1887. Report of the committee on the provincial museums of the United Kingdom. *Report of the British Association for the Advancement of Science 1887*. London: 97-130.

British Tourist Authority.1988. *Annual Report for the year ending 31st March 1988*. British Tourist Authority, London.

British Tourist Authority/English Tourist Board Research Services. 1986. *Heritage and Leisure Attendances 1985*. BTA/ETB Research Services, London.

1989. *Heritage and Leisure Atendances 1988*. BTA/ETB Research Services, London.

1990. *Sightseeing in Britain 1989*. BTA/ETB Research Services, London.

Brooks, S. 1985. L.A.M.A.S.: A Victorian Establishment. *Transactions of the London and Middlesex Archaeological Society* 36: 203-222.

Burt, J. 1983. Archaeology and public values, with reference to the magazine Popular Archaeology. *Archaeological Review from Cambridge* 2(1): 33-40.

Butcher, B. and Todd, J. 1981. *Electoral Registration in 1981*. HMSO, London.

Cameron, D.F. 1971. The Museum, a Temple or the Forum. *Curator* 14(1): 11-24.

Carr, E.H. 1961. *What is History?* Penguin Books, Harmondsworth.

Central Statistical Office. 1990. *Social Trends 20*. HMSO, London.

Chadwick, A. 1980. *The Role of the Museum and Art Gallery in Community Education*. Department of Adult Education, University of Nottingham.

Chippendale, C. *et al*. 1990. *Who Owns Stonehenge?*. Batsford, London.

Clark, J.G.D. 1947. *Archaeology and Society*. Second, revised edition. Methuen & Co Ltd, London.

Clarke, D.V. 1984. Basic archaeology. The 8th Beatrice de Cardi Lecture. *Council for British Archaeology Report No. 34*. C.B.A., London: 68-76.

Clarke, J. and Critcher, C. 1985. *The Devil Makes Work. Leisure in Capitalist Britain*. Macmillan, London.

Cleere, H. 1986. Amateurs and professionals in British archaeology today. In Dobinson, C. and Gilchrist, R. (Eds.) *Archaeology, Politics and the Public*. York Unversity Archaeological Publications: 22-24

Cole, J.R. 1980. Cult archaeology and unscientific method and theory. In Schiffer, M.B. (Ed.) *Advances in Archaeological Method and Theory Volume 3*. Academic Press, New York: 1-34

Crawford, O.G.S. 1921. *Man and His Past*. Humphrey Milford and Oxford University Press, London.

Crook, J.M. 1972. *The British Museum*. Penguin Press, Harmondsworth.

Crowther, D.R. 1983. Swords to ploughshares: a nationwide survey of archaeologists and treasure-hunting clubs. *Archaeological Review from Cambridge* 2(1): 9-19.

Cruickshank, G. 1972. Jewry Wall Museum, Leicester: trial by questionnaire. *Museums Journal* 72(2): 65-7.

Cumming, E.M. and Henry, W. 1961. *Growing Old*. Basic Books, New York.

Cunliffe, B. 1982. Archaeology and its public. The 6th Beatrice de Cardi Lecture. *Council for British Archaeology Report No. 32*. C.B.A., London: 59-64.

Daniel, G.F. 1950. *A Hundred Years of Archaeology*. Duckworth, London.

Davis, F. 1979. *Yearning of Yesterday. A Sociology of Nostalgia.* Macmillan, London.
Dellheim, C. 1983. *The Face of the Past. The Preservation of the Medieval Inheritance in Victorian England.* Cambridge University Press, Cambridge.
Demoule, J-P. 1982. La prehistoire et ses mythes. *Annales* 37: 741-59.
Dickerson, A. 1990. Strategies for Inclusion. *Museums Journal* 90(11): 33.
Digby, P.W. 1974. *Visitors to Three London Museums.* HMSO, London.
Dillman, D.A. 1972. Increasing mail questionnaire response in large samples of the general public. *Public Opinion Quarterly* 36: 254-7.
 1978. *Mail and Telephone Surveys: the Total Design Method.* John Wiley, New York.
 1983. Mail and other self-administered questionnaires. In Rossi, P.H., Wright, J.D. and Anderson, A.B. (Eds.) *Handbook of Survey Research.* Academic Press, London: 236-45.
Dimaggio, P. and Useem, M. 1978. Social class and arts consumption: the origin and consequences of class differences in exposure to the arts in America. *Theory and Society* 5: 141-61.
Dixon, B. Courtney, A.E., and Bailey, R.H. 1974. *The Museum and the Canadian Public.* Culturcan Publications, Toronto.
Doughty, P.S. 1968. The public of the Ulster Museum: a statistical survey. *Museums Journal* 68(1): 19-25 and 68(2): 47-53.
Eco, U. 1986. Travels in Hyper-reality. In Eco, U. (Ed.) *Faith in Fakes.* Secker and Warburg, London.
Eisenbeis, M. 1972. Elements for a sociology of museums. *Museum* 24(2): 110-19.
English Tourist Board 1978. *Sightseeing in 1977.* English Tourist Board, London.
 1979. *English Heritage Monitor.* English Tourist Board Development Planning Department, London.
 1982a. *Visitors to Museums Survey 1982.* Report by English Tourist Board Market Research Department and NOP Market Research Limited. English Tourist Board, London.
 1982b. *Sightseeing in 1981.* English Tourist Board, London.
 1983. *Survey of Visits to Tourist Attractions.* English Tourist Board, London.
 1989. *English Heritage Monitor.* BTA/ETB Research Services, London.
Erdos, P.L. 1970. *Professional Mail Surveys.* McGraw-Hill, New York.
Erwin, D. 1971. The Belfast public and the Ulster Museum: a statistical survey. *Museums Journal* 70(4): 175-79.
Feder, K.L. 1984. Irrationality and popular archaeology. *American Antiquity* 49(3): 525-41.
Feist, A. and Hutchinson, R. 1989. *Cultural Trends* 1989 (4). Policy Studies Institute, London.
Festinger, L. 1957. *A Theory of Cognitive Dissonance.* Row, Peterson and Co., Evanston, Illinois.
Fewster, C. 1990. Beyond the Showcase. *Museums Journal* 90(6): 24-27.
Fowler, P.J. 1977. *Approaches to Archaeology.* Adam and Charles Black, London.
 1981. Archaeology, the public and the sense of the past. In Lowenthal, D. and Binney, M. (Eds.) *Our Past Before Us: Why Do We Save It?.* Temple Smith, London: 56-69.
 1986. The past in public – roots for all or life with dried tubers? In Dobinson, C. and Gilchrist, R. (Eds.) *Archaeology, Politics and the Public.* York University Archaeological Publications: 6-13.
 1989. Heritage: A Post-Modernist Perspective. In Uzzell, D. (Ed.) *Heritage Interpretation Volume 1. The Natural and Built Environment.* Belhaven Press, London: 57-63.

Fox, A.J. and Goldblatt, P.O. 1982. *Longitudinal Study. Sociodemographic mortality differentials*. Office of Population and Census Surveys. HMSO, London.

Fritz, J.M. 1973. Relevance, archaeology and subsistence theory. In Redman, C. (Ed.) *Research and Theory in Current Archaeology*. John Wiley and Sons, New York: 59-82.

Gero, J.M. 1985. Socio-politics and the woman-at-home ideology. *American Antiquity* 50: 342-50.

Giddens, A. 1976. *New Rules of Sociological Method*. Hutchinson, London.

1979. *Central Problems in Social Theory*. Macmillan, London.

Goldthorpe, J., Lockwood, D., Bechhofer, F. and Platt, J. 1969. *The Affluent Worker in the Class Structure*. Cambridge University Press, Cambridge.

Goyder, J. 1982. Further evidence on factors affecting response rates to mailed questionnaires. *American Sociological Review* 47(4): 550-53.

Goyder, J. and Leiper, J. 1985. Decline in survey response: a social values interpretation. *Sociology* 19(1): 55-71.

Grana, C. 1971. *Fact and Symbol: Essays in the Sociology of Art and Literature*. Oxford University Press, Oxford.

Gray, P.G. and Gee, F.A. 1967. Electoral registration for parliamentary elections; an enquiry made for the Home Office. *Government Social Survey* (SS391). HMSO, London.

Greene, J.P. 1978. A visitor survey at Norton Priory Museum. *Museums Journal* 78(1): 7-9.

Greenwood, T. 1888. *Museums and Art Galleries*. Simpkin Marshall, London.

Gregory, T. 1983. The impact of metal detecting on archaeology and the public. *Archaeological Review from Cambridge* 2(1): 5-8.

1986. Whose fault is treasure-hunting? In Dobinson, C. and Gilchrist, R. (Eds.) *Archaeology, Politics and the Public*. York University Archaeological Publications: 25-7.

Griggs, S.A. and Alt, M.B. 1982. Visitors to the British Museum (Natural History) in 1980 and 1981. *Museums Journal* 82(3): 149-55.

Griggs, S.A. and Hays-Jackson, K. 1983. Visitors' perceptions of cultural institutions. *Museums Journal* 83(2/3): 121-25.

Grimshaw, R. and Lester, P. 1976. *The Meaning of the Loch Ness Monster*. Centre for Contemporary Cultural Studies, Birmingham.

Hall, S., Clarke, J., Jefferson, T. and Roberts, B. 1976. *Resistance Through Rituals*. Hutchinson, London.

Hancocks, A. 1987. Museum exhibition as a tool for social awareness. *Curator* 30(3): 181-92.

Hawkes, J. 1967. God in the Machine. *Antiquity* 41: 174-80.

Heady, P. 1984 *Visiting Museums. A Report of a Survey of Visitors to the Victoria and Albert, Science, and National Railway Museums for the Office of Arts and Libraries*. Office of Population and Census Surveys, HMSO, London.

Heberlein, T.A. and Baumgartner, R. 1978. Factors affecting response rates to mailed questionnaires: a quantitative analysis of the published literature. *American Sociological Review* 43(4): 447-62.

Hedges, B. 1977. *Presentation of Response Rates*. Methodological Working Paper No. 1, Social and Community Planning Research, London.

Held, D. 1980. *Introduction to Critical Theory*. Hutchinson, London.

Henry, H. 1953. We cannot ask 'why?'. In Henry, H. (Ed.) *Perspectives in Management and Marketing Research*. Crosby Lockwood, London: 293-311.

Hewison, R. 1987. *The Heritage Industry*. Methuen, London.

1989. Heritage: An Interpretation. In Uzzell, D. (Ed.) *Heritage Interpretation Volume 1. The Natural and Built Environment*. Bellhaven Press, London: 15-23

Hindle, B. 1978. How much is a piece of the True Cross worth? In Quimby, I.M.G. (Ed.) *Material Culture and the Study of American Life.* W.W. Norton, New York: 5-20.

Hirsch, F. 1977. *The Social Limits to Growth.* Routledge, London.

HMSO 1981. *A Heritage For Scotland. Scotland's National Museums and Galleries: the Next 25 Years.* HMSO, Edinburgh.

1990. *Report of the Parliamentary Select Committee on Museum Admission Charges.* HMSO, London.

Hobsbawm, E. 1972. The social function of the past. *Past and Present* 55: 3-17.

Hobsbawm, E. and Ranger, T. 1983. *The Invention of Tradition.* Cambridge University Press, Cambridge.

Hodder, I. 1982. Theoretical archaeology: a reactionary view. In Hodder, I. (Ed.) *Symbolic and Structural Archaeology.* Cambridge University Press, Cambridge: 1-16.

1984a. Archaeology in 1984. *Antiquity* 68: 25-32.

1984b. Ideology and power – the archaeological debate. *Environment and Planning D: Society and Space* 2: 347-53.

1986. *Reading the Past.* Cambridge University Press, Cambridge.

Hoinville, G., Jowell, R., *et al* (Eds.) 1978. *Survey Research Practice.* Heinemann Educational Books, London.

Hood, M.G. 1981. *Adult Attitudes Toward Leisure Choices in Relation to Museum Participation.* Unpublished PhD, Ohio State University.

1983. Staying away – why people choose not to visit museums. *Museum News* 61(4): 50-57.

Horkheimer, M. and Adorno, T. 1973. *Dialectic of Enlightenment.* Allen Lane, London.

Horne, D. 1984 *The Great Museum.* Pluto Press, London.

Hough, M. and Mayhew, P. 1983. *The British Crime Survey: First Report.* Home Office Research Study No. 76. Home Office Research and Planning Unit. HMSO, London.

Hudson, K. 1975. *A Social History of Museums.* Macmillan, London.

1981. *A Social History of Archaeology.* Macmillan, London.

Impey, O. and MacGregor, A. (Eds.) 1985 *The Origins of Museums.* Clarendon Press, Oxford.

Jameson, F. Postmodernism, or the cultural logic of late capitalism. *New Left Review* 146: 53-92.

Jenkins, R. 1982. Pierre Bourdieu and the reproduction of determinism. *Sociology* 16: 270-81.

Jowell, R., Witherspoon, S. and Brook, L. (Eds.) 1987. *British Social Attitudes. The 1987 Report.* Gower Publishing Co., Aldershot.

Kelly, J. 1982. *Leisure.* Prentice-Hall, London.

1983. *Leisure Identities and Interactions.* Allen and Unwin, London.

Kim, J.O. and Mueller, C.W. 1978. *Introduction to Factor Analysis.* Quantitative Applications in the Social Sciences No. 13. Sage, London.

Klein, R. 1974. Who goes to museums? *Illustrated London News* April 1974: 27-29.

Leone. M.P. 1973. Archaeology as the science of technology: Mormon town plans and fences. In Redman, C.L. (Ed.) *Research and Theory in Current Archaeology.* John Wiley and Sons, New York: 125-50.

1981a. Archaeology's relationship to the present and the past. In Gould, R.A. and Schiffer, M.B. (Eds.) *Modern Material Culture: The Archaeology of Us.* Academic Press, New York: 5-14.

1981b. The relationship between artifacts and the public in outdoor history museums. *Annals of the New York Academy of Sciences* 376: 301-14.

Levine, P. 1986. *The Amateur and the Professional. Antiquarians, Historians and Archaeologists in Victorian England 1838-1886.* Cambridge University Press, Cambridge.

Lewis, G.D. 1975. The museum and its public. In *Museums as an influence on the Quality of Life*. Proceedings of a conference held by the Group for Educational Studies in Museums, 6-11 April 1975: 19-23.

1984. Collectors, collections and museums in Britain to 1920. In Thompson, J. (Ed.) *Manual of Curatorship*. Museums Association and Butterworth's, London: 23-37.

Linsky, A.S. 1975. Stimulating responses to mailed questionnaires: a review. *Public Opinion Quarterly* 38: 82-101.

Loomis, R.J. 1973. Please, not another visitor survey. *Museum News* 52(2): 21-26.

Lowenthal, D. 1985. *The Past is a Foreign Country*. Cambridge University Press, Cambridge.

MacCannell, D. 1976. *The Tourist: A New Theory of the Leisure Class*. Schocken Books, New York.

Marcuse, H. 1968. *One Dimensional Man*. Sphere Books, London.

Marx, K. and Engels, F. 1864 (1965). *The German Ideology*. Lawrence and Wishart, London.

Mason, T. 1974. The visitors to Manchester Museum: a questionnaire survey. *Museums Journal* 73(4): 153-57.

Mayrand, P. 1985. The new museology proclaimed. *Museum* 37(4): 200-201.

McKechnie, G. 1974. *Manual for the Environmental Response Inventory*. Consulting Psychologists Press, Palo Alto, California

McManus, P. 1989. What people say and how they think in a science museum. In Uzzell, D. (Ed.) *Heritage Interpretation Volume 2. The Visitor Experience*. Belhaven Press, London: 156-65.

McWilliams, B. and Hopwood, J. 1973. The public of Norwich Castle Museum 1971-72. *Museums Journal* 72(4): 153-56.

Meltzer, D.J. 1981. Ideology and material culture. In Gould, R.J. and Schiffer, M.B. (Eds.) *Modern Material Culture: The Archaeology of Us*. Academic Press, New York: 113-25.

Merriman, N. 1989. Museum Visiting as a Cultural Phenomenon. In Vergo, P. (Ed.) *The New Museology*. Reaktion Books, London: 149-171.

Michell, J. 1969. *The View Over Atlantis*. Garnstone, London.

Middleton, V. 1990. *New Visions for Independent Museums in the U.K.*. Association of Independent Museums, London.

Miles, R.S. (Ed.) 1982 *The Design of Educational Exhibits*. George Allen and Unwin, London.

Millas, J.G. 1973. Museums and lifelong education. *Museum* 25 (3): 157-64.

Miller, D. 1982. Structures and strategies: an aspect of the relationship between social hierarchy and cultural change. In Hodder, I. (Ed.) *Symbolic and Structural Archaeology*. Cambridge University Press, Cambridge: 89-98.

Moore, H. 1982. The interpretation of spatial patterning in settlement residues. In Hodder, I. (Ed.) *Symbolic and Structural Archaeology*. Cambridge University Press, Cambridge: 74-79.

Morris, C.J. 1981. Townscape Images: A study in meaning. In Kain, R. (Ed.) *Planning for Conservation*. Mansell, London: 259-87.

Moser, C. and Kalton, G. 1971. *Survey Research Methods in Social Investigation*. Heinemann Educational Books, London.

Murray, J. and Stockdale, D. 1990. *The Miles Tae Dundee. Stories of a City and its People*. Dundee Art Galleries and Museums, Dundee.

Museums and Galleries Commission. 1984. *Eleventh Report 1978-1983*. HMSO, London.

Museums Association. 1945. Museums and art galleries. A national service. *Museums Journal* 45(3): 33-45.

Myerscough, J. 1988. *The Economic Importance of the Arts in Britain.* Policy Studies Institute, London.

National Audit Office. 1988. *Management of the Collections of the English National Museums and Galleries.* HMSO, London.

National Research Center for the Arts. n.d. *Museums USA.* National Endowment for the Arts, Washington, DC.

Nederhof, A.J. 1985. A comparison of European and North American response patterns in mail surveys. *Journal of the Market Research Society* 27(1): 55-63.

Niehoff, A. 1968a. Characteristics of the audience reaction in the Milwaukee Public Museum. In Borhegyi, S.F. and Hanson, I.A. (Eds.) *The Museum Visitor.* Publications in Museology No. 3. The Milwaukee Public Museum: 10-12.

1968b. Audience reaction in the Milwaukee Public Museum: the winter visitors. In Borhegyi, S.F. and Hanson, I.A. (Eds.) *The Museum Visitor.* Publications in Museology No. 3. The Milwaukee Public Museum: 22-31.

NOP Market Research 1982. *A Report on a Survey Carried out for English Tourist Board on Museums.* NOP Market Research Ltd., London.

Norusis, M.J. 1985. *SPSS-X Advanced Statistics Guide.* McGraw-Hill, London.

Ollerearnshaw, S. 1990. Colour Conscious. *Museums Journal* 90(11): 31-33.

OPCS 1980. *Classification of Occupations.* HMSO, London.

1984. *Electoral Statistics.* HMSO, London.

1990. *General Household Survey 1988.* HMSO, London.

O'Neill, M. 1990. Springburn: A Community and its museum. In Baker, F. and Thomas, J. (Eds.) *Writing The Past In The Present.* St David's University College, Lampeter: 114-126

Ovenell, R.F. 1985. *The Ashmolean Museum 1683-1894.* Clarendon Press, London.

Pallottino, M. 1968. *The Meaning of Archaeology.* Thames and Hudson, London.

Parker, S. 1976. *The Sociology of Leisure.* George Allen and Unwin, London.

1983. *Leisure and Work.* George Allen and Unwin, London.

Parkin, F. 1972. *Class Inequality and Political Order.* Paladin, London.

Pearce, S. 1986a. Thinking about Things: Approaches to the Study of Artifacts. *Museums Journal* 85(4): 198-201.

1986b. Objects High and Low. *Museums Journal* 86(2): 79-82.

1986c. Objects as Signs and Symbols. *Museums Journal* 86(3): 131-35

1990. *Archaeological Curatorship.* Leicester University Press, Leicester.

Peirson Jones, J. 1990. Interactive video and the Gallery 33 Project. *Museum Development* June 1990.

Pennsylvania Museum 1930. Pennsylvania Museum classifies its visitors. *Museum News* 1: 7-8.

Piggott, S. 1950. *William Stukeley: an Eighteenth Century Antiquary.* Clarendon Press. Oxford.

Pitt-Rivers, A.H.L.F. 1891. Typological museums, as exemplified by the Pitt-Rivers Museum at Oxford, and his provincial museum at Farnham, Dorset. *Journal of the Society of Arts* 40: 115-22.

Plumb, J.H. 1969. *The Death of the Past.* Macmillan, London.

Prince, D.R. 1982. Countryside interpretation: a cognitive evaluation. *Museums Journal* 82(3): 165-70.

1983. Behavioural consistency and visitor attraction. *The International Journal of Museum Management and Curatorship* 2(3): 235-47.

1985a. The museum as dreamland. *The International Journal of Museum Management and Curatorship* 4(4): 243-50.

1985b. Museum visiting and unemployment. *Museums Journal* 85(3): 85-90.

and Higgins-McLoughlin, B. 1987. *Museums UK: The Findings of the Museums Data Base Project.* Museums Association, London.

and Schadla-Hall, R.T. 1985. The image of the museum: a case-study of Kingston upòn Hull. *Museums Journal* 85(2): 39-45.
1987. On the public appeal of archaeology. *Antiquity* 61: 69-70.
Prown, J.D. 1983. Mind in matter. An introduction to material culture theory and method. *Winterthur Portfolio* 17: 1-19.
Rahtz, P.A. 1985. *Invitation to Archaeology*. Basil Blackwell, Oxford.
Rapoport, R. and Rapoport, R. 1975. *Leisure and the Family Life Cycle*. Routledge and Kegan Paul, London.
Roberts, K. 1981. *Leisure*. 2nd Edition. Longman, Harlow.
Schuman, H. and Presser, S. 1981. *Questions and answers in attitude surveys: experiments on question form, wording and context*. Academic Press, London.
Scott, C. 1961. Research on mail surveys. *Journal of the Royal Statistical Society* 124: 143-205.
Selkirk, A. 1982. The war against archaeology. *Current Archaeology* 85: 35-6.
Shanks, M. and Tilley, C. 1987. *Reconstructing Archaeology*. Cambridge University Press, Cambridge.
Shelton, A.A. 1990. In the lair of the monkey: notes towards a postmodernist museography. *New Research in Museum Studies* 1: 78-102
Shils, E. 1981. *Tradition*. Chicago University Press, Chicago.
Stebbins, R. 1979. *Amateurs: On the Margin Between Work and Leisure*. Sage, Beverley Hills, California.
Stone, P. 1986. Are the public really interested? In Dobinson, C. and Gilchrist, R. (Eds.) *Archaeology, Politics and the Public*. York University Archaeological Publications: 14-21.
Sudman, S. 1983. Applied sampling. In Rossi, P.H., Wright, J.D. and Anderson, A.B. (Eds.) *Handbook of Survey Research*. Academic Press, London: 145-194.
Sudman, S. and Bradburn, N.M. 1979. *Improving Interview Method and Questionnaire Design*. Jossey-Bass, San Francisco.
Suggitt, M. 1990. Emissaries from the Toy Cupboard. *Museums Journal* 90(12): 30-33
Szacka, B. 1972. Two kinds of past-time orientation. *Polish Sociological Bulletin* 1-2: 63-75.
Taylor, S.M. and Konrad, V.A. 1980. Scaling of dispositions toward the past. *Environment and Behaviour* 12: 283-307.
Teruggi, M.E. 1973. The round table of Santiago (Chile). *Museum* 25(3): 129-33.
Thompson, J.B. 1984. *Studies in the Theory of Ideology*. Polity Press, Cambridge.
Tilley, C. 1982. Social formation, social structures and social change. In Hodder, I. (Ed.) *Symbolic and Structural Archaeology*. Cambridge University Press, Cambridge: 26-38.
Toffler, A. 1970. *Future Shock*. Bantam Books, New York.
Touche Ross. 1989. *Museum Funding and Services – The Visitor's Perspective*. Touche Ross Management Consultants, London.
Tuan, Y-F. 1974. *Topophilia: A Study of Environmental Perception, Attitudes and Values*. Prentice-Hall, Englewood Cliffs, New Jersey.
UNESCO 1972. *Convention on the Protection of the World Cultural and Natural Heritage*. UNESCO, Paris.
1982. *World conference on cultural policies. The Final Report*. UNESCO, Paris.
Veblen, T. 1899. *The Theory of the Leisure Class*. Republished 1973. Houghton-Mifflin, Boston.
von Daniken, E. 1970. *Chariots of the Gods*. Bantam Books, New York.
1972. *Gods from Outer Space*. Bantam Books, New York.
Wallace, M. 1981. Visiting the past: history museums in the United States. *Radical History Review* 25(3): 63-96.

Walsh, K. (forthcoming). *The Representation of the Past.* Routledge, London.
Watson, P., Leblanc, S. and Redman, C. 1971. *Explanation in Archaeology. An Explicitly Scientific Approach.* Columbia University Press, New York.
Williams, R. 1961. *The Long Revolution.* Chatto and Windus, London.
Williamson, T. and Bellamy, L. 1983. *Ley Lines in Question.* World's Work, Kingswood.
Willis, P. 1977. *Learning to Labour: How Working Class Kids Get Working Class Jobs.* Saxon House, Farnborough.
Wittlin, A. 1949. *The Museum: Its History and its Tasks in Education.* Routledge and Kegan Paul, London.
1970. *Museums: In Search of a Usable Future.* MIT Press, Cambridge, Massachussetts.
Woodall, J.N. and Perricone, P.J. 1981. The archaeologist as cowboy: the consequence of professional stereotype. *Journal of Field Archaeology* 8: 506-8.
Wright, P. 1985. *On Living in an Old Country: The National Past in Contemporary Britain.* Verso, London.
1987. Treasure island. *New Society* 21st August: 14-17.

Index